TM

19/07

SEX, SCANDAL, AND CELEBRITY IN LATE EIGHTEENTH-CENTURY ENGLAND

Sex, Scandal, and Celebrity in Late Eighteenth-Century England

Matthew J. Kinservik

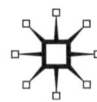

SEX, SCANDAL, AND CELEBRITY IN LATE EIGHTEENTH-CENTURY ENGLAND

First published in 2007 by
PALGRAVE MACMILLAN™
175 Fifth Avenue, New York, N.Y. 10010 and
Houndmills, Basingstoke, Hampshire, England RG21 6XS.
Companies and representatives throughout the world.

PALGRAVE MACMILLAN is the global academic imprint of the
Palgrave Macmillan division of St. Martin's Press, LLC and of
Palgrave Macmillan Ltd. Macmillan® is a registered trademark in the
United States, United Kingdom and other countries. Palgrave is a
registered trademark in the European Union and other countries.

For permission to use in altered form some material published
previously, I wish to thank the Lewis Walpole Library (*"The Production
of a Female Pen": Anna Larpent's Account of the Duchess of Kingston's
Bigamy Trial of 1776*, copyright © 2004 Yale University), the editors
of *The Review of English Studies* ("Censorship, Sodomy, and Satire in
Samuel Foote's *The Capuchin* [1776]"), and the editors of *The British
Journal of Eighteenth-Century Studies* ("The Politics and Poetics of
Sodomy in the Age of George III").

ISBN-10: 1-4039-7992-8
ISBN-13: 978-1-4039-7992-6

Library of Congress Cataloging-in-Publication Data

Kinservik, Matthew J., 1967–
   Sex, scandal, and celebrity in late eighteenth-century England /
Matthew J. Kinservik.
      p.cm.
   Includes bibliographical references and index.
   ISBN 1-4039-7992-8 (alk. paper)
      1. Bristol, Elizabeth Chudleigh, Countess of, 1720–1788.
2. Kingston, Evelyn Pierrepont, Duke of, 1711–1773–Relations with
women. 3. Trials (Bigamy)–Great Britain–History–18th century.
4. Scandals–Great Britain–History–18th century. 5. Mistresses–
Great Britain–Biography. I. Title.

DA483.C6K56 2007
364.1'83092–dc22   2007060056

A catalogue record for this book is available from the British Library.

Design by Macmillan India Ltd.

First edition: June 2007

10 9 8 7 6 5 4 3 2 1

Printed in the United States of America.

For Mara

CONTENTS

List of Illustrations

WORKS FREQUENTLY CITED

Gervat   Claire Gervat, *Elizabeth: The Scandalous Life of the Duchess of Kingston* (London: Century, 2003).

Hervey   Augustus Hervey, *Augustus Hervey's Journal*, ed. David Erskine (London: William Kimber, 1953).

HLRO   House of Lords Record Office.

Larpent   *"The Production of a Female Pen": Anna Larpent's Account of the Duchess of Kingston's Bigamy Trial of 1776*, Miscellaneous Antiquities, no. 17, ed. Matthew J. Kinservik (New Haven, CT: The Lewis Walpole Library, Yale University 2004).

LMA/DL   Diocese of London court records in the London Metropolitan Archives.

Mavor   Elizabeth Mavor, *The Virgin Mistress: A Study in Survival* (Garden City, NY: Doubleday & Co., 1964).

Melville   Lewis Melville [pseud.], *Trial of the Duchess of Kingston* (Edinburgh and London: William Hodge & Company, Ltd., 1927).

NA/C   Chancery records in the National Archives, London.

NA/KB   King's Bench records in the National Archives, London.

Pearce   Charles E. Pearce, *The Amazing Duchess*, 2 vols., 2nd ed. (London: Stanley Paul & Co., 1911).

Walpole   Horace Walpole, *The Correspondence of Horace Walpole*, ed. W. S. Lewis, 47 vols. (New Haven, CT: Yale University Press, 1937–1983).

Whitehead   Thomas Whitehead, *Original Anecdotes of the Late Duke of Kingston* (Bath, 1792).

A Note on Sources

The story of Elizabeth Chudleigh's bigamy has been told several times, usually in biographical accounts. The most thorough and reliable of these are Charles E. Pearce's *The Amazing Duchess* (1911), Elizabeth Mavor's *The Virgin Mistress* (1964), and Claire Gervat's *Elizabeth: The Scandalous Life of the Duchess of Kingston* (2003). For obvious reasons, these biographies repeat many facts and anecdotes of Elizabeth's life. In my retelling of Elizabeth's marital and legal history in chapters 2–5, I have relied on these sources a great deal, but in order to avoid redundant notation of common facts, I have used the endnotes only to document a direct quotation or a fact from a particular biography. Similarly, when explaining English marriage law in the eighteenth century, my primary sources were Lawrence Stone's *Road to Divorce* (1990), *Uncertain Unions* (1992), and *Broken Lives* (1993); Martin Ingram's *Church Courts, Sex and Marriage in England, 1570–1640* (1987); and R. B. Outhwaite's *Clandestine Marriage in England, 1500–1850* (1995). As with the biographies, I have generally used endnotes only to cite quotations and material peculiar to one of these texts.

Acknowledgments

I am very grateful for the tremendous support I received while researching and writing this book. The project began to take shape during a fellowship at the Huntington Library. I was able to complete this book thanks to subsequent research fellowships at the Lewis Walpole Library and the Beinecke Library (Yale), the Houghton Library (Harvard), the Clark Library (UCLA), and the Harry Ransom Humanities Research Center (University of Texas at Austin). The University of Delaware supported me with a generous General University Research Grant and sabbatical that allowed me to do important archival research in England.

While working on this book I have met many new friends and colleagues to whom I am greatly indebted for their advice and support. Chief among these are David Turner, Romita Ray, Heather McPherson, and John Beynon (alias, the BBGOF), and Maggie Powell and her staff at the Walpole Library, who put up with all of us with good humor in the summer of 2001. For the opportunity to share my work in progress, I want especially to thank Maggie Powell, Joe Roach, Jill Campbell, Ruth Yeazell, and everyone who attended the Country House Weekend at the Walpole Library in March 2002, and Felicity Nussbaum, George Haggerty, and everyone I met at the Southern California eighteenth-century studies colloquium in the spring of 2004.

As always, I am grateful for the incisive comments of Rob Hume, Judy Milhous, Don-John Dugas, and Paul Cannan. At Delaware, McKay Jenkins offered crucial advice and encouragement about the nature and shape of this book at an early stage, and Jerry Beasley, Don Mell, and many other colleagues in the English Department have been as supportive and helpful as ever. My greatest debt, however, is to my wife, Mara Gorman, whose superb editing, sense of literary style, and generous help have truly made this book possible.

Introduction: 15 April 1776

Anna Porter, the eighteen-year-old daughter of an English diplomat, was up by 5:00 a.m. on the morning of 15 April 1776. She had no choice, really. For an eighteenth-century lady, dressing well took time. One's figure had to be contracted and enhanced in all the right places in order to show off fine clothes to their best advantage. So to be dressed properly, she had to allow herself plenty of time to put on the complicated essentials such as a whalebone corset, with its many laces to thread and tie.

Once her clothes were sufficiently arranged, Anna had to visit her hairdresser. On an ordinary day she would have dressed her own hair, but this was no ordinary day. Today she would wear her hair in the highest fashion, which meant piling it in a steep rise from her forehead and decorating it with fruit, flowers, and ribbons. At the queen's birthday party earlier in the year, one woman's headdress was described as terminating "in a lofty peak, like a grenadier's cap, with a bouquet on top of it all."[1] Another woman wore her hair splayed out in wide plaits, resembling a lady's fan. These headdresses could add two feet to a lady's height, and they required elaborate preparations to hold their shape, not something a lady could do for herself. Anna was not alone in making her preparations. All over London and Westminster, hairdressers were up early, helping the fine ladies look their finest. Apart from the unusually early hour, they faced an added challenge because newspaper notices had warned ladies not to wear their hair so high that it obstructed the view of others in Westminster Hall that day.[2] Seating was limited and space was tight, so fashion would have to be tempered by these realities.

By 7:00 a.m., Anna was finally dressed and anxious to leave the house. To pass the time, she took up a pen and began an excited and rambling letter to a friend:

> I can absolutely settle to nothing.—No Chaos ever equalled my head at present, & I will venture to pronounce the heads of half the People in this great Town. This day the Duchess of Kingston is tried for Bigamy— the whole Town has talked of nothing else, for this week past.[3]

She had barely finished writing these sentences when the summons to depart came. At last, she was off to Westminster Hall, where the duchess's trial would take place before an illustrious jury, the House of Lords. Before entering the Hall, however, Anna would meet her party at a coffeehouse adjacent to the House of Lords, overlooking Old Palace Yard and the entrance to the Hall. Although she was neither an aristocrat nor a part of the fashionable set, the "bon ton," as it was called, Anna did have connections enough to attend the trial at the invitation of Lady Bathurst. This was something of a coup. As a guest of Lady Bathurst, she would enjoy one of the best seats in the house that day, for Henry Bathurst was the Lord High Steward, the presiding judge. He would be at the center of things, seated on the woolpack, the traditional seat of judgment for a peer (or in this case a peeress). But he also had a private box for his wife and her friends. It held thirty-six people, and of the four thousand spectators in the Hall, they would have some of the most prominent seats.

The route to Westminster usually bustled with horse carts and draymen, but today, by order of the House of Lords, the road had been cleared all the way from Charing Cross to Old Palace Yard (Trafalgar Square to Big Ben) in order to make way for the thousands of coaches and chairs that would flood into the area. The Palace Guards were on hand to help with crowd control and their smart appearance lent even more pomp to the occasion. Most of the tickets were distributed to the lords and other dignitaries, and those that were being sold fetched as much as twenty guineas, so only the rich and very well connected could get inside the Hall to witness the trial. For the rest, there was the pleasure of watching a parade of the finest collection of vehicles they had ever seen in one place, not to mention the thrill of celebrity-gazing as the ticketed spectators left their coaches and entered the Hall. Like the crowds who watch the movie stars arrive at the Academy Awards nowadays, Londoners gathered early and stood along the length of the route, straining for a view.

Lady Bathurst had rented a private room in the coffeehouse for the duration of the trial and she treated her thirty-five guests to a breakfast before they went into the Hall. Anna Porter feasted on the spectacle outside instead of the breakfast inside. Resuming her letter to her friend, she described how from an upper window in the coffeehouse, she enjoyed the display:

> I amused my self in seeing the Peers & Peeresses coming into the Hall from their Carriages, which were mostly elegant ones, & the Horses full harnessd & ornamented.—Every thing was orderly & quiet in Palace Yard, & the Guards were very diligent & drawn up under arms.—which was a pretty sight. (83)

Across town, Lord Bathurst was hosting a breakfast of his own at home in Great Russell Street. If the hairdressers of London were up early, the cooks and scullery maids got no sleep at all. They were busy preparing elegant meals like the one Bathurst gave to his gentlemen attendants, featuring cold tongue and rich wines. As Lord High Steward, he had twenty attendants during the course of the trial (Anna's brother was one of them) so this was no small affair.

The same scenes were playing out all over the metropolis during the five-day duration of the trial. At the Adelphi Building, the fashionable new residential block on the Strand, the home of the great actor David Garrick, was also bustling early. His wife was attending the trial with the young playwright Hannah More, to whom Garrick had generously given his ticket. By 7:00 a.m. the ladies were, like Anna, fully dressed and had their hair done. An hour later they were at the Duke of Newcastle's house, which adjoined Westminster Hall. They were particularly lucky because the duke's house had an entrance directly into the large gallery that he had reserved for his guests. This spared them the trouble of making their way into the Hall through the crowd in Old Palace Yard. Hannah boasted to a friend: "You will imagine the bustle that must attend five thousand people getting into one Hall, yet in all this hurry we walked in by these means as tranquilly as at any other time to drink tea."[4] She was certainly luckier than Edward Pigott, whose commonplace book describes the same scene from down below. Pigott attended two days of the trial at the cost of two hats—he lost each of them while elbowing his way through the doors with a hundred other people vying for good seats.[5]

With the breakfasts over, the spectators began to take their places inside the Hall. The scene that greeted them was breathtaking.

Ordinarily, Westminster Hall was the seat of the most important courts in England, which were scattered throughout the cavernous medieval building. The courts were separated by partition walls that did not even begin to reach the vaulted ceilings; instead, they merely demarcated each court's space. The sound traveled from court to court, and along the sidewalls were bookstalls, where vendors hawked books to passersby and friends met to talk. Like the English legal system itself, the Hall was an improvised affair, adapted over the years to suit the changing needs of the legal profession and the nation. But on this day, everything was different.[6]

The law courts and bookstalls had all been removed and in their place was a huge scaffolding that contained the private boxes and galleries where the four thousand ticketed spectators would sit. The scaffolding was handsomely ornamented with crimson cloth and it rose from the floor to the rafters around the entire perimeter of the Hall. It had taken so long to build that the trial was delayed from January until 15 April, the earliest completion date the master carpenter thought feasible. It was actually done two weeks before the trial, allowing those who could not afford tickets to the trial itself to pay a modest fee to gawk at the structure in the empty Hall. Public curiosity was so intense that in one week the doorkeeper pocketed £500, a small fortune.

The carpenters would have done well to take a bit more time with the job. In their haste, they neglected to lay a floorboard in one of the galleries, causing a spectacular accident. As the spectators were taking their seats, one young woman fell through the cavity, landing on two people below, injuring them both and flattening the woman's headdress. Another woman fell part way into the hole and got stuck there, her legs dangling down.[7]

But for the most part, the scene was splendid and dignified. And little wonder, not only was the Hall full of the elite of Great Britain, but they were all in their finest dress. What had drawn them all to Westminster Hall?

The last peeress to stand trial before the House of Lords was the Countess of Somerset, who had been tried for murder nearly two hundred years earlier. That trial had been sensational, but a bigamy trial promised to provide an even better show. And looking at the Hall that morning, nobody could doubt that this was as much a show as it was a trial. There were aristocrats of every rank, famous actors and artists, princes of the blood, foreign dignitaries, and the queen herself—and that was just the audience. The principal actors had not yet entered the courtroom.

Bathurst, as Lord High Steward, had one of the most important parts to play. He was the presiding judge during the trial and was also the man most responsible for making it into the social and media event that it had become. When the House of Lords debated the mode of trial for the duchess, he took every opportunity to magnify the size and grandeur of the process. Now the day had come and it was fulfilling his every expectation.

After breakfast, Bathurst and his attendants traveled to Westminster in magnificent style. His entourage included "five new carriages, four painted green, and the fifth white, with the arms of the family of Bathurst, and the motto 'Tien ta Foy' ["Keep the Faith"]; all the coachmen and footmen having new liveries. Next followed the state coach in which was the Lord High Steward."[8] Luckily for Bathurst, the crowds around Westminster Hall were so thick that traffic advanced very slowly, because when his state coach came within thirty yards of the Hall, it came to a crashing halt as its axle broke underneath it with what must have been a deafening crack. Bathurst must have been shaken and embarrassed by the abrupt end of his stately approach, but he was not injured. Emerging from the vehicle, the Lord High Steward regained his dignity as best as he could and made his way to the House of Lords, where he joined his attendants and the peers of the realm to prepare for their state procession into the Hall.

The prisoner arrived more discreetly. Rather than take her coach, which was blazoned with the Kingston arms and ducal coronets, the Duchess of Kingston opted for the anonymity of being carried in a chair. Eighteenth-century crowds were not above pelting the coaches of aristocrats with mud and eggs when the spirit moved them, so the duchess's prudence was warranted. But pity the two chairmen who had to carry her from Kingston House, Knightsbridge, to Westminster Hall, a distance of nearly two miles.

At 11:00 a.m., the moment that everyone had been waiting for finally arrived: the procession of the lords into the Hall. It was so long and complicated an affair that many of the spectators had purchased a guide called *Ceremonial for the Trial of a Peer*, which explained the order of the dignitaries and included a diagram of the Hall and a seating chart. First came the Lord High Steward's gentleman ushers, who filed slowly past the empty throne, all twenty of them removing their hats and bowing low in turn, as if the king were actually present. This gesture was repeated by every member of the procession, drawing its duration out considerably. Behind them came the eldest sons of the peers and those lords who were still minors and so could not serve on a jury. Next came the clerks of the legal counsel and the Masters of Chancery, two by two, dressed in their legal caps and bands.

But all this was merely the preamble to the main event, the entrance of the lords. As they entered, two by two, the Garter King at Arms called out each lord's name as he passed. First came the junior barons, who were distinguished by having just two bands of ermine trimmed with gold on the right arm of their dark red ceremonial gowns. The earls came next, with three bands, and then came the dukes, who had four bands. Most of these men had not worn their ceremonial dress since the last great state trial: Lord Byron's manslaughter case a decade earlier. When the dukes had reached their seats, the Duke of Cumberland entered. As a prince of the blood he walked alone, the train of his robe borne by an attendant. Edward Pigott thought the duke's entrance was overly theatrical, commenting, "The Duke of Cumberland, who is said to walk well, walks like a theatrical dancer, which I think does not become a nobleman."[9]

Two heralds followed in ceremonial dress with the arms of England on them, followed by four sergeants-at-arms, carrying maces. The Garter King at Arms came next, exceeding the heralds in finery, with the Usher of the Black Rod, the ceremonial attendant of the House of Lords on state occasions. Between them walked Bathurst, the Lord High Steward. Bathurst was distinguished by his large black hat, which made him look to Anna Porter like a Quaker, not nearly so dashing as Black Rod, whom she considered to be "tres bien habilee" (84). Black Rod then reverenced on his knee three times before the Lord High Steward and presented him with his long white staff of office.

If the lords made an impressive spectacle with their procession, the audience rising to the rafters all around them returned the favor. A newspaper report describes the effect of this collection of power and wealth:

> Imagination can hardly picture a more solemn, august, and at the same Time brilliant appearance than the court in Westminster Hall cut yesterday, as soon as the Lord High Steward and the lords had taken their places. Several foreigners of the first distinction were present, and they confessed they never had a conception that such an assemblage of grandeur, splendor, and beauty could be collected in so narrow a space. It was computed that no less than 4,000 persons were present, that out of that number 2,500 were ladies, and that the jewels they wore were worth upwards of four millions of money.[10]

Another reporter noted that the afternoon sun made those jewels shine so brightly that the east side of the hall looked ablaze. James

Boswell was agog, noting that he "did not think there had been so many fine women in the universe."[11] A mixture of high seriousness and high fashion, the scene was everything Bathurst had dreamed it would be, and everything the Duchess of Kingston had feared. With his staff in hand and the jury seated, Bathurst ordered the herald to call the prisoner into the courtroom.

Although the duchess dreaded the scene that awaited her, she was prepared for it. Following Black Rod into court, she entered with a procession of her own. She could not match the size and splendor of the lords' entrance, but she could compete with them on the symbolic level. Whereas the lords' procession pronounced grandeur and power, hers would display the injured innocence of a weak, unwell, and victimized widow whose only comfort was God.

The duchess came first, dressed in a long black mourning gown, hoopless and trimmed with black flowers. She wore her hair discreetly low and without powder, and her head was covered with a black hood. Anna Porter thought the long hood gave the duchess a handsome appearance, resting on her shoulders like it did on Mary, Queen of Scots in the old pictures. This may have been intentional: the Duchess of Kingston could have done worse than to dress like that romantic, widowed queen who died a martyr. Her outfit was completed with long black gloves and a fan. She was followed by three female companions in white satin dresses—her personal chaplain, her physician, and her apothecary—who were on hand to minister to her physical and spiritual needs during this crisis. Nor was the duchess entirely without friends who were willing to stand by her. The Duke of Newcastle, Lord Mountstuart, and James LaRoche, who stood her bail, accompanied her to the prisoner's bar.

The duchess's entrance caused a commotion in the Hall, prompting the heralds to read the proclamation for silence several times. Lady Harrington, who was, as the eighteenth-century phrase goes, "no better than she should be," was disgusted by the duchess's dramatic entrance: "The devil confound her! How brazen the wretch looks!"[12] Hannah More was also unimpressed. She thought that the duchess possessed "but small remains of that beauty of which kings and princes were once enamoured . . . She is very large and ill shaped. There was nothing white but her face, and had it not been for that she looked exactly like a bale of Bombazine."[13] Anna Porter was inclined to be more generous. She thought that the duchess looked "unconcerned, seemingly unaffectedly so" and concluded that "she really looked handsome" (84).

When the duchess reached the bar, she made the customary three reverences to the lords, but then she fell to her knees and remained there. More than a polite curtsy, she was abjecting herself before Bathurst and the lords as if to show how absolutely she was in their power. Abruptly and without compassion, the Lord High Steward called out, "Lady, you may rise." She did so, dropping a polite curtsy, which the jury returned with a bow. The Lord High Steward then addressed the duchess in a short speech that pointed out how serious a crime she stood accused of and what dangerous consequences it threatened to both domestic and national happiness. He ended by assuring her that "awful however as your situation is, you have, as a support under the weight of it, the reflection of being tried before the most honorable and impartial tribunal any court could boast." She replied in a modest yet assured voice:

> As I am innocent of the crime laid to my charge, I therefore have no fears arising from any other cause than that of appearing before so awful a tribunal. I beg that if I fail in any ceremonial observance, it might be imputed to the real cause of my present situation and not misconstrued as a disrespect to an assembly the most honorable in the world, to appear before whom I have traveled in a litter from Rome in a very dangerous illness, knowing that my life, my honour, and my fortune could not be placed in hands so just and sacred as yours.[14]

Bathurst replied tersely, "Madam, you will do well to give attention while you are arraigned on your indictment." And with that exchange, the trial had begun.

The trial of the Duchess of Kingston is a fascinating event. A celebrity show trial of the first order of magnitude, it serves as a reminder that the current age did not invent media intrusions into the private lives (and courtroom ordeals) of the rich and famous. We are merely updating the techniques. But the trial is more than just the high point of drama in the life of an eighteenth-century eccentric, and its significance far exceeds the biography of the Duchess of Kingston.

While the Second Continental Congress was assembling in Philadelphia, where they would soon formally declare American independence, their counterparts in London had stopped business to hear a sex trial. As one historian incredulously notes, the duchess's trial "occasioned greater popular interest and larger aristocratic crowds in the galleries than any debates on the American war."[15] But this is not really surprising. A major sex scandal at home is always going to engage more attention than a war half a world away—especially a war whose successful resolution seems assured. In the fall of 1775 and the spring of 1776, few in England seriously thought that the North American empire was actually in jeopardy. The conflict was important, certainly, and it demanded attention from the king and his ministers. But the nation had other concerns to attend to, and the Duchess of Kingston's bigamy trial merited and received a lot of that attention.

Nor were the two events wholly unrelated. When great threats are perceived abroad, nations often look for enemies within, and to some people, the duchess's bigamy represented a threat to the political order that was just as real as that of George Washington and his rebel army. Americans took up arms against the British government, but the duchess's bigamy threatened the system more subtly by tampering with the lineal succession of a noble line. Bigamy involving a noblewoman was more than just a sex crime, it was a dangerous political act. During and after her trial, many commentators located the source of the American Revolution not with the Sons of Liberty in Boston, but with sexually loose noblewomen— especially the Duchess of Kingston—whose immorality constituted a sort of treason and encouraged others to assault the empire.

This attitude is expressed most powerfully in the opening pages of *The Court of Adultery* (1778):

> Long has our flag triumphant rul'd the seas,
> And prostrate Kings obey'd our dread decrees;
> From *Andalusia*'s rock to *India*'s shore
> Both Arts and Arms confirm'd our sov'reign pow'r.
> Now view the sad reverse; hear War's alarms;
> On ev'ry side advance the adverse arms.
> *Britannia*'s foes the Eastern Phoebus lights,
> On *Britannia*'s num'rous foes the Western sets.
> The angry Gods on you adult'rous race
> Pour down this vengeance, and our arms disgrace.[16]

In this poem, as in many other poems, newspaper paragraphs, and pamphlets, the distressing state of the British Empire in the 1770s is regarded as divine judgment on a nation whose ruling elite could be characterized by sexual depravity and the violation of bourgeois values.

The trial also matters because of the gender and rank of the defendant. Trials of peers were not entirely uncommon: the House of Lords had heard two of them in the 1760s alone. But putting a peeress on trial was a very rare event, and doing it in so public a manner was entirely without precedent. The lords had their reasons. Throughout the 1770s, the sexual indiscretions of British aristocrats had become increasingly well publicized, bringing the entire class into real disrepute. The decade began with the trial of George III's brother, the Duke of Cumberland, for having "criminal conversation" with a married noblewoman. He was convicted and forced to pay £10,000 in damages to the lady's husband. This was just the first of a number of high-profile adultery cases that amused and alarmed the nation. The fashionable *Town and Country Magazine* began running a regular column that featured a new upper-class sexual exposé each month, and transcripts of adultery trials became a popular form of soft-core pornography. This bad publicity led one contemporary essayist to damn the ruling class wholesale, complaining: "Instead of subjecting themselves to the laws, they take measure of their own appetites and passions, and then make laws to fit them, which laws, though neither founded in justice nor enacted by legal authority, too often prevail over, and insult, both justice and authority."[17]

According to some historians, the 1770s mark the beginning of a bourgeois assault on what critics perceived to be a system of aristocratic privilege that licensed flagrant violations of sexual norms. Nicholas Rogers claims that prior to 1770, "public figures had rarely been taken to task for their private vices . . . But thereafter an increasingly vocal middle-class public preferred sobriety and regularity in their leaders."[18] Anna Clark has identified the early reign of George III as the pivotal moment in British history when sex scandals became a major feature of political life.[19] The extent to which this bourgeois criticism focused on the marital irregularities of the upper class in the 1770s can be seen in a series of essays that appeared in the *Covent Garden Magazine* in 1774. In the February and March issues, there was a mock proposal that England establish a law of "triennial marriages," which would terminate all marriages after three years unless they were renewed by both parties. The author of the proposal reasons that the king "could not possibly have any objection, as by this means he might marry his own wife again, and disannul the marriages of his two brothers."[20] The May issue claims that a law was debated in the time of Charles II to legalize bigamy in England. The author goes on to discuss how easily an aristocratic couple can obtain a divorce, and ends by claiming to have a list of ladies of quality who are adulterers and by laying odds on how many earls, viscounts, and barons will be divorced by the end of the year (166).

In this context, the Duchess of Kingston was the perfect scapegoat for an aristocracy in disgrace: she was a commoner by birth who had a scandalous past and was now without the protection of her noble husband. Like setting a controlled fire to save the entire forest from destruction, the British aristocracy sacrificed the duchess in hopes of drawing attention away from the rest of them.

But the duchess's trial is also significant for what it started, not only for what it finished. Although the duchess's case ended on 23 April, over the course of the next year she would be involved in two other lawsuits that scandalized the nation and took up the valuable time of important people when they could least afford it. One was a libel case against the duchess's publicist, the Reverend William Jackson, editor of the *Public Ledger*. The other was a case for attempted sodomy against the famous actor and theatrical patentee Samuel Foote, who also happened to be a bitter enemy of the duchess. Sodomy was a capital crime, but by the 1770s, libeling someone as a sodomite was too, so the stakes in both suits were extremely high. These cases are directly linked to the Duchess of Kingston and her bigamy trial, but the full story of all three has never been told. That is what this book will do.

The story is improbable. The surprising events and eccentric characters at times make it seem like a Restoration sex comedy. But we would be wrong to regard it as merely a salacious costume drama. Rather, it is a cautionary tale of what can happen when a free society tries to police the bedroom too closely. We hear a lot about the social cost of divorce nowadays, but as the duchess's story shows, the inability to escape an unhappy marriage could lead to desperate measures, including bigamy. Bigamy was widespread in the eighteenth century among the more anonymous lower classes because divorce was not legal in England until 1857. The duchess's case was scandalous because she was an aristocrat, not because she was a bigamist.

And although divorce, rather than bigamy, is a social concern today, sodomy has remained a subject for debate throughout history and there have always been strong political and cultural forces at work to demonize homosexual sex as a threat to holy matrimony. As this book will show, the so-called defense of marriage has a long history, and it is not an illustrious one.

In the process of telling this story, a very different picture of the supposedly rational and decorous Age of Enlightenment emerges. This period is frequently regarded as a time when virtue and good sense prevailed over superstition and ancient prejudices. But the old days begin to look like good old days only when time obscures the messy details. By taking a close look at some of those details, we will see how the Age of Reason dealt with sex and passion.

CHAPTER 1

DISGRACING HER GRACE

After the Duke of Kingston's death in 1773, three years before his widow's trial, Elizabeth Pierrepont, dowager Duchess of Kingston, found that her exalted rank did not guarantee her friends, or even respect. Although she had been a duchess for only four years, she acted as if she had been born into the aristocracy and had a naive faith that her exalted rank would guarantee her the polite respect of her peers. She would soon learn that class solidarity was a fleeting thing among the British aristocracy and that wealth and celebrity were double-edged swords.

As the chief beneficiary of the duke's will, she was now one of the richest single women in the world. She had vast resources and no check on them, for not only was her husband dead, so were his parents, her parents, and her brother. In a society that defined women primarily by their protective relationships with their male relations, the duchess was now in a much different position from anything she had ever known. But instead of exulting in her new state like a merry widow in a comic play, she mourned the duke loudly and felt exposed before the world.

Without the duke's protection, Elizabeth found herself the subject of a torrent of unflattering gossip. Her excessive displays of grief over his death were the source of great amusement to her aristocratic peers. The late eighteenth century has been called an age of "sensibility," a time when the spontaneous overflow of powerful emotions was encouraged, but for the upper echelons of society, self-control was a mark of good breeding. As the sophisticated Lord Chesterfield advised his son, laughter is evidence of a loss of self-control: "a man of parts and fashion is therefore only seen to smile, but never heard to laugh."[1] However, there was one type of laughter that courtiers and aristocrats allowed themselves: the derisive sneer at those who broke the rules and made spectacles of themselves. The Duchess of Kingston, in her mourning, was one such spectacle. The respectable Mary Delany summed up the prevailing attitude toward the duchess when commenting on her journey from Bath (where the duke died) to London: "Her widowed Grace fell into fits at every turn on the road from Bath—true affection and gratitude surely cannot inhabit such a breast."[2]

This sort of extravagant behavior had characterized the duchess throughout her life. In 1749, when she was a twenty-seven-year-old Maid of Honour to the Princess of Wales, she attended a masquerade dressed in a gown so transparent that her breasts were plainly visible. Upon arriving at the party, she is reputed to have said, like Iphigenia, "I am ready for the sacrifice!" The other Maids of Honour refused to speak with her that evening, and the bluestocking, Elizabeth Montagu, sniffed that she was "so naked the high priest might easily inspect the entrails of the victim."[3] But the men took a kinder view. When George II saw her in that costume, he begged to fondle her breasts, prompting her to take him by the hand and say, "Sire, I shall put it to a far softer place." She then placed it on his forehead.

This anecdote characterizes the key elements of the duchess's personality better than any other: she craved both notoriety and social distinction, but she was not always prudent enough to achieve the first without risking the latter. And her wit and beauty earned her more male admirers than female friends. For ambitious women in the eighteenth century, this was sometimes the case. And Elizabeth Chudleigh was an ambitious woman. She was born in 1721 to an army captain who was fortunate enough to become lieutenant governor of the Chelsea Hospital, but who was far from rich. When he died, he left his widow and children with little. Had Elizabeth been a different person, she might have reconciled herself to a life of genteel poverty or, perhaps, used her great beauty to attract a rich merchant and lead a comfortable life as a private citizen. But her ambition was to be a fine lady, and a famous one at that.

As a young woman, she had attracted the attention of William Pulteney, the Earl of Bath, and his influence was enough to secure her an appointment as a Maid of Honour to the Princess of Wales in 1744. She was twenty-two years old, and while the post paid her the generous salary of £200 a year, it was more welcome because it provided her with her first title (the modest "honorable") and it put her on display for the bachelors of exalted rank in the Prince of Wales's court. She even caught the eye of some married men, including George II.

She also captured the attention of Evelyn Pierrepont, the Duke of Kingston, one of the richest and most handsome bachelors in England. She became his mistress in the early 1750s, and after nearly twenty years of trying she persuaded him to marry her in 1769. This was the attainment of her life's dream. She was a duchess, she was fabulously rich, and she was, at last, respectable. But when the duke died four years later, leaving her a rich duchess, she seemed to lose her respectability, and it was not long before her right to call herself a duchess came under attack.

This attack came in the form of a lawsuit in the Court of Chancery, where important civil cases were heard. When the Duke of Kingston died, he specifically disinherited Evelyn Meadows, his eldest nephew and presumptive heir. The ostensible reason was a dishonorable discharge from the army, but Meadows was a grasping and treacherous young man whom everyone seemed to loathe. Whatever the cause, he was disinherited and forced to content himself with a paltry £500. (The title died with the second duke and was never an issue.) This was insulting to Evelyn, but the worst blow was felt by the entire family. The duke had left everything to his wife: his money was hers outright and the revenue from his vast estates belonged to her so long as she did not remarry.

The Meadows family could absorb the shock of Evelyn's disgrace (he had not brought them glory in the past), but losing the money and land was unacceptable. In May of 1774, seven months after the duke's death, they began a Chancery suit to invalidate the will on the grounds that the Duchess of Kingston was not his legal wife. They claimed to have incontrovertible evidence proving that she had married him while her first husband was still living. This was worse than gossip. Being the subject of nasty letters is one thing, but being involved in a Chancery suit was something altogether more serious. It would be reported in the newspapers, fueling more gossip of course, and it would almost certainly be a lengthy and expensive process. Long before Dickens wrote *Bleak House*, in which a Chancery suit over a disputed will drags on for generations, that court had earned a reputation for inefficiency. But there was an upside to this: the duchess had virtually inexhaustible financial resources, and since she was just fifty-three years old, time worked to her advantage as well. In a long Chancery suit, she could outlast and outspend the Meadowses.

The publicity, however, would be a bitter pill to swallow. And the duchess did herself no favors by reacting to news of the suit like a guilty woman. She had just returned to Kingston House from wintering in

Rome when she was informed of the event, having missed her lawyer's letters about it on her way home. In a panic, she fled. So great was her hurry, in fact, that instead of waiting for the next packet boat, she was rowed out to a merchant ship that was just getting under sail for Calais. This ignominious trip to Calais delighted her detractors, giving them plenty to write about. The duchess huddled with her lawyers in France, wrote self-pitying letters to her sympathetic friends, and then left for Rome, where she arrived in November 1774.

While she nursed her wounds in the Eternal City, the Meadows family was opening a second front in its legal campaign against her. On 4 December, they persuaded a grand jury that they had shown sufficient cause to pursue a criminal case of bigamy against the duchess. She was duly indicted for that crime at the Quarter Sessions in Hicks' Hall in the county of Middlesex, a charge she would have to answer before the end of the next June. If she failed to appear, she would be declared an outlaw, a presumptive judgment of guilt.

The news arrived in Rome in less than a month, reaching the duchess on New Year's Day. Initially, she was not sure how to respond. She thought of petitioning the king for a *noli prosequi* ruling, one that would quash the prosecution outright. She also considered paying off the Meadows family. There were hints that £10,000 would placate them, a vast sum, but one that she could afford, especially if it meant avoiding a trial and the shameful publicity that it would generate. The lawsuits probably were meant to bring her to an accommodation with the family who would content themselves with some of the money now and the promise of the rest of it after the duchess died. If that was so, the Meadows family had underestimated her anger and determination.

After some consideration, she decided that she would return immediately to England and answer the charge. This meant that she had to undergo a dangerous Alpine crossing in winter, when the threat of blizzards and avalanches was highest. It also meant physical agony for the duchess, who was suffering from a painful abscess in her side. When it burst early in the journey, she was forced to abandon her coach and be carried in a chair from Florence to Bologna. That she was willing to undertake such a journey is testament to how high the stakes had been raised by the criminal charges. She reached Calais by late March 1775 and met with her lawyers to craft her legal strategy. At that point she was afraid to return to England, fearful that when she disembarked she would be jailed without the possibility of bail until her trial was over.

Among the lawyers who met with her was William Murray, the Earl of Mansfield and Lord Chief Justice of England. He was the most respected lawyer in the country, the highest-ranking judge, and Elizabeth's personal friend. Mansfield assured her that she would not be imprisoned. He also advised her to obtain a writ of certorari, moving the case from the Middlesex Quarter Sessions to the Court of King's Bench. Wealthy criminal defendants often removed their cases to King's Bench, where the steep legal fees forced many plaintiffs to abandon their prosecutions. King's Bench was especially attractive to Elizabeth because it was presided over by Mansfield himself. She had every reason to expect that it would provide a more discreet and favorable hearing than the busy Middlesex Sessions.

Comforted by Mansfield's friendship and legal counsel, the duchess returned to England and appeared before him in the Court of King's Bench in Westminster Hall on 24 May. She posted bail and promised to answer the charges whenever a trial date was set. Her spirits were only boosted a month later when the prosecution in Chancery was abruptly dismissed by the Lord Chancellor. Upon hearing the news, she wrote to a friend that "the Court strongly and obviously convinced of my innocence, decided in my favour. This decree pronounced by the Lord Chancellor is so complete and so decisive that I find myself out of danger from the malice of my enemies from now on."[4] She was wrong on every count. The Lord Chancellor, Henry Bathurst, was not convinced of her innocence, and his decree did not put her out of danger from her enemies. Indeed, Bathurst himself was soon to become one of her most dangerous and intractable foes.

At this point, the duchess thought that her rank was going to be her salvation. She truly believed that although she might be the object of aristocratic ridicule in private, class solidarity counted for something, and she could rely on her peers to save her from the shameful designs of the Meadows family. When news of her criminal indictment first reached her in Italy, she expressed shock that "in a free country like ours . . . the testimony of its lowest subjects, which can be bought for a louis d'or can summon a person from Rome to London."[5] Since that time, the actions of Mansfield and Bathurst had seemed to confirm that her status as a duchess—the highest rank a woman could hold short of being a princess—would ultimately save her. The Meadows family, she implied, were buying testimony to fabricate a case against her. And they were proving to be annoyingly persistent, refusing to abandon the criminal case even though the civil judgment went against them. In an attempt to intimidate the Meadowses and (she thought) ensure the most favorable hearing possible, the duchess took a fateful step in November 1775. Betting that class solidarity would work to her advantage, she removed the criminal case from the friendly venue of the Court of King's Bench to the House of Lords. It was a step she would regret to her dying day.

Although Bathurst and Mansfield presided over the civil and criminal courts of the first instance, those courts were still part of the common law system in England. To outsiders, their work could be dauntingly inscrutable. Apart from the jargon that the lawyers used, technicalities and legal fictions abounded, turning even the simplest cases into confusing and dull affairs that could drag on for ages and bore even the most interested parties. These factors, along with the heavy hand that eighteenth-century judges were allowed in controlling debate and instructing juries, would have worked to the duchess's benefit. Indeed, they already had in Chancery.

But instead of taking comfort from her victory, she was emboldened by it. She knew that standing trial before a jury of her peers was her right as a British subject, and that as a duchess, she had the privilege of demanding that her jury be the peers of the realm, the House of Lords. The lords, she figured, would kill the prosecution, and she would avoid a criminal trial altogether.[6] But by making the trial the lords' business, she raised the stakes not just for the Meadows family, but also for every one of her jurors. Now the case ceased to be a private criminal prosecution and took on the character of a state affair. It was fraught with symbolic value that remained muted when it was in the law courts, but became pronounced when it became the business of the House of Lords. Class solidarity would, in fact, dictate how the lords would hear the case and rule on it, but that would mean protecting themselves, however hypocritical this might be, and throwing the duchess to the wolves.

At the duchess's request, Bathurst introduced a motion to remove her case from King's Bench to the House of Lords. She realized her mistake immediately. When the lords began the task of deciding how to try a peeress, something that had not been done for nearly two hundred years, two factions emerged, one led by Mansfield, the other by Bathurst. Mansfield remained the duchess's friend and advocate, but Bathurst was nothing of the sort. For the next six months, he would use every opportunity to craft the trial into a painful and humiliating affair for her. Even before the debate began, Bathurst was lobbying to have the case heard with the maximum publicity: a show trial in Westminster Hall. Shocked by this betrayal, the duchess complained to the Duke of Portland that she might become "a Publick Spectacle to Gratify the Vanity of Lord C[hancellor Bathurst]."[7]

The Earl of Mansfield was a tall, sedate, and genteel man. Although he was not born into the nobility (he was elevated to a peerage by

George III), he wore his title well. He had kind eyes, an aquiline nose, and a reserved air that permitted just a hint of an indulgent smile. He looked and acted every inch a patrician. Not only was he the most respected jurist of his day, but he was much respected for his personal probity and his skills as a debater. As a young man, he is said to have practiced public speaking in front of a mirror while being coached by his friend Alexander Pope.[8] One admirer characterizes Mansfield's powers of persuasion in almost musical terms:

> His lordship is certainly one of the greatest orators this country ever beheld. His powers of discrimination are equaled by none of his contemporaries . . . His judgement is no less sound upon many occasions, than his genius is extensive and penetrating: for as he pours forth at pleasure strains of the most bewitching and persuasive oratory; so his dexterity in bringing every thing offered on the other side within a narrow compass, and either entirely defeating its intended effect, or breaking its force, is hardly credible, but by such as have heard him.[9]

When the House of Lords took up the issue of the duchess's trial on 20 November 1775, he was the first to rise to the duchess's defense.

In the measured and reasonable tones that he always used, he admonished his colleagues to quash the prosecution altogether. The trial, he suggested, was a waste of time and money, a cruel exercise in futility:

> It may be worth your lordships' while to look forward to the consequences. It will be understood by all Europe, should your Lordships think proper to have the Duchess of Kingston tried in the Hall, a Lord High Steward appointed, and all the Formalities consequent on that Mode of Trial adopted: It will be understood, I say, that something very serious may be the Consequence of her possible Condemnation. But let us, my Lords, before we sanction all those Solemnities, look forward to the probable Consequences.[10]

Mansfield had a point. The trial was frivolous because even if Elizabeth was found to be a bigamist, she would suffer no penalty for her crime. The man she was accused of having married first, Augustus Hervey, was the Earl of Bristol. Therefore, the only legal consequence of a conviction would be a demotion from being Duchess of Kingston to being Countess of Bristol. She would still be a peeress of the realm, and that entitled her to plead benefit of clergy, an ancient loophole that exempted certain defendants—like peers and peeresses—from prosecution for their first felony. Mansfield reasonably asked the lords whether they should bother with a trial at all, "*Cui bono?* [Who profits?] What utility is to be obtained, suppose a conviction be the result? The lady makes your lordships a *curtsey*, and you return a *bow*."[11]

All this genuflection, suggested Mansfield, would be a silly conclusion to a frivolous trial. It would embarrass the duchess, certainly, but it would also be an embarrassment to the nation. At a time when there were concerns of more manifest importance, such as the rebellion in America, surely a trial like this should not "encroach on the national business."[12] He ended by moving that if a trial was deemed necessary, it should take place within the month and behind closed doors in the lords' parliamentary chamber.

The motion passed, and for the moment it looked as if Mansfield's vaunted powers of persuasion had spared the duchess a trial in Westminster. But there was a backlash immediately. A few days later, the *St. James's Chronicle* printed an angry letter denouncing Mansfield's speech and motion. Signed "A Friend to real Virtue," the writer was particularly upset with Mansfield's suggestion that the prosecution be quashed. The letter insisted that just because the duchess would escape punishment even if convicted, the trial must go on, reasoning that if she were really innocent, she would never consent to avoiding a trial. What had she to lose? A conviction would cost her nothing, but avoiding the trial would leave the charge of bigamy unresolved, something no innocent woman could tolerate.

When the lords took up the issue again on 8 December, Bathurst made his move. Conceding that the trial could produce no legal consequences for the duchess, Bathurst still maintained that bigamy was, in his opinion, "the blackest crime which came within the benefit of clergy, and the most grievous consequences attended the conviction."[13] He was referring, of course, to the shame that the conviction would produce. For that reason alone, he suggested, the house needed to reconsider its decision of just a few days ago. He introduced several issues for them to debate so that they could "give the greater dignity to their proceedings." This was code for making the trial into a public spectacle.

The questions he put forward gave every indication that he intended to humiliate the duchess: Should she be imprisoned for the duration of the trial? If so, he thought sending her to the Tower of London was most appropriate since that is where state prisoners were usually held. Should she be made to kneel before the jury? Should she be permitted to sit during the trial? (In the eighteenth century, it was customary for defendants to stand throughout the course of a trial. This is the origin of the phrase "to stand trial.") Should there be a formal procession of the lords into the court, accompanied by the Palace Guards "to add grater solemnity as well as dignity to the business?"

Bathurst lacked the grace and rhetoric of a Mansfield. He was a small, rail-thin man who spoke tersely and gained his points by political maneuvering, not by charming his audience. While Mansfield was the most respected legal mind of the day, Bathurst was frequently ridiculed as a vacant-minded, venal fool. His appointment as Lord Chancellor shocked the nation's political circles. According to one legal historian, during the eighteenth century, the Lord Chancellor was "for the first time unquestionably recognized as the head of law— not indeed in any precise sense of ministerial responsibility, but as the most respected and influential judge in the kingdom."[14] Naturally, this appointment went to men with great legal minds, but Bathurst was universally considered to have been an exception to that rule. Nevertheless, he proved a formidable opponent to Mansfield during the debate over the trial. At the end of his catalog of questions, he resorted to the oldest parliamentary move in the book: he suggested forming a committee to take up the issues. When the house agreed, Mansfield must have known there was trouble ahead.

The committee worked quickly and presented its recommendations to the house on 13 December. On the issue of imprisonment, they suggested that the duchess should be taken into the custody of the Gentleman Usher of the Black Rod before the trial. If it lasted longer than a day, she should be sent to the Tower of London. The duchess was stung anew by Bathurst's maneuvering, sarcastically later calling it "a friendly step of the Chancellor towards sending the dutchess to the Tower."[15] But she still had some true friends in the House of Lords. Mansfield rose immediately to her defense. The duchess, he said, was unwell, and her health might not withstand imprisonment, not even in the genteel apartments of the Tower. He suggested that they leave the entire issue open, waiting to see her state of health at the start of the trial before deciding. Since she was hardly a flight risk, the lords agreed.

But although Mansfield won the battle over imprisonment, he was losing the war over the venue. The newspapers reported, "In the Course of the Debate, it appeared to be the prevailing Opinion that Westminster-Hall is the properest Place for the Trial. It was urged that the Offense was of the deepest Dye; that Bigamy in some Cases might have worse Consequences than Murder; that therefore the Trial ought to be as public and notorious as possible."[16] Because the Duchess of Kingston's bigamy potentially complicated the succession of not one but two noble titles, her trial was one of those cases that was worse than murder. This was no private marital conflict, they said, it was a matter of state.

Bathurst ended debate by observing again that although the duchess would avoid the legal penalties of imprisonment and branding on the hand, she would suffer a terrible humiliation and would never "dare to show her head after such a solemn condemnation." Of course, she would suffer the same humiliation if acquitted, but that seemed not to matter. The day ended with a motion to take up the matter again on 14 December.

On 13 December, Mansfield's faction tried to preempt the debate. He argued that the committee had exceeded its charge by recommending that the trial be moved to Westminster Hall. But the Bathurst group countered that the committee had no choice. The Board of Works had advised them that the House of Lords was simply too small to contain "all the Attendants who must necessarily, and of right, appear at the trial, besides strangers."[17] This was specious reasoning: the size of the venue would dictate the grandeur of the proceedings, not vice versa. The Bathurst faction was presuming a full-blown state ceremony and then using that to justify moving the trial to Westminster Hall. Most worrisome, however, was the phrase "besides strangers." This meant spectators, and Westminster Hall could hold a lot of them.

When the lords reassembled on 14 December to settle the matter of venue, Mansfield and the duchess's other allies knew their cause was lost. But that did not stop them from trying. Lord Gower moved that they defer the issue until the state of the duchess's health stabilized. Her doctors had testified that she was too ill to stand trial now, so the proceedings had to be deferred anyway. Then Lord Sands tried to move the issue to a new committee. These delaying tactics were in vain. Lord Lyttelton put an end to the debate in a speech that indicated just how much contempt the Bathurst faction felt for the duchess:

> If, said his Lordship, there had been any particular Claim of Virtue and Modesty in the Lady, which might entitle her to particular indulgence from their lordships, he should then be inclined in Favour of a Lady, for once to depart from the usual Mode of trying Peers for capital Crimes in Westminster; but as no such Thing was pretended, he thought the Lady's Reputation required that if she was acquitted, her Innocence should be made as public as possible.[18]

This was like the devil preaching against sin. Lyttelton's reputation for immorality was well known, and when commenting on the proceedings in the House of Lords, Horace Walpole scoffed that Lyttelton was "as bashful as [the duchess] herself."[19] That Lyttelton could deliver such a potent attack is proof that the Duchess of Kingston had a very weak hand, indeed. In the eyes of most, she was neither virtuous nor modest, and so she deserved no special considerations because of her gender.

Now the duchess's situation looked truly desperate. If there was going to be a trial, it was going to be big. And that "if" was beginning to look more like a "when." On 22 December, her fate was sealed. In a last-ditch effort, her lawyers made an application to the Attorney General, Edward Thurloe, to stop the prosecution. But Thurloe refused to intervene, so now all that was left was to prepare a defense and steel herself for the crisis of a public trial in Westminster Hall.

How had it come to this? How had the class solidarity that she had relied on evaporated so quickly? And why was Bathurst leading the charge? As Lord Chancellor, he had ruled decisively in her favor in June, ending the civil suit. What had changed now to make him push for such a grand trial?

Perhaps Bathurst was motivated by the prospect of being named Lord High Steward and presiding over the trial. As Lord Chancellor of England, he was already a powerful man, but as Lord High Steward for the duration of the duchess's trial, he would truly be without peer. This ancient office was suspended in the reign of Henry III because it concentrated too much power over judicial, civil, and military affairs in one person. It was only temporarily reinstated for special occasions, such as the trial of a nobleman or woman. At the outset of the trial, the Lord High Steward would be handed a white staff, signifying his tenure as Lord High Steward; at the conclusion, he would break it across his knee, voluntarily relinquishing his great authority.

Several weeks after Bathurst prevailed in persuading the lords to move the trial to Westminster Hall, he was named Lord High Steward. He kissed King George III's hand at the king's levee on 9 February in gratitude. In early April, he received the official commission, described in the newspapers as being "engrossed with Letters of Gold, and the Skin finely adorned round the Edges with the King's Arms curiously coloured, and different Kinds of Foliage and Fruit."[20] These formalities were meant to impress upon the world the seriousness of Bathurst's commission, but they also glossed over the fact that Bathurst had spent months doing all he could to craft the duchess's trial into a process that could only end in her conviction and utter disgrace.

Anyone following the newspaper reports of the trial preparations knew that Bathurst was leading the effort to make the trial as embarrassing as possible for the Duchess of Kingston. And some doubted Bathurst's high-minded motives. Was he acting as a defender of public virtue and the established order, or did he have other, more private reasons for his campaign against the duchess? Some suggested that money was his real aim. As Lord High Steward, he was due to receive £1000 per day. By making the trial so public, he raised the stakes for everyone involved, thereby ensuring it would not be a speedy matter; rather, it would take at least a week, considerably enriching him with each passing day. He quickly answered these charges, suggesting his salary was being inflated. He pointed out that the High Steward for Lord Ferrers's murder trial in 1760 earned just £1000 even though it lasted three days.

If not money, then perhaps personal animus motivated him. An early biographer of the duchess suggested that he was taking advantage of his position to settle a long-standing grudge against her. According to this source, Bathurst had once sought to buy a valuable piece of Crown land at Hyde Park Corner, but he wished to do so anonymously, so he had the land grant made out in the name of his mistress, a Mrs. Gilbert. However, he then neglected to assign the grant to himself before he began building a new house on it. When Mrs. Gilbert shared this secret with her close friend, the Duchess of Kingston, the latter advised her to "Keep in with him, let him complete [the house], and then you may take possession; it will be your own . . . he will bleed freely."[21] The house in question is better known today as Apsley House (Bathurst was also Baron Apsley), where the Wellington Museum is now housed. The story of Mrs. Gilbert and the land grant may be apocryphal, but the Lord High Steward was certainly no friend to the lady on whom he was to sit in judgment.

Bathurst's motives might be guessed at, but they did not explain why a majority of the rest of the peers agreed to make the trial a state occasion. If convicted, the duchess would not be branded on the hand and imprisoned, the standard punishment. She would not even lose her inheritance, for the Duke of Kingston took care to write his will in such a way that would allow Elizabeth to retain control of his estate during her lifetime even if she were proven not to have been his legal wife. Knowing all this, why would the House of Lords bother with the trial at all? The North American empire was, after all, in need of their attention. Lieutenant General Howe and his troops were in the process of being driven from Boston by George Washington's army. In Canada, Governor Carleton was also under siege in Quebec City from a rebel force led by Benedict Arnold. With such matters to attend to, why did the House of Lords think it worthwhile to devote six months of debate and planning to a bigamy trial that served no legal purpose?

The answer to these questions is that the importance of Elizabeth's trial was symbolic, not legal. She was a scapegoat for the sexual indiscretions of the upper class at a time when they needed such a victim. It was an exercise in hypocrisy, and nothing proved this more clearly than the fact that among her jurors would be the Duke of Cumberland. He was the king's brother, and in 1770 he was tried in the Court of King's Bench for having "criminal conversation" with Lady Grosvenor. Mansfield presided as judge. As Lord Chief Justice, he had heard a great many of these "crim, con." cases in his career—rich and noble husbands suing the lovers of their adulterous wives for monetary damages. But none had been as embarrassing as the Duke of Cumberland's. During the course of the trial, eyewitness testimony revealed that not only had the duke made a pander of his valet, a shocking impropriety because he was, in essence, putting himself in the power of a servant, but he had also disguised himself as "one 'squire Morgan, who was a little foolish in his mind" so that he could visit Lady Grosvenor incognito.[22] And if that were not embarrassing enough, his love letters to Lady Grosvenor, which were intercepted and copied by her husband, were read aloud in court and the details of their being caught in bed together were revealed with relish. The result of all these revelations is best summed up by an anonymous poet, who writes:

> To Greatness born, but fated to be mean,
> In public laugh'd at, and despis'd unseen;
> Spur'd on by Passion, and by Folly led,
> A Heart all flutter, and a thoughtless Head;
> The growing Subject of keen Ridicule,
> A Knave to Women, and to Knaves a Fool.[23]

As this quotation demonstrates, Cumberland's sexual crime was compounded by his disregard for his own exalted rank.

The Cumberland affair shocked and amused the nation, and it ushered in a decade of obsessive interest in, and vilification of, upper-class sexual misbehavior. Newspapers and magazines began reporting the details of adultery trials in greater detail than ever before. The trial transcripts became a popular form of "soft-core" pornography.[24] For Cumberland and the royal family, the trial was a disaster. The duke was forced to pay £10,000 in damages to Lord Grosvenor and the royal family did what it could to limit the public relations damage. The Lord

Chamberlain forbade any reference to the affair on the public stage, which was under his strict control, but the press was free, and so readers were treated to a flood of trial reports about the case, including transcriptions of all the love letters. The next year Cumberland married Ann Horton, an attractive young widow who was better known for her long eyelashes than her discretion. The king considered the match "a disgrace to the whole family."[25] He held out no hope that with matrimony might come maturity, and the Duke and Duchess of Cumberland lived down to his expectations.

The hypocrisy of the process against the Duchess of Kingston was not confined to her noble jury. Among the lawyers who would prosecute the duchess was Edward Thurloe, the attorney general who had refused to halt the prosecution in December. Like Bathurst, Thurloe enjoyed neither the rhetorical polish nor the reputation for moral probity that Mansfield did. One commentator described him this way:

> His voice is harsh, his manner uncouth, his assertions made generally without any great regard to the unities of time, place, or probability. His arguments frequently wild, desultory, and incoherent. His deductions, when closely pressed, illogical; and his attacks on his adversaries, and their friends, coarse, vulgar, and illiberal, though generally humorous, shrewd, and *pointedly severe*.[26]

In terms of style and substance, Thurloe was Mansfield's opposite and he promised to be a caustic and unpredictable opponent.

If Thurloe's professional reputation was "pretty notorious," as some claimed, his personal reputation was even worse. A few years earlier, he was featured in the "Tête à Tête" column in the fashionable *Town and Country Magazine*, a regular feature that retailed the sex lives of the rich and famous to a prurient reading public. There was plenty to reveal about the sexual exploits of the "Amorous Advocate," as the magazine called him, but the piece focused mainly on his current affair with a coffeehouse barmaid called "The Temple Toast." It explained how he seduced and impregnated her, removing her to Dulwich for the lying in. His bastard child died soon after birth, and Thurloe then moved the "Temple Toast" back to London, where she could receive the obstetric care she required. The magazine thought she deserved a marriage proposal, but Thurloe disagreed.[27] Instead, he moved on to new conquests, as a critical poem explains:

> Thurloe, great master in seduction's wiles,
> With art, damn'd art, the simple maid beguiles.
> The spoils obtain'd, he throws the conquest by,

Each grace, each beauty, fades before his eye;
Another conquest fires his daring mind,
And leaves no traces of the last behind.[28]

This sort of criticism did little to reduce his effectiveness in either the courtroom or the bedroom. And it did nothing to soften the tone he was going to use with the duchess.

By the time her trial began, the Duchess of Kingston knew better than to hope for anything short of abusive treatment. She was nearly incapacitated by the prospect of being made a spectacle for the amusement and scorn of the very people whose acceptance she craved the most, the peers and peeresses of England. She had spent her life scrambling in any way she could to rise from her impoverished lower gentry roots to the upper branches of the British aristocracy. It is not an exaggeration to say that no eighteenth-century woman took more outlandish and daring steps to attain a title than Elizabeth did. To lose the title of duchess would be a social death that she could not suffer without a fight. And to have it taken from her in so public and pompous a manner by men she was proud to call her peers only made the process more painful. She knew that if the lords convicted her and she became Countess of Bristol, it would only clear the way for the Earl of Bristol to win speedy passage of a parliamentary divorce. When that happened, she would be plain Miss Chudleigh again. True, she would retain her inheritance from the Duke of Kingston no matter what the outcome, but that would be little comfort.

As the duchess stood in the prisoner's dock on the first day of her trial, it might have seemed to her that all of fashionable London was staring at her, but there were some notable exceptions. David Garrick, the great actor, chose not to attend. And the Duchess of Devonshire, leader of the fashionable "ton," was not there (although the papers assured readers that she was planning to attend on the second day). But the most conspicuous absence was the king's. The newspapers hinted that he was planning to attend the trial incognito, but that would have been impossible. He was a tall man whose bulging eyes and weak chin made him unmistakable in any disguise.

Although the king refused to dignify the trial with his presence, he secretly approved of it. As the House of Lords debated the trial preparations in December, the duchess wrote a desperate letter to the king, begging him to halt the prosecution. In it, she pointed out that Mansfield "has publicly declared that the law stands in my favour; and as he is the greatest judge and the ablest lawyer that this country ever boasted of, His Majesty is justified to all nations in not suffering an unhappy woman to die under persecutions."[29] She ended by asserting that the king would not

> suffer a peeress to be disgraced with a trial, and break the heart of a most faithful and loyal subject, when every mouth will speak his praise for having rescued me from the hands of my enemies without doing an injury to any mortal. Be persuaded, my Lord, that I will not dishonour your friendship, for good actions are the best contradiction to bad words.

By referring to herself as a "peeress," she was hoping to make the king act out of class solidarity, and by asserting a "friendship" with him, she was trying to suggest a cordial personal history. But she failed on both counts. George III never answered the letter and he refused to interfere with the trial.

The king was, in fact, privately glad that the trial was promising to become a spectacle. He and Queen Charlotte were no friends of the Duchess of Kingston. When she and the duke were presented at court a week after their marriage, the king and queen were duped into wearing their wedding favors, corsages distributed by the newlyweds to be worn in their honor. Like many courtiers, the king and queen seriously doubted the legality of the marriage, and by wearing the favors, they unwittingly gave the impression that they condoned the match. The queen, in particular, was furious with the duchess. When news of her legal troubles first broke, the queen expressed her pleasure that the duchess's infamy would at last be brought to light. On the first day of the trial, the queen was in attendance, representing the royal family despite being heavily pregnant.

In important ways, the Duke and Duchess of Kingston were the antithesis of the royal couple. George and Charlotte married for dynastic reasons, setting aside love in favor of the perceived interests of England. But once married, they settled into a highly contented domesticity. Well before Victoria and Albert, George III and Queen Charlotte sought to be a model couple for the nation to imitate. They had a great number of children, and their frugality was such that the public prints lampooned them as an old farm couple who dined on boiled eggs at a simple table. A French visitor to England during this period said that if "any king ever deserved the love of his people, it is George III. He leads, at his rural seat near Richmond (a seat much inferior in magnificence and lustre to that of many noblemen) a life of the most regular simplicity; which he divides entirely between the queen and his books."[30]

The Duke and Duchess of Kingston cut a different figure. Although the duke was a modest man, he was fabulously rich and he spent his treasure on his acquisitive mistress, who later became his wife. At the time of their marriage, she was reputed to have owned more jewels than any other woman in England. Unlike the king, the duke lived his life for pleasure, not participating much in the political life of the nation, as might be expected from one of his rank and wealth.

While the duke was alive, class solidarity meant that neither the king nor anyone else would challenge the marriage, but after he died few cared to stand in the way of a thorough disgracing of her Grace of Kingston.

But what had brought the duchess to the point of begging her sovereign to save her from being put on trial before the nation and the world? What had she done to make herself so vulnerable to the charge of bigamy? She had, after all, married the Duke of Kingston in London by special license of the archbishop of Canterbury, not exactly an anonymous match in a country parish. If she was, in fact, a bigamist, how could this very public marriage have occurred? Where was her supposed first husband and why did he not intervene?

Marriage in eighteenth-century England was frequently a slipshod and random business, not at all like the idealized image of a happy couple standing at the church door under the benevolent approval of parents and priest. The strict rules established by the Church of England for marrying were observed more in the breach than in the practice. More often, people improvised ceremonies both in and out of church, with and without a priest's or parent's sanction. The system permitted innovation and manipulation of marriage practices, and few people exploited the opportunities it offered more than the woman who became Duchess of Kingston.

CHAPTER 2

THE CLANDESTINE MARRIAGE

Of Elizabeth Chudleigh's two weddings, the first was by far the more romantic. It took place under cover of darkness, late on a summer night in a remote family chapel in the Hampshire countryside. She was twenty-three, the groom was twenty, still a minor in the eyes of the law. Later in life, she claimed that it was all "such a scrambling shabby business" and "so much incomplete" that she doubted whether the ceremony constituted a legal wedding at all.[1] But that was the cynical voice of age speaking about an event that had proved to be a disastrously bad decision. The wedding was rushed and secret, but to the young couple those elements only added to the excitement of a clandestine marriage, a secret love match that defied social conventions and the desires of their parents, but one that was perfectly legal—and binding.

The marriage can only have been a love match because by any rational measure, it made no sense at all. Just five months before the marriage, Elizabeth was named Maid of Honour to the Princess of Wales. This coveted position put her at the center of fashionable life in London and it provided the handsome salary of £200 per year, which promised financial stability to Elizabeth and her widowed mother. But to keep the job, she had to remain a maid, literally an unmarried woman who still possesses her maidenhead. There were no Matrons of Honour at court. What, apart from love, would cause her to do the one thing that could jeopardize the position that she and her mother relied on?

In the summer of 1744, Elizabeth was an extremely eligible young lady. She was vivacious, witty, and very attractive. She stood just over five feet tall but probably seemed taller because of her graceful deportment—throughout her life she was considered an accomplished dancer. Early portraits show her to have been slim as a young woman, and her skin was very fair, a quality much prized in those days. Long, thick auburn hair framed her soft features and delicate chin, making her face a perfect oval. But her most prominent feature was her eyes. They were a grayish-blue, topped by full, arched brows, and they give her an air of wry humor and confidence in virtually every existing portrait, from the 1740s to the 1780s. Certainly she could have found a husband at court who could marry her publicly and support her in style—if only she had waited.

Elizabeth went on to become thoroughly savvy and manipulative, but in the summer of 1744 she was a young woman just entering the exalted circles of London high society. She had virtually nothing in the way of an education and had spent her life up to this point in the company of her widowed mother. They lived mostly in London, taking in lodgers at one point, but while Elizabeth would have been used to the excitement of city life, that is no guarantee that she was worldly. By the summer of 1744, she had spent only a small part of one season at court before the beau monde left the heat of London for the countryside in late spring, not to return until the following autumn. Instead of being invited to the country home of another courtier or going to the expensive and fashionable retreats of Bath or Tunbridge Wells, Elizabeth went with her aunt, Mrs. Hanmer, to Lainston, a sleepy hamlet in the Hampshire countryside where her cousin, John Merrill, had a house. In a few years, she would be famous, the subject of court gossip and a number of engravings sold in the public print shops. But for now, she had to content herself with visiting her cousin for the summer in the company of her aunt.

Although one of Elizabeth's biographers calls Lainston a "harmonious addition to the landscape," this is damning the place with faint praise.[2] It must have seemed a dull and lonely exile from the court life that Elizabeth had just gotten a taste of. She would have been primed to view it this way by scores of poems and plays that ridiculed the rural life. John Merrill's big, old-fashioned house at Lainston, populated by Elizabeth and her aunt, sounds remarkably like the sort of countryside exile described by Harriet, the spirited heroine of Sir George Etherege's Restoration comedy, *The Man of Mode*. Testing her lover's resolve, Harriet dares him to quit London and follow her into the country:

> To a great rambling lone house, that looks as it were not inhabited,
> the family's so small; there you'll find my mother, an old lame aunt,

and myself, sir, perched up on chairs at a distance in a large parlour; sitting moping like three or four melancholy birds . . . pity me, who am going to that sad place. Methinks I hear the hateful noise of rooks already—kaw, kaw, kaw—there's music in the worst cry in London![3]

The only thing missing in Elizabeth's case was her mother, who evidently stayed in London that summer, foolishly trusting Elizabeth to the care of her aunt.

To break the tedium, there were the Winchester Races, an annual event that briefly brought the fashionable world to nearby Winchester every June for three days of racing, dancing, and (inevitably) flirting. It was there that Elizabeth met Augustus John Hervey. Before two months passed, they were married.

Hervey was a naval lieutenant with a smooth tongue and an impressive pedigree, but no fortune. He was the second son of John, Lord Hervey, and grandson to the Earl of Bristol. As a second son, he would not inherit the family title. Upon the old man's death, the title would go to his father and then to his older brother, George. Because of the law of primogeniture, only the eldest sons of the English aristocracy inherited the family title and estates. Younger brothers could only hope to inherit the title if their older male siblings died before having any male heirs. Because both his father and his elder brother, who was just three years older than Augustus, stood between him and the title, becoming the Earl of Bristol seemed a remote prospect. So like many younger brothers of noble families, he chose to pursue a genteel profession

When he was just twelve years old, he joined the navy as a midshipman and was promoted to lieutenant within a year. He was probably tutored at home as a boy, but his real education came in the service, where he had spent eight years before meeting Elizabeth Chudleigh in the summer of 1744. As a result, he would have seemed older, more worldly than the average twenty-year-old, and his years at sea provided him with good stories to impress young ladies like Elizabeth. He was also handsome. An early portrait shows him cutting a dashing figure in his naval uniform of blue coat and breeches, silver waistcoat, and black tricorner hat, all edged with gilded silk. He looks young and self-assured, the sort of man who would stand out in the crowd at the Winchester Races.

Hervey was also attractive to Elizabeth because he represented a sort of dangerous glamor. His father, Lord Hervey, was the most famous courtier of the eighteenth century. A member of George II's Privy Council, Lord Hervey enjoyed a lavish pension of £1000 per year from the king, and he was particularly doted on by the queen, who loved him better than her own son. But then the Hanoverians never did care much for their own children. The queen once famously said that the Prince of Wales was "the greatest ass, the greatest liar, the greatest canaille, and the greatest beast in the world and I heartily wish he was out of it."[4] In his place, she favored Lord Hervey.

Lord Hervey was an effeminate man who, despite having fathered eight children, is generally considered to have been bisexual and to have had a penchant for wearing makeup. He was best known for having gotten on the wrong side of Alexander Pope, the greatest poet of the era, who called him, "this Bug with gilded wings, / This painted Child of Dirt that stinks and stings."[5]

And Augustus's father had other, more powerful and bitter enemies than Pope. Chief among them was William Pulteney, the Earl of Bath. Pulteney was a political opponent of Lord Hervey, and the rancor between them was so great that it culminated in a sword fight that took place in the Green Park in January of 1731. While both men were wounded, Hervey escaped death only because Pulteney slipped when charging at his opponent, ready to run him through. At that point, their seconds intervened and put an end to the duel. Pulteney was a friend of Elizabeth's father, and it was through his patronage that she became a Maid of Honour in the spring of 1744. Even though Lord Hervey had died the previous year, being courted by his son must have seemed like an illicit romance to Elizabeth: with some exaggeration, she could imagine them as star-crossed lovers whose powerful emotions overcame the dynastic rivalry of their families.

Exactly how the lovers met and how their courtship progressed is a mystery. The only hints come from the testimony of a servant who was called on to prove their marriage more than thirty years later in the bigamy trial. Evidently they had some social dinners together at John Merrill's house, no doubt in the company of Elizabeth's cousin and aunt. And Augustus took the Lainston group to tour the *Victory,* a naval ship docked at Portsmouth. But apart from this, nothing is known for certain.

These blanks can be filled in by looking at how other couples of a similar social status romanced each other. While it is natural to think that young people nowadays are more promiscuous than their eighteenth-century ancestors, young adults in the 1740s enjoyed great freedom to pursue sex and romance. Premarital sex was very common throughout the period, and while this originally stopped short of intercourse, by the 1740s that had begun to change. Out-of-wedlock births and pregnant brides were becoming much more common, especially among the poor. For Elizabeth's and Augustus's social class, however, the taboo against intercourse was probably strong enough to make them wait until after the marriage ceremony. In 1747, one young man whose fiancée made him wait until after the wedding complained that the wedding day was being put off by people who were "not so eager for a f—k as I am."[6] But if he was anything like his peers, he probably enjoyed everything short of a "f—k" before going to the altar.

If Elizabeth and Augustus were anything like other young couples of their social class, they took advantage of opportunities to meet each other frequently, and often privately. The well-documented courtship of Arthur Collier and Elizabeth Moseley provides some clues to how these relationships progressed.[7] Collier and Moseley met in Bath in 1746 and pursued a romance behind the backs of Moseley's elderly parents. Arthur was a civil lawyer at Doctor's Commons, the church court in London where, years later, he would play a key role in helping Elizabeth to disavow her marriage to Augustus. But in the 1740s, he was a young lawyer looking for a wife. Moseley was allowed to attend the public rooms and walks of Bath without her parents, which was not unusual, and this gave her the opportunity to meet and begin a romance with Collier. They soon began meeting privately in the Abbey and for walks in the fields around town. Before long, they met at his lodgings, although he took care that his landlady be on hand to chaperone their dates. But within the year, they were secretly engaged and meeting in each other's bedrooms (he would visit Moseley after her parents went to bed), and they were almost certainly engaging in some form of sex.

Because they had made a promise to each other that they would marry, Moseley, like most women of the time, felt free to have sex with Collier. She was certainly more audacious than most of her peers by sneaking him into her bedroom while her parents were asleep in the same house, but she was not unusually promiscuous. Many courting couples engaged in what was known as "bundling;" that is, they stayed up all night together—sometimes with parental consent—and engaged in mild forms of sexual activity. This could go on for months before marriage and it was something done by all social classes except the very highest nobility. The fact is that many young men and women of the eighteenth century expected some physical intimacy with a prospective spouse before the wedding night, and in that regard, they were not much different from young couples today.

We may think of the age as a decorous time when imperious fathers dictated marriage choices to their children, but in fact many young people expected to have time to get to know their future mates—and to approve of them. More than a few wished to take the initiative of mate selection rather than let their parents arrange things for them. For those who lacked the nerve or the opportunity to approach the opposite sex the way Collier and Moseley did, there was the Ladies' and Gentlemen's Register Offices. This was the world's first dating service, begun in London in 1750. In a pamphlet advertising the business, the proprietors explained that many men were too busy and women too shy to initiate successful courtships without a little help.[8] Their remedy was to create two offices where single people could go (one for men, the other for women) and enter their names and personal information into a book. Registration cost a guinea, which was a lot of money, an indication that this service was intended only for people of some means. Indeed, the personal information form that participants filled out asked only for their age, height, complexion (a code word for physical attractiveness), and fortune. Obviously, if you did not have a fortune, you were not going to seem very attractive to the other clients. The proprietors said that they got the idea from a friend who found his wife by placing an advertisement in the *Daily Advertiser*, which may have been the first successful personal ad ever.

To preserve decency, the rules of the service were strict. There were two separate offices for men and women. Only men were allowed to inspect the women's register and vice versa, and the register books were open for inspection only during limited hours two days a week. If a client saw a likely prospect, he or she could arrange for a date at the cost of another guinea (to be split by the couple). They would meet between seven and nine at night in a private room in a "respectable" public house, similar to a modern-day restaurant. The lady could be veiled, if she chose, and the man could not compel her to show her face. The man had to check his sword at the door with a guard, who stood outside. And just to make sure nothing indecent occurred inside, the door to the room did not have a lock.

The elaborate rules were necessary because this was a highly unusual business venture and the proprietors had to take pains to advertise their respectability. But its existence shows that single people in eighteenth-century England—women as well as men—expected a surprising degree of freedom in initiating and pursuing courtships.

Not everyone was pleased by this state of affairs. One writer thundered against parents and guardians who let their children go on unchaperoned dates:

> I have often been astonished how any man or woman could be so great a stranger to the knowledge of life, as to trust a young daughter

or niece, in a little *bawdy vehicle*, along with a rampant rake, able and ready to ravish a whole boarding school, and to take a country jaunt ten or twenty miles distant, when every jolt on the road, not only gives a kind of titillation, but even the situation itself affords the most favourable opportunity, for a fellow to rob a girl of all that's dear to her. What dreadful execution hath been done by *play, masquerade* and *opera* tickets, especially, when in the hands of skilful *engineers*. Not to mention dancing-bouts and other merry-makings, which seldom prove such innocent recreations, as some weak and credulous parents imagine them to be.[9]

Almost every social occasion gave couples the opportunity to get to know each other better—in more ways than one.

Elizabeth and Augustus may have lacked operas and masquerades, but they met in the romantic atmosphere of the Winchester Races. Horse races in the eighteenth century were exciting affairs with more than a hint of danger and intrigue to them. They were not decorous, like the races at Ascot have become; rather, they were raucous and a bit chaotic. Rich and poor, nobles and commoners mingled in an atmosphere that celebrated high stakes and bold strokes. Describing a visit to such a race, a French tourist to England explained that "a considerable number of the inhabitants of London, and all the neighboring gentry" were on hand for race day. And the horses ran right through the center of it all: "There are neither lists nor barriers at these races; the horses run in the midst of the crowd, who leaves only a space sufficient for them to pass through; at the same time, encouraging them by gestures and loud shouts."[10] It was in this charged atmosphere that Elizabeth and Augustus first laid eyes on each other.

A servant testified that they had some chaperoned dates after the races, and judging from the standards of the day, they probably had several unchaperoned ones as well. Given the haste with which they jumped into bed the minute their wedding was over, it is safe to assume that they were not entirely chaste during their courtship but that they saved full intercourse for the night of 4 August.

That night, John Merrill and his aunt, Mrs. Hanmer, went out for dinner, leaving the servants with nothing to do, presumably encouraging them to be out of the house. Merrill employed a butler, a maid, two housemaids, a laundrymaid, and a kitchenmaid, none of whom knew that there was to be a marriage in the house that night. Only Ann Cradock, Mrs. Hanmer's maid, was trusted with the secret, and it must have been exciting for her. Like a busy hoyden in an eighteenth-century comedy, she served the lovers a candlelight dinner out of the housekeeper's room before their secret wedding. Sadly, when testifying to these events three decades later, she mentioned no details except that both Elizabeth and Augustus were fond of greengages, the sweet, firm, green plums that ripen at that time of year. It is tempting to think of the lovers seducing each other from across the table, eating greengages like forbidden fruit and laughing with excitement over the bold step they were about to take.

Merrill and Mrs. Hanmer returned to the house around 8:00 p.m., and sometime after dark, the party discreetly made their way through the garden to a small family chapel at the back of the house. There they were met by Mr. Mountenay, a friend and houseguest of Merrill, and the Reverend Thomas Amis, the Rector of Lainston. The parish that Amis served was a small one: it consisted only of Merrill's house. If the parish was not really a parish, the chapel that everyone assembled in was not a really a church; rather it was a private devotional space intended for family use only.

The marriage that took place in that chapel was almost a parody of the Church of England's "Form of Solemnization of Matrimony." *The Book of Common Prayer* is very explicit about the conditions under which a marriage can take place and about the liturgy for holy matrimony. As Reverend Amis strained to read the service in the dim light of that chapel, illuminated only by a single wax candle stuck in the crown of Mountenay's hat, he must have been conscious of how far this ceremony deviated from the prescribed form. And yet Ann Cradock later swore that the marriage was done according to the liturgy in *The Book of Common Prayer*.

The service began by noting that no marriage is to take place until the banns have been published on three successive Sundays or holy days. The banns were a declaration of a couple's intention to marry, and "publishing" them normally took the form of the rector naming the couple in church, instructing the congregation: "If any of you know the cause or just impediment, why these two persons should not be joined together in holy Matrimony, ye are to declare it."[11] In an age before reliable public-record keeping, the banns served to publicize a wedding beforehand and thereby allow disapproving parents or even current spouses to prevent the wedding.

When Reverend Amis began the ceremony, his first words must have produced either some embarrassment or guilty amusement from the party:

> Dearly beloved, we are gathered together here in the sight of God, and in the face of this Congregation, to join together this Man and this

Woman in holy Matrimony, which is an honourable estate instituted
of God in the time of mans innocency, signifying unto us the mystical
union that is betwixt Christ and his Church . . . and therefore is not
to be enterprized, nor taken in hand unadvisedly, lightly, or wantonly,
to satisfy mens carnal lusts and appetites, like brute beasts, that have
no understanding; but reverently, discreetly, advisedly, soberly, and in
the fear of God.

After summarizing the reasons for which marriage was instituted
(to produce children, prevent fornication, and provide mutual comfort), the rector ended with an injunction to the "congregation" at
Lainston that "if any man can shew any just cause why they may not
lawfully be joined together, let him now speak, or else hereafter for
ever hold his peace." Merrill and Mountenay held their peace, as did
Ann Cradock and Mrs. Hanmer, who sat in the aisle, apart from the
huddled group, perhaps in protest of a marriage that she thought was
being undertaken too unadvisedly, lightly, and wantonly.

After hearing no reason why Augustus and Elizabeth should not
be married, Reverend Amis led them in their vows and in placing a
ring on Elizabeth's hand, invoked the example of Isaac and Rebecca,
who "lived faithfully together, so these Persons may surely perform
and keep the vow and covenant betwixt them made (whereof this
Ring given and received is a token and pledge) and may ever remain
in perfect love and peace together, and live according to thy laws,
through Jesus Christ our Lord. *Amen.*" Then he turned to the table
(Anglican houses of worship feature a plain table instead of an altar)
and sang either Psalm 67 or 128, both of which praise the procreation
of children. After that the couple kneeled before the priest and he led
the small group in the Lord's Prayer and a prayer for children. We can
safely assume that Reverend Amis omitted the optional sermon that
follows these prayers and proceeded on to the biblical lessons about
the proper duties of husbands and wives.

The woman's duty according to Saint Peter is particularly rich in
regard to Elizabeth and Augustus's marriage. If Reverend Amis chose
this passage, he would have told Elizabeth, "Saint Peter doth also
instruct you very well, thus saying, Ye wives be in subjection to your
own husbands." And he would have warned her to take more care of
her soul than of her body:

Let it not be that outward adorning of plaiting the hair, and of wearing of gold, or of putting on of apparel; but let it be the hidden man
of the heart, in that which is not corruptible, even the ornament of a
meek and quiet spirit, which is in the sight of God great price. For after

this manner in the old time, the holy women also who trusted in God, adorned themselves, being in subjection unto their own husbands; even as Sara obeyed Abraham, calling him lord.

If she heard these words that evening, Elizabeth soon forgot them. Her marriage with Augustus Hervey would be characterized by the reverse of these pious instructions, just as the clandestine ceremony violated many of the precepts of the Church of England.

After instructing Elizabeth in her duty, Reverend Amis dismissed the party and the wedding was over. Elizabeth Chudleigh was now Elizabeth Hervey. The whole ceremony would have lasted no more than ten minutes. Ann Cradock was sent out of the chapel first to make sure that the garden was clear, allowing the rest to sneak from the chapel to the house undetected by the servants, who were not in on the secret. It must have been thrilling for the maid to be involved in such a secretive business, especially because she was chosen from all the servants to play such a key role.

This was not a "shabby scrambling" wedding, as Elizabeth later characterized it; rather, it was highly dramatic and self-consciously theatrical. The whole thing reads like a scene from a play: two young lovers defying the wishes of their families and the expectations of society so that love can conquer all. The private candlelight dinner beforehand and the excitement of the secret ceremony in a darkened chapel added to the romance. The poignancy of late summer and the fact that Augustus was days away from shipping off for a tour of duty made everything about the marriage seem urgent and passionate.

One of Elizabeth's biographers calls the wedding a "particularly wretched" affair, but to the bride and groom it probably seemed dangerous, exciting, and illicit.[12] In their eyes, the secret wedding was a heroic act in defense of true love. This was not a dynastic union arranged by parents to further family interests, nor was it a desperate decision to avoid being an old maid. People in the eighteenth century tended to marry in their late twenties, which means that Elizabeth and Augustus, both very attractive and young, must have been convinced that they had found the love of their lives and that they needed to marry before family and social pressures could pull them apart.

This is not hard to understand. First loves can seem desperately serious, even without the added urgency of raging hormones, which was clearly a factor in Elizabeth and Augustus's case. Ann Cradock testified that they went directly from the chapel to the bedroom. She saw them bedded herself, and Merrill and Mountenay were probably on hand as well. It was customary to see the couple to the marriage bed and throw the bride's stocking across the bed, symbolizing fertility. Mrs. Hanmer was not there for the bedding, and when she learned that the newlyweds were already in bed, she charged into the room and insisted that they get up. One can imagine their reluctance, but they obeyed her—at least until she went to sleep for the evening. Then they leapt right back into bed together and remained there all night, until awoken by Ann the next morning. They spent the next several nights together and, a few days later, were awoken one last time by Ann, who came to make sure that Augustus was up in time to leave for Portsmouth, where he was to board ship for a tour of duty in the Caribbean. Elizabeth wept inconsolably as Augustus tore himself away from the marriage bed and left love for duty.

It is hard to believe Elizabeth's claim, that she doubted whether the marriage to Augustus Hervey was legal or not. Nothing about her actions after the wedding suggests that she doubted its validity, and the particular care that she took to be married by a priest, in a chapel, and according to the Church of England's marriage rite meant that there really could be no doubt about the legality of the marriage. A historian of eighteenth-century marriage has recently observed that "as a result of the glaring defects in the laws of marriage, very large numbers of perfectly respectable people in the seventeenth and early eighteenth centuries could never be quite sure whether they were married or not."[13] But Elizabeth and Augustus were not among that number. To their later regret, the elaborate nature of their secret wedding was proof that they took pains to have a ceremony that would result in a legally binding marriage.

To be married in England in 1744, they did not need to go to such lengths. They could have stood in the house in Lainston and in the presence of any two adults—Ann Cradock and the kitchenmaid would have sufficed—and declared their union. Elizabeth could have said, "Augustus, I am your wife," to which he would reply, "Elizabeth, I am your husband." And that would do it. In the eyes of God, they would be man and wife, and their declaration before two witnesses would be defensible in the local Consistory Court (or church court), which had jurisdiction over the validity of marriages.[14]

Or they might have been more tentative and made their vows in the future tense before two witnesses, "Augustus, I *will be* your wife," and "Elizabeth, I *will be* your husband." This would have contracted them to each other in a legally binding way until they were married in a ceremony in church—or at least until they had sex. When a future tense vow of marriage existed, the marriage became valid when the couple had sexual intercourse. So Elizabeth and Augustus could have made a future tense promise of marriage in front of the servants, jumped into bed, been awoken by Ann Cradock in the morning, and (presuming there was some physical evidence of intercourse during the night) they would be man and wife.

This may sound far-fetched, but it is perfectly true, as Thomas, Lord Onslow, learned to his dismay a decade earlier. Onslow was taken with the charms of someone he later referred to only as "A. M—d," an Irish beauty who traveled to London in search of a rich husband. He pursued her for months, but she kept putting him off by telling him that he may have her "as soon as I pleased, after the Man in Black has said Grace."[15] What Onslow wanted was (as Willmore puts it in Aphra Behn's play *The Rover*) the honey of matrimony without the sting, so while he never absolutely refused marriage, he evaded the issue, hoping that he could convince her to have sex without getting married.

One evening he found himself at a party with the young lady and a group of her friends. They decided to play *Questions and Commands*, which Onslow happily agreed to, "imagining it would give me an Opportunity of taking several little Liberties, which I durst not have presumed to take at another time" (5). As it turned out, Onslow was being set up by the Irish lady. The leader of the game, called the Queen, ordered him to take the lady's hand and repeat with her the words of the Church of England marriage rite. He did so "very willingly, having a Mind to see how far the Jest wou'd be carry'd, and whether I might not obtain that of her in a Frolick, for which I had long sued in vain" (5). Once they had repeated the marriage vows, Onslow said, "Madam, . . . you know what follows Matrimony." The ladies answered, "Ay, ay, answered the Ladies, there is a Bed in the next Room, let us put the Bride to Bed, and then throw the Stocking" (5). But they were prevented by Queen, who insisted that Onslow must make some marriage settlement upon his lady, "then let him consummate as soon as he will." Onslow pleaded with her, "Lord, Madam . . . Your Majesty does not consider that we ought to have a Lawyer here to draw the Writings, which would take up a great deal of Time, and I hope you would not oppose my Happiness so much as to delay it so long, now the Lady is willing" (5). The Queen laughed at this and said that he ought to settle at last £500 per annum on her and give her a bond for £10,000 until formal articles could be drawn up. Onslow foolishly signed a note to that effect so that he could get into bed with the Irish beauty: "I hasten'd to her; they threw the Stocking, and then left us to ourselves; *the Reader may guess the Rest*" (6).

While the reader might be able to guess the rest, Onslow failed
to. Miss "A. M—d" now began calling herself Lady Onslow and
she came after him, insisting that the mock ceremony constituted an
actual wedding and demanding her alimony of £10,000. Once word
of the sham marriage got out, Onslow became a laughing stock.
A ballad was published about the affair, called *The Mock-Marriage:
or, A Lady and no Lady* (1733). It ridiculed Onslow for being such
a dupe and anticipated that the lawyers in the church courts (called
"civilians") would be kept busy by the case:

> He marry'd in Haste, and repents it at Leisure,
> Having met with a Tartar, instead of a Treasure;
> And when 'tis too late does bewail the curs'd Seizure,
> > *Which No-body can deny, &c.*
> And now there is Work for Civilians cut out,
> A Tryal, so noted, you need never doubt,
> Will in Country and Town make a damnable Rout,
> > *Which No-body can deny, &c.*[16]

The affair was also the subject of a short musical piece called *The
Promised Marriage; or, the Disappointed Lady,* which was inserted at
the end of a play that season and dedicated to Onslow. The public
shame associated with this mock marriage was infuriating to Onslow,
but the legal demands should have come as no surprise to him.

Being tricked into a clandestine marriage while playing a parlor
game was very unusual, which is why Onslow's case aroused so much
publicity. But clandestine marriage itself was very common, and in
the 1730s and 1740s, its popularity was growing rapidly. For various
reasons, English men and women in the eighteenth century were
generally averse to public weddings. This was especially true of the
upper classes. For a society that was increasingly characterized by
conspicuous consumption and ostentatious display, this seems surprising. Perhaps the rich just wished to display themselves on their own
terms and in front of their own kind. Being forced by the church to
be a spectacle for the entire parish may have offended upper-class
sensibilities. Or maybe the widespread practice of premarital sex made
couples wary of publishing the banns and enduring three weeks of
ribbing about what they were doing at night. Whatever the reasons,
the novelist Fanny Burney spoke for her age when she confided to
her diary, "I don't suppose anything can be so dreadful as a publick
Wedding."[17] As a result private marriages were very popular, and not
just among the rich. For those with something to hide, like Elizabeth
and Augustus, privacy was not enough; they required secrecy.

Elizabeth's reason for secrecy was simple: if she married publicly, she would lose her job. Since Hervey had no fortune and since Elizabeth's mother relied on her income, she could not afford a public wedding or public knowledge of her marriage. She was not alone in keeping her marriage secret in order to keep her job. Apprentices were very fond of clandestine marriages because the terms of their apprenticeships stipulated that they remain single. If they married publicly, they would ruin their career prospects and drag their new spouses (and sometimes unborn children) down with them. The apprenticeship system frequently put young people into this bind because it allowed them unusual freedom from parental supervision at a young age, since virtually all apprentices lived in their masters' homes, which allowed them to socialize with other young people of the opposite sex. While this freedom might lead to sex and romance, the system technically made marriage impossible. Clandestine marriage was a way around the rules, and many young people, like Elizabeth Chudleigh, took advantage of it.

Why Elizabeth kept her mother in the dark is a mystery. Perhaps she felt thatHervey was an impressive enough catch for her mother to approve of the wedding after the fact. Or maybe she worried that the animosity between her patron, the Earl of Bath, and Augustus's father would turn Bath against her and her mother. It is also possible that she just did not care what her mother thought. Now that she was the breadwinner with an impressive job, Elizabeth might have felt that her mother had no place giving her advice about who she ought to marry. Mrs. Hanmer was uncomfortable with the wedding, but evidently not enough to let her sister know it was going to happen.

Augustus had family reasons for wanting to keep his wedding a secret. Although his father was dead and he was not the heir to the earldom of Bristol, he was still part of an important family. His grandfather almost certainly expected to be consulted about his choice of a marriage partner. When the match became common knowledge among the upper class a few years later, his brother wrote to him and said that if the rumors of his marriage were true, he would try to broker a reconciliation between Augustus and the old Earl, who was upset about the matter. His mother's reaction is not known, but since mothers were usually more deeply involved in the courtship and marriage decisions than fathers were, she must also have felt disappointed.

It would have been much worse if Augustus were first in the line of succession. Noble families sometimes took great steps to rescue their eldest sons from clandestine marriages. The most unusual case of this sort involved Sir John Rudd, a sixteen-year-old baronet who secretly married a servant girl named Lettice Vaughan in 1720.[18] When Rudd's family learned what he had done, they shipped him off to Holland. Five years later, the Rudd family executed an elaborate hoax, publishing an obituary for Sir John in the newspaper (he was still alive, living abroad) and going into mourning for him. His younger brother, an Oxford student, falsely assumed the title of baronet. Lettice believed the news of her husband's death and ended up marrying another man a few years later. The Rudd family, seizing this opportunity, revealed that Sir John was still living and then sued Lettice for adultery in the church courts. They won, and Sir John was able to obtain a parliamentary divorce on the grounds of his wife's adultery. It was a lengthy, expensive, and thoroughly mean process, but it shows the lengths to which at least one family would go to undo a foolish marriage.

How was it that marriage law and practices in England were so loose and prone to manipulation? This was partly owing to the state church—the sacred nature of the marriage bond led the Church of England to insist that the sole criterion necessary for two people to be married in the eyes of God and the church was mutual consent. If both freely chose to devote themselves to each other, if they were not too nearly related, and if neither was already married to another person, then no worldly power could stand in the way. Neither parliament nor parents could infringe on the "natural right" to choose a spouse.

The irony is that the Church of England came into existence because Henry VIII chafed under the pope's rule and broke from Rome so that he could marry and unmarry at will. The church he founded obviously took a more serious view of holy matrimony. But because England had broken away from the Catholic Church, the nation did not benefit from the updating of marriage laws that took place in the Council of Trent in 1563. Even Protestant nations in Continental Europe followed the Catholic Church's lead in banning clandestine marriages and in requiring parental consent for minors to marry. Only in England could two teenagers secretly tie the knot and be sure that it remained tied even after their parents found out: Romeo and Juliet would have been better off in Shakespeare's London than in his Verona.[19]

This is not to say that the Church of England had no rules about marriage. There were plenty of them; the church just did not enforce them effectively. To be married according to the rules, the couple had to have a wedding in the parish where one of them was a resident. The wedding was to take place between the "canonical hours" of 8:00 a.m. and noon. Marriages were discouraged during Lent. If the male was younger than fourteen or the female younger than twelve, they needed their parents' permission. A clergyman had to read the marriage rite from *The Book of Common Prayer*. And the banns had to be read on three successive Sundays prior to the marriage. For those who dreaded publicity, the banns could be waived by obtaining a license from a clergyman instead. These licenses ostensibly did the same thing as the banns, confirmed that both parties were eligible to be married. Finally, the marriage had to be entered into the parish register.

But all these rules aside, the church recognized the validity of marriages made in many other ways, so long as both parties consented to the match and were free to marry. This is why the mere espousal of marriage ("Augustus, I am your wife") constituted a legal marriage in England. These "spousal" matches were not uncommon in the seventeenth century, but by the time Elizabeth and Augustus decided to marry, their legal validity was being undermined in the church courts. Sometimes they were determined to constitute a marriage, sometimes not. To play it safe, most couples who chose to marry secretly did what Elizabeth and Augustus did: they approximated the regular marriage ceremony as best they could, given their need for speed and secrecy. This is why their ceremony took place in the chapel at Lainston and involved a clergyman, witnesses, and *The Book of Common Prayer*, and this is why it is unlikely that Elizabeth was telling the truth when she claimed that she felt uncertain about the marriage later.

For many couples, a romantic family chapel was not an option. Instead, they came in droves to the Fleet Prison in London where destitute clergymen had set up marriage shops, offering to marry all comers for a fee. This open violation of the church's rules made the parsons vulnerable to prosecution and a £100 fine, a vast sum for clergymen who commonly earned less than half that amount per year. But since they were already imprisoned for debt, the threat of a fine was no deterrent. If being married in a prison was too unpalatable, then a couple could go to one of several churches in London called "Peculiars," which were not subject to the rule of any bishop. Together with the Fleet, these London marriage shops did a thriving business, performing an astonishingly high number of marriages each year.

When these marriage shops were outlawed in the early eighteenth century, the business shifted to the Rules of the Fleet Prison, an area just outside the prison where convicts could obtain a license to live, escaping the squalor inside. Being outside the prison also presented the opportunity to advertise. The practice was so brazen that one writer complains of seeing signs on the street reading "Do you want a parson?" and "Will you be married?"[20] An estimate places the number of marriages done this way at nearly a fifth of all marriages in the entire nation.

By the 1740s, the situation was becoming a national scandal, and foreign visitors like Blanc were critical of the situation. In *Letters on the English and French Nations*, l'abée le Blanc had this to say about clandestine marriage in England:

> [England] is a country of liberty; and this liberty is stretched so far as to do silly things almost without incurring censure. Decorum is little respected, and vice is render'd familiar. Our laws have wisely provided all possible means to prevent children marrying without the consent of their parents; lest they should enter into engagements prejudicial to themselves, and dishonourable to their families. Youth is too blind, and too much abandoned to its passions, to discern its true interest. The laws of England are very different: they tend to favour even the most indecent marriages.[21]

One of George II's chaplains agreed. In 1750, the Reverend Henry Gally complained that "of late years indeed this pernicious Practice has been carried on with such a barefaced contempt of public authority, as cannot be accounted for but by its being practiced in a country, where liberty, even mistaken liberty, is the darling principle."[22]

Both men recognized one source of the problem: the ungovernable English citizenry's inclination to do what it liked with little interference from the state. England was a very loose, poorly policed society in the eighteenth century. London even lacked a metropolitan police force of any kind until the 1740s, when the novelist and magistrate, Henry Fielding, organized the "Bow Street Runners," a small force that operated out of his Bow Street office, near the piazza in Covent Garden.

Clandestine marriage became so widespread and was so generally tolerated because reform was consistently prevented by political turf battles. The House of Lords tried repeatedly to outlaw the practice because they worried that their children—especially their eldest sons—would be seduced into marriage by fortune hunters. But these reform measures were always voted down in the House of Commons, which was populated by ambitious men who either wanted to marry up themselves or who wanted their children to marry into the nobility. Henry Fox's elopement and secret wedding to Lady Georgiana Caroline Lennox in 1744 was the most scandalous example of this political logjam. Fox was a young member of parliament and Lady Caroline was the daughter of the powerful Duke of Richmond.

Their marriage was a famously happy one, but it never would have happened if men like Fox had not resisted changing the marriage laws in parliament.

The other opponent of change was the Church of England, which jealously guarded its legal jurisdiction over the validity of marriages. In theory, the church was opposed to state action regarding marriage because it was a holy bond that politicians should not tinker with. The lords wanted to control marriage for dynastic and financial reasons, and to the church, this was a perversion of the holy purposes of marriage. But in more practical terms, the church feared losing revenue and authority to the civil government in England. Selling marriage licenses so that the banns would not have to be published was a big business in the church. Many people who married clandestinely took the pains to purchase a license from the officiating clergyman. Reform of the laws threatened this lucrative source of revenue.

But the big reason why the church opposed change was because it threatened the church court system. These Consistory Courts were an ancient part of the legal system in England, along with the Common Law courts (which tried civil and criminal cases) and Equity courts (which tried financial cases). The church courts ruled on the validity of marriages and, therefore, they profited from the legal fees associated with clearing up the messes that the loose marriage system inevitably created. In other words, the church and Commons had a vested interest in the marriage system remaining chaotic and unstable while the House of Lords had a vested interest in cleaning things up. This messy situation of competing interests among the rulers of the church and state had existed for centuries and was a source of real annoyance to the lords. Elizabeth failed to realize the depth of this annoyance when she had her bigamy case removed to the House of Lords. By doing so, she gave the lords a spectacular opportunity to embarrass not just her, but also the antiquated church court system. She thought she was making a power play, but in fact, she made herself a pawn in a much larger institutional struggle.

In August 1744 major reform of marriage laws was still a decade away, so Elizabeth and Augustus, like thousands of lovers each year, took advantage of the freedoms unique to English men and women. Like the romantic heroes and heroines of countless eighteenth-century plays and novels, they threw caution to the wind and risked all for love. But they did not live happily ever after. It took less than two years for them to kick themselves, wondering what had possessed them in the summer of 1744. They were beginning to realize that while marriage in eighteenth-century England was an easy thing to get into, it was virtually impossible to get out of.

The Hon:ble Miss Chudley,

Unknown, after Reynolds. *The Honble. Miss Chudley.* Mezzotint, 38 × 26.3 cm, sheet. In *Horace Walpole and His World*, 4:129. Courtesy of The Lewis Walpole Library, Yale University

CHAPTER 3

MARRIAGE À LA MODE

At the end of Elizabeth and Augustus Hervey's brief honeymoon in Lainston, they parted company reluctantly. During the bigamy trial three decades later, Ann Cradock testified that she had the sad duty of waking the pair at five o'clock a few days after the wedding: "Entering the chamber, I found them both fast asleep; they were very sorry to take leave."[1] As Hervey left that morning, he sent Ann back inside to give Elizabeth "all the comfort I could which I accordingly did and found her in a flood of tears."

With Hervey's departure, the fleeting period of their marital bliss came to an end. Although they would meet secretly as man and wife over the next few years and even produce a child, the story of their marriage is an unhappy one. At the end of 1748, they separated as secretly as they had married, but whereas their marriage was legitimate, the separation was not. They remained married until Hervey's death in 1779, a few months after their thirty-fifth wedding anniversary.

Augustus Hervey was not alone in being released from an unhappy marriage only by death. Because divorce was illegal until 1857, English men and women of the eighteenth century regarded marriage as the most important decision of their lives, and not simply for reasons of wealth and class. The romantic novels and plays of the time frequently dealt with the making of a proper marriage, pitting the wishes of true lovers against the dictates of their stern parents, and almost always championing the cause of true love. Judging by the popular culture, marriage without love could only lead to trouble.

Hervey and Elizabeth parted sometime in early August 1744, but Hervey spent the next few months in port, not actually setting sail for his Caribbean tour of duty until the middle of November. Despite the delay, the couple seems not to have seen each other before his departure. He was second lieutenant on the *Cornwall*, the flagship of a small fleet sent to protect British traders from French and Spanish privateering in the Caribbean. The region had been the site of a low-intensity conflict since 1739 when the "War of Jenkins's Ear" began. This war got its unusual name from an incident in which Robert Jenkins, the British captain of the merchant ship *Rebecca*, had his ear cut off during a search of his ship by Spanish coast guards. Some doubted Jenkins's story, which allegedly took place eight years earlier, but war hawks trotted him around London and he was more than happy to display the severed remainder of his ear and tell his tale of Spanish cruelty. Despite the efforts of Sir Robert Walpole, the prime minister who had given the nation more than two decades of peace and prosperity, the sensation of Jenkins's ear led to a declaration of war. This small war ostensibly ended in 1742, but the much larger War of Austrian Succession had begun in 1740, pitting Britain against Spain and France and ensuring that the Caribbean remained a problem spot.

For navy men such as Hervey, war was a welcome state of affairs because it meant employment at full pay and the prospect of rich prizes. The risks of eighteenth-century naval combat were counterbalanced by the prospect of quick riches in the form of prize money. Any ship of an enemy nation was a potential "prize" that could be confiscated and sold along with its contents, the proceeds of the sale being split between the government and the sailors. As a second lieutenant on the *Cornwall*, Augustus stood to share one-eighth of any prize money with the other lieutenants and the master. Three years earlier he had served on a ship that took a prize, netting him £1500, a handsome sum that allowed him to live well and to impress young ladies such as Elizabeth Chudleigh. If he was to keep his new wife in any style, it was going to be with the help of future prize money.

But for Hervey, this was a frustrating tour of duty that mostly involved idling in Port Royal, Jamaica. In his journal, he complains that despite the state of hostilities with France and Spain, "we remained as idle in the harbour, as inactive as to the fleet, as had it been a profound peace, and only so many ships stationed there for their amusement."[2] In despair, he resigned his commission and set sail for England on 23 June 1746, arriving in London in mid-August. By Hervey's own reckoning, he was not worth more than £300 at this point, and his reliable income was a meager £50 annuity from his father's will. He badly needed to find either loans or a new naval commission, or both. Instead, he found unsettling news.

His older brother, George, told him that both he and his grand-father, the old Earl of Bristol, had heard rumors of Hervey's marriage to Elizabeth. Worse still, George said that when he approached Elizabeth with the rumor, she did not deny it. Assuming that they were married, George had gone to the cantankerous earl and persuaded him to receive Elizabeth into the family if Hervey confirmed the marriage. This was no small feat, given the old man's bad temper and self-righteousness, but it was not inducement enough to make Hervey own up to the marriage—not even privately to his brother. Before he said anything, he wanted to meet his wife and find out where their relationship stood. Why had she told his brother of the marriage? Was it still a general secret? Had she been faithful to him? Were they still in love? Unfortunately, Hervey's journal, which begins in 1746, makes no mention of any letters passing between him and Elizabeth during his time at sea, so the state of their relationship is a mystery to us, as, indeed, it may have been to him. Shocked by George's inquiries, Augustus said nothing, and his brother let the matter drop, "perceiving I was unwilling to keep up that topic, which indeed I had no reason to continue till I knew how things were and were likely to be."[3]

Hervey got an inkling of how things were a few days later when he visited Lady Townshend, an old family friend, on 22 August. Apart from filling him in on news of his family, Lady Townshend also made "some innuendos that were sufficient to ground some sort of suspicions in me that Miss Chudleigh's conduct was not altogether as Vestal-like as I might have wished."[4] In his journal, Hervey claims that he did not take alarm at these innuendos, choosing instead to wait until he met Elizabeth, whom he had not seen for two years. Then he could judge her conduct for himself. But when she failed to turn up in London after his arrival, he began to grow uneasy and to suspect "there might be something in the reports I had heard of her conduct."

Elizabeth had spent the past two years ingratiating herself to the Prince and Princess of Wales, quickly becoming a favorite among the Maids of Honour. They held court at Leicester House, a modest mansion in Leicester Square that the prince leased in 1743. Because it only had six bedrooms, Elizabeth and the other Maids of Honour actually lived in rented lodgings nearby. This unusual arrangement was the result of the prince and princess being evicted from St. James's Palace by George II. The king and queen were furious with Prince Frederick for secretly spiriting Augusta away from Hampton Court on the night she went into labor so that she could give birth to their first child in St. James's Palace. Queen Caroline, convinced that Frederick was impotent, doubted his paternity and insisted on being present at the delivery. When a messenger finally awoke her with the news of the princess' labor, she cried out, "My God, my nightgown!" One of her ladies-in-waiting replied, "Your nightgown, madam, and your coaches too. The Princess is at St. James's."[5]

When the king sent the prince and princess packing, he forbade them to remove any furniture from St. James's, not even trunks to pack their clothing in, sputtering, "A basket is good enough for them." When Frederick leased Leicester House, it was déjà vu all over again, for his father had leased the same house when he was evicted from St. James's Palace by George I. But Frederick's years in Leicester House were different. Unlike his surly, graceless father, he was an amiable man who enjoyed company, patronized the arts, and (oddest of all for a Hanoverian) loved his children intensely. He possessed that most-valued eighteenth-century attribute, good nature, and preferred an easy familiarity to stifling decorum. At St. James's, George II's court life was characterized by tedious card parties and the king's embarrassingly vicious outbursts against the queen. Leicester House, by contrast, was famous for its conviviality.

As a Maid of Honour, Elizabeth attended upon a princess who was just two years older than she. Augusta was noted for her moral probity throughout her life; Horace Walpole referred to her as "Lady Prudence" in his letters. But her Maids of honour enjoyed a different reputation. Elizabeth's secret aside, these were among the most eligible unmarried women in London, constantly on display and mixing in the best company. When the princess went to the opera or to a masquerade, they went with her. When a dinner party at Leicester House lasted until five in the morning, as was often the case, they were part of the company. Elizabeth's appointment transformed her life from one of humble obscurity to one of prestige and privilege. Like the other Maids of Honour, her love life became the object of public speculation, and like them she enjoyed the social whirl of court life and the unique freedoms it offered her as an (ostensibly) unmarried young woman. Because Elizabeth's family background was less illustrious than that of many of the other maids, mixing with flirtatious young dukes and earls must have been a heady experience during these early years. Collectively, the Leicester House Maids of Honour were known for their beauty and their high spirits, which were a little too high for some. One of their coach drivers reportedly told his son that he could do what he wished with his life so long as he did not marry a Maid of Honour.

In the summer of 1746, Augustus Hervey may have been wishing that his father had given him the same advice. If Elizabeth's absence in Devonshire led him to doubt her fidelity to their marriage bed (such as it was), it also seems to have prompted him to stray from it himself. As he was a handsome young man without employment and the company of a wife, he says that it was "not surprising I got hold of some things." These "things" were two Italian opera singers, Signora Galli and Signora Campioni. Because the latter was being kept by Count Hasslang, the imperial ambassador, her favors cost Augustus nothing, so he chose to "stick to her" (44).

These were far from Hervey's last extramarital affairs. Over the next several years he would accrue a huge number of lovers in his many ports of call, earning him the sobriquet "the English Casanova." But the sexual double standard was strong, and what he found "not surprising," even natural, in his own conduct was troubling when it came to his wife's.

The two were finally reunited on 16 October, when Elizabeth returned to London and sent for Hervey to meet her secretly at her aunt Hanmer's house. The reunion was testy. Elizabeth complained that he should have traveled to Devonshire to see her, which was not a very reasonable complaint when one considers that he had just made a nine-week journey across the Atlantic. But the argument was not very serious. As Hervey explains, "Being both very young, this little quarrel passed off, nor did we let it break in on our pleasures. We often met at Mrs. Hanmer's (who was not in Town) about midnight, and passed together quite uninterrupted till 4 or 5 in the morning, and this continued whilst I remained in Town" (44).

Apart from their secret meetings, Elizabeth and Hervey saw very little of each other. One of her biographers paints a picture of Hervey at this time as a disgruntled stalker, turning up at every opportunity to spoil Elizabeth's fun, but the truth is that Hervey was the one who was avoiding Elizabeth, not the other way around. He explains, "I very seldom met her at any public place, as I avoided it, having been told some secrets by many people." Just what these secrets were is left vague, but they had something to do with Elizabeth "being much more taken up with her pleasures, with the Court and with particular connections than she was with our attachment" (44). This is a reference to Elizabeth's affair with the Duke of Hamilton.

James, the sixth Duke of Hamilton, was one of the most eligible bachelors in London that summer. He was handsome and very well connected (his great-aunt was the Prince of Wales's powerful mistress), and at twenty-one, he had just come into his inheritance. But he was also a fool. A Scot, he flirted with Jacobitism at the very time that the Jacobite army invaded Britain through Scotland and made its daring plunge toward London in the spring of 1745, only to be turned back at the bloody battle of Culloden. Jacobitism had a strong romantic pull for many in England (including Augustus Hervey's mother) but it was a hopeless cause, and adhering to it demonstrated a stout heart but a soft head. When Hamilton came to London in August 1746, he was there partly to plead for the lives of some of the captured rebel lords (who were hanged anyway) and partly to court Elizabeth Chudleigh.

Like almost everyone else in fashionable circles, Hamilton was unaware that Elizabeth was actually Mrs. Augustus Hervey. When Elizabeth is mentioned in letters and diaries dating from these early years of the marriage, there is no indication that her secret had become common knowledge among the fashionable set. Elizabeth may have performed her conjugal duties with Hervey under cover of darkness, but in the light of day and under the eyes of the court, she was returning Hamilton's attention and favors. Yet Hervey not only ignored this behavior, he also paid off Elizabeth's debts (contracting debts of his own to do so) and gave her an onyx watch set with diamonds. As her husband, he was legally obligated to pay her debts, but since the marriage was secret, his doing so seems quite generous, especially given the shaky state of their relationship.

Perhaps he paid her debts as a way to salve his conscience. Judging from a partially deleted diary entry, Hervey continued his affair with Signora Campioni even after Elizabeth returned to town. He seems to have spent one of his final nights in town in bed with the singer, and he gave her a parting gift of a diamond ring.

All this largesse was made possible by loans Hervey contracted from family members and bankers. He was able to obtain the loans on the promise of future prize money because he had recently been named Master and Commander of the *Porcupine*, a sloop soon bound for duty in the Leeward Islands. With this command came the courtesy title of "captain" and the promise of at least a quarter share of any prizes taken.

Hervey took his leave of Elizabeth and London and set sail from Deptford on 17 November 1746. Before the *Porcupine* made its way into the Channel, however, he had received letters from Elizabeth's aunt, Mrs. Hanmer, who complained to him about her niece frequently receiving the Duke of Hamilton, presumably at Mrs. Hanmer's house, where she had received Hervey's midnight visits for the past month. Alarmed by this, he sent a parting letter to Elizabeth reprimanding her for carrying on with Hamilton.

Hervey was not gone long. After less than a month at sea, the *Porcupine* had managed to take a troublesome French pirate ship as a prize, a bit of good fortune that netted Hervey £149. Upon bringing the prize to Plymouth on Christmas Day 1746, Hervey received even more good news: Admiral John Byng had just promoted him to the rank of post-captain and ordered him to join the Mediterranean fleet aboard the *Princessa*. Now he was a captain in earnest and bound for a tour of duty in the prize-rich Mediterranean. If his personal life was disordered, his professional life seemed to be looking up.

As the *Princessa* was being fitted up for the tour, Hervey passed his time in London from January to May 1747. In his journal, he says that he spent every evening that he was in London with Elizabeth, but he says nothing about their meeting in public and he complains of being tired of London and anxious to set sail. This is understandable. As long as he had no fortune, he could not publicly own up to his marriage and establish a life for himself and Elizabeth in London. The prospect of a properly furnished house in a respectable part of town, a coach and horses, and a decent amount of disposable income certainly seemed closer now that he was a captain headed for the Mediterranean; but for the moment, he was still virtually broke and could pay Elizabeth's ever-mounting debts only by contracting more debts of his own. As he explains in his journal, at this period he was "trusting to the chance of war and success of prizes to be able to repay it all" (44).

He saw Elizabeth with an almost marital regularity during this period, but all was not well. He complains that he "still found there was some underhand game going on that I did not comprehend. I found great mysteries, great falseness, and every mark of what I wholly disapproved" (48). He may have been suspicious, but what Hervey did not comprehend is how far Elizabeth's affair with the Duke of Hamilton had progressed. And judging from his journal entries, he seems to have been unaware that she was also being courted by Peregrine Bertie, the third Duke of Ancaster. Ancaster was a thirty-two-year-old widower from a wealthy and very powerful family, making him in some ways a better catch than Hamilton. In a letter written many years later, Elizabeth explains that there was "not one but two Dukedoms . . . at my option; but I have no regret on that Subject for neither of the two would have made me happy."[6] Despite this airy assertion, her refusal of their proposals must have been mystifying to them and painful to her. Already she had cause to regret her rash marriage.

Instead of becoming a duchess at the age of twenty-six (around the average age that English women got married in those days), Elizabeth was the secret wife of the Honorable Captain Hervey. And before he left for the Mediterranean in June 1747, they both knew that she was well on her way to becoming the mother of his first child. When he left for his tour of duty, she excused herself from court and retreated to Chelsea for her lying-in.

This was certainly not a planned pregnancy. Sensational accounts of Elizabeth's life attribute it to marital rape: Hervey, inflamed with jealousy, locked her in a room at her mother's house and attacked her. But the only evidence of this is that Elizabeth is reported to have said that she and Hervey had "an assignation with a vengeance" during this period.[7] But if they did spend every night together, as Hervey claims in his journal, then they were probably having sex regularly and taking measures to avoid a pregnancy.

However Elizabeth may have felt about her marriage, her husband, and her future prospects, there is no suggestion that she tried to terminate the pregnancy, even though it threatened to expose her marriage and cost her the title of Maid of Honour. Quite the opposite. Elizabeth arranged to leave London for Chelsea, where she grew up. More surprisingly, she seems to have told the Prince and Princess of Wales about her pregnancy because the *accoucher*, or male midwife, who attended at the baby's birth was none other than Caesar Hawkins, surgeon to the Prince of Wales. Revealing the pregnancy also probably required that she reveal her marriage to Hervey. This might have been a risky move, but Elizabeth was a special favorite of the princess, who stood by her in this time of crisis and generally helped to quell unflattering rumors about her. Clearly, the expectation was that Elizabeth would leave the child in someone else's care and resume her position as Maid of Honour—at least until Hervey returned from sea and they could decide the future of their marriage.

Lying-in at Chelsea would give Elizabeth privacy from the prying eyes at court, and it would keep her mother from learning of the pregnancy. For while the Princess of Wales knew that Elizabeth was expecting, her mother was ignorant about both her marriage and the pregnancy. Chelsea was a safe place, for as Ann Cradock explained years later, Mrs. Chudleigh could never bring herself to visit Chelsea since it was where her husband and son were buried. Before long, it would be where her grandson was buried, too.

There was no question that the pregnancy and birth had to be hushed up, but to face this prospect without the support of a husband or mother must have been difficult for Elizabeth. Indeed, this was the second great rite of passage that she would undergo secretly and, inevitably, shamefully. If marriage was said to mark the passage from girlhood to womanhood, pregnancy and childbirth changed one from a woman into a mother. Elizabeth gained little satisfaction from the first change, and she would derive even less from the second.

Leaving London for the country is the opposite of what a fine lady in eighteenth-century England normally did. For women of rank, childbirth—especially the birth of the first child—was a very public affair. When the woman was well into her final trimester, she was taken on a bumpy coach ride to her London townhouse for the lying-in. The London papers announced the arrival of fashionable women, complete with liveried entourages, to town for the "Great Event," as it was often called. The street in front of the house was covered in straw to muffle the sound of horse hooves and rolling carriages, and partly to announce to the world that birth was imminent. When the baby was born, a blue or pink silk ribbon was tied around the door-knocker, proclaiming the birth and gender to the world. One historian of eighteenth-century childbirth notes that the laying of straw was "rather awkwardly reminiscent of the manger."[8] In Elizabeth's case, this would have been a bitterly ironic association since she was still ostensibly a *Maid* of Honour.

Elizabeth's exile to Chelsea was a far cry from the fashionable lying-in that a London lady would experience, but it was not as dreary as the process some in her situation underwent. A generation later, Elizabeth's niece by marriage, Lady Elizabeth Foster, became pregnant by the Duke of Devonshire, the husband of her best friend, Georgiana, the famous Duchess of Devonshire. Lady Elizabeth took pains to remain away from England and to have the baby secretly. Well into her third trimester, she traveled a hundred miles by open boat to Salerno with her brother, Lord Hervey. Her physical discomfort was compounded by the shame of going disguised as the wife of her servant and the mistress of her own brother. She described the situation this way:

> My heart almost failed me as I traversed the little streets, narrow and dim, leaning on my servant and compelled to pass myself off as his wife and the light o' love of my lord and brother. With no woman at hand, encumbered by the weight of my child, enfeebled by long ill health, fearing every person I met, and, for the first time in my life, wishing only to hide myself, I arrived at last.[9]

Lady Elizabeth gave birth to a baby girl after a few weeks and had to leave the baby with strangers to make an arduous journey to visit her brother in Naples just six days after the birth so that her absence would not be commented on. Her servant discreetly provided flannels to absorb any milk that leaked from her breasts, and after a few weeks he fetched the baby girl.

The example of Lady Elizabeth shows how dire the need for secrecy was in such cases and how humiliating the ordeal could be for the unlucky woman. At least Elizabeth Chudleigh remained in England, lying-in near her girlhood home, perhaps in the company of women she knew from her early years. We know for certain that she was attended at the birth by Caesar Hawkins, who later testified to the fact, adding "I was desired to attend, with a view and purpose that I might be a witness to the birth of that child."[10] Evidently with Hervey away at sea and their marriage in bad shape, Elizabeth wanted a reputable witness on hand to confirm the birth in the event that the child's legitimacy might one day be questioned in court.

The birth took place sometime in or around October 1747, and was as much a secret as her wedding three years earlier. Elizabeth was delivered of a boy, whom she named Augustus Henry Hervey who was baptized by his great-uncle, the Reverend Henry Aston, on 2 November at St. Luke's in London. Having Aston perform the baptism was one more way to ensure the legitimacy of young Augustus and to keep the birth a secret. But in the end, concerns about legitimacy and secrecy were unnecessary. The child grew sick very soon after birth and required the attention of Caesar Hawkins again, but not even the prince's surgeon could help. Augustus Henry died in January 1748 and was buried in Chelsea, not far from his grandfather and uncle.

The story of the baby's birth and death is usually dealt with lightly by Elizabeth's biographers. In a typical passage, one writer says that she "gave birth to a son, who conveniently died soon after his christening."[11] Another speculates that Elizabeth "was heartbroken, but possibly also a little relieved."[12] When Elizabeth returned to court the following spring, she evidently tried to quell the rumors of her having given birth by making light of them herself. One anecdote has her asking the witty Lord Chesterfield, "Do you know, my lord, that the world says I have had twins?" Chesterfield replied, "Does it? For my part, I make a point of believing only half of what it says."[13]

Elizabeth's social situation did not permit for postpartum depression, which strikes more than half of new mothers nowadays, and probably did then. If Elizabeth suffered from melancholy, she had to hide it behind a facade of genteel repartee and vivacity. She sought to cover up the birth (and perhaps to recover her health) by going to Bath in late December. Elizabeth Montagu wrote to a friend on

28 December 1747: "We have here Miss Chudleigh, and a very pretty daughter of Lord Chief Justice [Willes]; but they are ill provided with beaus, so that it is scarce worth their while to be so handsome."[14] That the pious Mrs. Montagu could be so totally unaware of Elizabeth's pregnancy is testament to Elizabeth's fortitude and powers of deception: just two months earlier she had given birth; the traditional recovery period for women of her social class would have ended about a month prior to her arrival in Bath. Yet Mrs. Montagu calls her pretty and pities her having no beaus to seduce.

Elizabeth's jollity and her visit to Bath aside, the birth and death of her child must have taken a mental and physical toll. The demand for secrecy fell particularly hard on Elizabeth, who was given to great emotional outbursts and fainting spells throughout her life. She has left no record of her feelings about the birth and death of her son, but as one historian has noted, "maternal loss might be no less agonizing for the absence of hysterical expression."[15] It is true that babies were much more prone to illness and death in the Georgian age than they are now, but the notion that parents did not develop strong emotional bonds to young babies is not supported by the firsthand accounts that survive. For instance, George III sired fifteen children, but when he lost his favorite son he said, "There will be no Heaven for me if Octavius is not there."[16]

Elizabeth obviously had an emotional investment in her baby, judging from the money she spent in preparation for his birth: she borrowed £100 from her aunt Hanmer to buy baby things. It is sad to think of Elizabeth, like any young mother, doing all that she could to prepare her layette; and it is sad to think that this was the only time she ever gave birth; but it is sadder still to consider that she had virtually nobody to confide in during this crisis. Ann Cradock, Mrs. Hanmer's servant, testified that Elizabeth came to her "in great grief" and told her that the baby, who looked "like Mr. Hervey," was dead.[17] His father never saw him.

While Elizabeth was in Chelsea undergoing the ordeal of giving birth to and then burying young Augustus, his namesake was making money and making love all over the Mediterranean. Between Lisbon, Leghorn (Livorno), and Florence, Hervey bedded six different women, opera singers and minor noblewomen among them, and spent lavishly in the process. He was able to do so because of the number of prizes he was taking as captain of the *Princessa*. These prizes enabled him to pay back the debts he had accrued on his last visit to London. Despite his philandering, he wasted no time in writing to Elizabeth, offering to pay her debts too. He sent £200 to her in August 1747, and a further £500 in May 1748, along with a promise that he would pay all her debts if she would let him know what they were. (Frustratingly, although his journal scrupulously records the amount of money he sent her, there is no mention of the baby at all.) This generosity was either an attempt on his part to salve a conscience troubled by his multiple adulteries or it was a genuine attempt to fulfill his duties in a marriage that he still hoped would work and someday become public. If Hervey's journal can be trusted, he claims that his inclinations at this time were "still to please her if I could" (44).

CHAPTER 4

THE SIREN'S VOICE

After the death of her baby, Elizabeth was a changed person. For the past three and a half years, she had lived at court, concealing a secret marriage, removed herself from court to have a secret baby, and twice refused the chance to become a duchess, for secret reasons. She was certainly a sadder person as 1748 began, but she was not in any position to let that show. Her only option was to keep her marriage a secret until Hervey's return from the Mediterranean, whenever that might be, and then see what they could do about it. At this point neither of them seemed ardently committed to the match, but the marriage had not yet broken down altogether. Within the year, it would.

Having recovered from the trauma of the previous autumn—or perhaps to help her recover from its lingering emotional and physical effects—Elizabeth went to Tunbridge Wells in the summer of 1748. There she threw herself into the fashionable spa's social mix with gusto, becoming the center of attention. Prior to this time, she had not aroused a great deal of public comment, but from this point until her death, she became one of the most talked-about women in Britain.

She was the undisputed center of attention at Tunbridge Wells that summer. Located thirty-five miles southeast of London, it was the favorite summer resort for the rich and famous during the age of George II. Unlike Bath, a spa town that was a thriving city in its own right, Tunbridge was a more intimate, less grand spot that flourished during the warm summer months and then was boarded up when fall came around. Like Bath, Tunbridge Wells was presided over by Richard "Beau" Nash, the pompous and foppish master of ceremonies who posted rules to ensure that polite society remained polite when it came together for dinners, balls, and gambling. To prevent dueling, men were prohibited from wearing swords. To limit the effects of gossiping, Nash warned "That all Whisperers of Lies and Scandal be taken for their Authors." In an age that prided itself on its refinement and good manners, Beau Nash was a sort of genial public censor, and in 1748, at the age of eighty, he was still in his heyday.

A guidebook from the time lays out a typical day in the life of the fashionable visitor. Many people woke early, appearing on the parade between 7:00 and 8:00 a.m. to drink the supposedly curative mineral waters or just walk for an hour or two. Gentlemen treated the ladies to breakfast in the tea rooms in small groups or gave a grand public breakfast "to the whole company without exception; which, in fine weather, is often given under the trees upon the open walk, and attended with music the whole time."[1] After breakfast the company went to chapel for morning service, took an airing in their coaches, or gathered in the bookshops or coffeehouses. After prayers, the public walks (now known as the Pantiles) became crowded with people, shopping, conversing, and gawking. The evenings were devoted to dancing and gambling in the public rooms, all of which ended strictly at eleven o'clock.

The relatively early end of the social day was a nod to the resort's ostensible function: it was a place for the sick to take the waters and convalesce. But in reality, it was a pleasure ground where minuets, horse races, and celebrity gazing took center stage. It was also a place to pursue romance. The same guidebook explains that the atmosphere was conducive to "the commerce of love and gallantry, and all those delightful sensations arising from a free intercourse between the sexes." Only in the coffeehouses were the sexes segregated (women were not allowed). Everywhere else, the sexes danced, gambled, ate, and flirted from sunrise to sunset.

For Elizabeth Montagu, Tunbridge was an "epitome of the world" where the classes, like the sexes, mingled happily in amusing fashion:

> Tunbridge seems the parliament of the world, where every country and every rank has its representative; we have Jews of every tribe, and Christian people of all nations and conditions. Next to some German, whose noble blood might entitle him to be Grand Master of Malta, sits a pin-maker's wife from Smock-alley; pick-pockets, who are come to the top of their profession, play with noble dukes at brag. (3. 90)

Although normally censorious, Mrs. Montagu let her guard down at Tunbridge and even enjoyed the flirting and outrageous dress of some of the younger women. Writing of the outrageous dress of

Lady Parker's daughters, she says, "One of the ladies looks like a state bed running upon castors; she has robbed the valance and tester of a bed for a trimming" (3. 93).

Elizabeth Chudleigh shone in this atmosphere. Along with the young dukes Hamilton and Ancaster, she also stole the hearts of some older, more famous men. Among those on hand to enjoy her charms this summer were some of the most famous names of the eighteenth century: David Garrick, the great actor; Samuel Johnson, the literary lion; William Pitt, the Prime Minister; Samuel Richardson, the sentimental novelist; and, of course, Beau Nash. A print entitled "The Remarkable Characters who were at Tunbridge Wells with Richardson in 1748" shows them all on the promenade, Elizabeth in the center, flanked by Pitt the Elder and Beau Nash.

Richardson was at the Wells for his health. Despite complaining that the fashionable young women were too forward and bold, he left behind this memorable testament to Elizabeth's charms:

> She is a lively, sweet-tempered, gay, self-admired, and, not altogether without reason, generally admired lady—She moved not without crowds after her. She smiled at everyone. Everyone smiled before they saw her, when they heard she was on the Walk. She played, she lost, she won—all with equal good humour.[2]

According to Richardson, Colley Cibber, the poet laureate and retired actor, was Elizabeth's chief admirer. He tells of Cibber promenading with Beau Nash every day on the lookout for Elizabeth, who was fifty years his junior.

Because of the great disparity in their ages, Richardson explains that Elizabeth's young admirers were not jealous of Cibber; rather, they often called him to her side to enjoy their repartee:

> She said pretty things—for she was Miss Chudleigh. He said pretty things—for he was Mr. Cibber; and all the company, men and women, seemed to think they had an interest in what was said, and were half as well pleased as if they had said the sprightly things themselves; and mighty well contented they were to be second-hand repeaters of the pretty things.[3]

Elizabeth and the company at Tunbridge Wells were enjoying themselves more than usual that summer, for the War of Austrian Succession was over and, although the peace had not been formalized in a treaty, the resolution was a happy one for Britain. It was during the public celebrations of the peace treaty the following spring that Elizabeth Chudleigh became a household name. But for the moment, she enjoyed being the toast of Tunbridge Wells, and no doubt did her best to forget the events of the previous autumn.

In the Mediterranean, Captain Augustus Hervey got his orders to return home along with the rest of the fleet. He arrived in London in December 1748 a very rich man, having earned some £9,000 in prizes during his tour of duty. His fortunes changed also with the death of his uncle Henry Aston, the man who had christened (and perhaps buried) young Augustus the year before. This meant that Hervey's older brother, George, was now next in line to become the Earl of Bristol, a title he inherited in 1751. Because George was unmarried, Augustus was now just two lives away from the earldom of Bristol.

This change in fortunes emboldened Hervey to deal with Elizabeth in a much different manner than he had the last time they were together. Instead of turning a blind eye to her affairs, he claims in his journal that he was now "very much displeased" with her. It seems that the gossipy Mrs. Hanmer had been telling tales on Elizabeth, inflaming Hervey's anger. Unfortunately, the journal is vague about the particulars, but Hervey was so put out by what he heard that it made him "mind several little circumstances that perhaps would otherwise have passed with me as nothing" (76).

Hervey's new wealth and the nearer prospect of becoming an earl had an effect on Elizabeth, too. Rather than staying away from Hervey, as she did the last time, she came to him with a list of her debts. By the end of December, he had paid out £800 to her creditors, but whereas before he claimed that he paid her debts in the hopes of pleasing her, now he did so in order to get rid of her. When he returned to London after a new year's visit to Admiral Byng at Finchly, he says that he "had come to some *éclairissments* as to Miss Chudleigh's conduct with her, which she did not approve" (77).

With his aunt, Mrs. Aston, serving as a witness, Hervey met with Elizabeth on 25 January 1749. He told her that he had resolved to go abroad and that from that day onward, he washed his hands of her and their marriage forever.

Obviously this was wishful thinking: Hervey was never able to extricate himself from his rash marriage to Elizabeth five years earlier. But the balance of power in their relationship had shifted so dramatically in his favor that he felt confident in sending her packing at the beginning of 1749. For her, this was unwelcome news. Although she may have been indifferent to Hervey by this time, she was the sort of person greatly attracted to money and status. For the first time in their marriage, he now had the former and was in a fair way to gaining the latter. Her reaction to his surprising declaration is not known, but she must have been greatly unsettled by it, not least because she relied on his money and goodwill to pay her considerable (and mounting) debts.

To make matters worse, his unilateral declaration that they were now separated was legally a moot point. She was still his wife, no matter what he said. Informal separations of the sort Hervey announced that day were not uncommon, but since English law gave the man almost total authority over his wife and her earnings, separations of this sort left women in a precarious legal position.[4] Elizabeth was now dependent on the goodwill of a husband who obviously disliked her. Hervey could return and demand her fidelity to their marriage bed at any time, and he could make their marriage public if he wished to. This was something Elizabeth would never do because it would cost her the position at court that was now her only means of support.

She must also have known that it was her own aunt who had betrayed her affairs to Hervey. What stake Mrs. Hanmer had in all this is unclear, but Hervey specifically records in his journal that the break came because he was upset by "many things I heard of Miss Chudleigh's conduct, especially from her own relations" (76). Her sexual indiscretions must have grown more audacious at this time, scandalizing even her own relatives. With Hervey's repudiation, Elizabeth might have swallowed her pride and attempted to win him back by charming him and promising to mend her ways. But that was not in her nature. Throughout her life she never made apologies for her conduct and was totally averse to moderation. She kept her eyes on the main chance and made no excuse for that. Characteristically, as 1749 began she threw caution to the wind and went from being the notable toast of Tunbridge Wells to being one of the most notorious women of her age.

With the announcement of the Peace of Aix-la-Chapelle in April 1749, the War of Austrian Succession came to a formal end, and London celebrated lavishly. Writing to a friend from Strawberry Hill, his Twickenham retreat, Horace Walpole told of the "torrent of diversions" that London was experiencing to celebrate the peace, including three weeks of masquerade parties. The first was held at Ranelagh Gardens, the famous pleasure ground on the banks of the Thames, not far from Elizabeth's girlhood home in Chelsea. Opened in the spring of 1742, Ranelagh featured neat gravel walkways flanked by elms and yew trees, flower gardens, a canal, and, most important of all, the rotunda. This was a large three-storey structure with two levels of boxes for dining and tea drinking, and a baroque pillar in the center where musicians performed. The chief entertainment at Ranelagh was promenading, walking up and down along the outdoor walks, or simply milling around the rotunda in an endless circle. It was primarily a place to see and be seen, although it was also a popular spot to listen to music (Mozart played the harpsichord and organ there in 1764 when he was just eight years old).

Ranelagh was also popular for its masquerades, and the most famous masquerade of the century took place there on 24 April 1749 to celebrate the peace. Advertised as a party in the "Venetian manner," the masquerade featured a gondola filled with musicians on the canal and temporary structures resembling the piazza di San Marco in Venice. Writing about that night, Walpole says that the masquerade was "the prettiest spectacle I ever saw: nothing in a fairy tale ever surpassed it."[5]

The huge garden was filled with masked partygoers milling about. Musicians were scattered all around, some playing French horns like huntsmen, others like peasants playing tunes on tabors and flutes as dancers circled a maypole. The rotunda was illuminated and the central column was made to look like a circular bower with potted fir trees reaching twenty to thirty feet high, surrounded by orange trees "with small lamps in each orange." The entire structure was decorated with floral garlands.

This masquerade ball marked the beginning of the "torrent of diversions" celebrating the end of the war. As Walpole put it to his friend, "We have at last celebrated the peace, and that as much in extremes as we generally do everything, whether we have reason to be glad or sorry, pleased or angry."[6] That spring nobody went to greater extremes than Elizabeth.

At a more exclusive subscription masquerade held at the King's Theatre in the Haymarket a week after the Venetian ball, Elizabeth appeared in the costume of Iphigenia, the daughter Agamemnon sacrificed during the Trojan War. Upon arrival at the masquerade, Elizabeth said, like Iphigenia, "I am ready for the sacrifice!" as she threw off her cloak, revealing a gown so transparent that it left nothing to the imagination and scandalized even her own jaded peers.

The costume's effect on the other partygoers was electrifying. Subscription masquerades were exclusive and expensive affairs and one could gain admission only with a ticket, and tickets for such events were available only to the rich and famous. Conventionally, women dressed up in "Van Dyke" costumes, approximations of seventeenth-century fancy dress that they knew from old portraits by artists such as Van Dyke. Mrs. Montagu described her dress for a correspondent in loving detail: "I was some days preparing for the subscription masquerade, where I was to appear in the character of the Queen Mother, my dress white satin, with fine new point for tuckers, kerchief, and ruffles, pearl necklace, and ear rings, and pearls and diamonds on the head, and my hair curled after the Vandyke picture."[7] Because such dresses were very costly, many women, like Mrs. Montagu, had their portraits painted in them.[8]

Masquerades were always criticized by moralists because the masking of identity supposedly led to sexual intrigue. But for the most part they were decorous affairs patronized by the social elite without any harm to their reputations (if not, the good Mrs. Montagu, who stayed until 5:00 a.m., would never have been there). That is why Elizabeth's costume was so scandalous—it confirmed what the moralists feared about masquerades, and it cemented a public perception of her as an audacious and lascivious woman.

The reign of George II was regarded by many people at the time as being more outrageous for its immorality than the fabled Restoration court of Charles II nearly a hundred years earlier. In fact, the mid-eighteenth century was a time of strong contrasts between vice and virtue, delicacy and grossness, prudery and obscenity. Elizabeth Chudleigh, perhaps more than anybody else, embodied these contradictions.

Far from being indelicate, she was famous in her day for fainting at the drop of a hat. At Tunbridge Wells, she fainted in the assembly room when a drunken man was wheeled in and dropped off a chair, looking for all the world as if he was a dead man. According to one person who was there, her delicacy was matched by eight other ladies who followed her example and dropped like flies. Six years later, she was removed from the King's Theatre in the Haymarket, kicking and shrieking in a hysterical fit. This time the other ladies chose not to compete with Elizabeth's over-the-top theatrics. And at her bigamy trial in 1776, she had to be removed from the courtroom; it was her last great public fit.

As her masquerade costume in the spring of 1749 shows, she could also be shockingly indelicate. But as the contemporary moralist John Brown wrote, these contradictory qualities were typical not just of Elizabeth but of the era in which she lived. It was an age of hypocrisy, a time of false delicacy, when refined manners glossed over sordid vices and follies. Using a metaphor that might have been inspired by Elizabeth's famous masquerade costume, Brown describes this charade:

> In ancient days, bare and impudent obscenity, like a common woman of the town, was confined to brothels: whereas the double-entendre,

like a modern fine lady, is now admitted into the best company; while her transparent covering of words, like a thin fashionable gauze delicately thrown across, discloses what it seems to veil, her nakedness of thought.[9]

At the subscription masquerade of 1 May 1749, Elizabeth Chudleigh not only caught the attention of the fashionable world, but also helped to define it.

She became famous, and infamous, as a result of the costume. Just as the images of her are unreliable, so are some of the anecdotes about what happened that evening. One story has the Princess of Wales angrily covering her nudity with a cloak. Mrs. Montagu said the other Maids of Honour tutted their disapproval and refused to speak to Elizabeth.

If the king was offended, he did not show it. Instead, he ordered another jubilee masquerade to be held on 8 May at Ranelagh in her honor. Retailing the courtly gossip of the week, Walpole tells a correspondent that the king was "so much in love" with Elizabeth that he presented her with a watch worth thirty-five guineas that he paid for out of his privy purse rather than charge it to his public account.[10] George II's attraction to Elizabeth was not short-lived. A year and a half later, he chose her mother, Mrs. Henrietta Chudleigh, to be the housekeeper at Windsor Castle, a lucrative post. At a royal reception in St. James's Palace in December 1750, the king claimed his reward for the appointment and kissed Elizabeth in front of the entire company. This was an unusual breach of decorum and one that fueled the gossip that Elizabeth had become his mistress. While there is no evidence that this ever happened, he clearly took no pains to disguise his passion for her. Just a few months later, Walpole writes that the king left a masquerade in a huff when he learned that Elizabeth was not there.

While Elizabeth's scandalous masquerade dress earned her the favors of the king, it drove Hervey even further away, as surely she knew it would. Perhaps that was the reason she chose the costume in the first place. In his journal, Hervey complains that he was tired of the country life in the summer of 1749, but was "so horridly vexed to go to London to see all that was going on there, that I determined to go abroad." Two days after Elizabeth made her splash as Iphigenia, Hervey wrote to the Admiralty, requesting permission to travel to France and Italy. As he was packing his bags on 2 June 1749, Elizabeth came to see him one last time, either with a new list of debts or with a plea of some other sort. Hervey does not say what she wanted, but he is clear about his response: "I was deaf to all the siren's voice" (84). Although his journal continues for another decade, this is the last reference he makes to Elizabeth. The next time they would meet was twenty years later, and then only to bring what they mistakenly thought was a legal end to their marriage.

For the next decade, Elizabeth and Augustus Hervey led separate lives, and not very virtuous ones at that. Hervey went to Paris, where he spent a year and a half living the high life. He was twenty-five, rich, and, judging from his success with women, as attractive as his wife. In all, his journal records nine different sex partners during this year and a half. Not all were disreputable: he had an affair with his mother's forty-three-year-old friend, Mme de Monconseil, and he fell passionately in love with Mme Susanne-Felix de Caze, a respectable married woman whom he met at a masquerade. She bore him a son on 12 February 1751, the first of his three known bastard children. Hervey obviously had no trouble forgetting all about his English wife.

While Hervey was enjoying himself in France, Elizabeth was making the most of George II's infatuation with her and looking out for new conquests. The two dukes who had courted her a few years earlier had moved on to other women. The Duke of Ancaster had made a respectable match in Newmarket the previous November. The Duke of Hamilton, by contrast, dismayed his family by marrying Elizabeth Gunning, a penniless Irish beauty, on Valentine's Day 1751, in a clandestine ceremony at Mr. Keith's chapel, the most notorious marriage shop in the liberties of the Fleet Prison. With the dukes spoken for, Elizabeth is rumored to have begun an affair with Admiral Howe, a considerable move up the naval chain of command from Captain Hervey. Wills Hill, Viscount Hillsborough, is also reported to have been a lover at this time; years later, as the Earl of Hillsborough, he would rise in the House of Lords in a vain attempt to persuade his colleagues not to hold Elizabeth's bigamy trial in Westminster Hall. But admirals and viscounts aside, it was not long before she counted another duke among her admirers, and this time she was determined not to let the prospect of becoming a duchess slip away. She may have been willing to shock society on occasion, but she had no intention of remaining merely a subject of gossip.

Evelyn Pierrepont, the second Duke of Kingston, was a forty-one-year-old bachelor when he and Elizabeth met sometime in 1752. Walpole called him a "very weak man, of the greatest beauty, and finest person in England," but added that his good looks were "at the fall of the leaf" in the early 1750s.[11] That Kingston was handsome is obvious from his portraits. He was tall and fair, but his most striking feature was his expressive blue eyes, set off by perfectly groomed brows that gave him an air of either interest or detached hauteur, depending on how you read his expression. Whether painted in a fine coat with his star and garter on his chest, or in riding clothes on horseback, he looked every inch the patrician. According to his valet, he was fastidious without being vain and took pains with his appearance. But then valets see the man in his most private moments. To the rest of the world, the Duke of Kingston looked and behaved like someone who was to the manner born.

Walpole is right in calling Kingston "very weak," and his weakness was of two sorts. He had so great a love of rural pleasures (hunting, fishing, and horseracing) that he never made much of the political power he might have wielded. A loyal Whig and Hanoverian, he raised a cavalry regiment to oppose the Jacobite Rebellion in 1745; and he did hold a succession of offices, such as Steward of Sherwood Forest and lord lieutenant of his native Nottinghamshire. But he favored play over work, so he was a political nonentity even though he might easily have become an influential figure on the national scene.

His other weakness was for married women. Like the voracious philanderer Hervey, Kingston, too, went to Paris at the tender age of twenty-five, but he was a monogamist. He fell in love with the Marquise de la Touche, one of the ornaments of the court at Versailles and the mother of three. At the duke's urging, she left her husband and children and followed him to England in 1737, where he installed her in his Nottinghamshire home, Thoresby. Lord Hervey, Augustus's father, told a friend that Mme de la Touche's flight "makes some talk here, but much more noise at Paris. Her husband pursued her, but concluding she was gone to Calais, missed her."[12] A prosecution was begun against the duke in the Parlement of Paris, but the French King Louis XV put a stop to the proceedings. Depending on whom you believe, once in England, Mme de la Touche was either beloved by the local gentry, serving as unofficial duchess to the duke or she lived in a lonely exile, a duke's whore ignored by respectable people. But given Kingston's famous good nature and the generally lax moral attitudes of the day, she was probably more welcomed than shunned in her adopted home.

By 1749, Kingston had begun to tire of his French mistress. That year, Lady Mary Wortley Montagu commented in a letter that the Marquise had moved to London and was living in the home of the duke's sister, Frances Meadows. This was probably the idea of Lady Frances's husband, Philip, who was keen to keep the duke involved with a mistress and far from a wedding altar. If the duke remained unmarried and had no legitimate heir, then Philip's sons would stand to inherit the duke's fortune. It was Philip who would later pursue Elizabeth all the way to Westminster Hall in an effort to disinherit her after the duke's death. But Lady Mary attributed the move in 1749 to Frances Meadows, commenting, "I think Lady F. Meadows pays very dear for whatever advantages she may gain. But interest is so commonly preferr'd to Honor, I do not doubt her conduct will be applauded by many people."[13]

Despite the Meadows family's efforts to ensure their inheritance in 1749 (the first of many to come), the duke was on the verge of replacing the Marquise de la Touche with another married woman, the Honorable Elizabeth Hervey.

How and when Elizabeth first met the duke is unknown, but rumors of their affair began in 1752. Writing at that time, Lady Jane Coke gossiped about the duke's attention to Elizabeth and said, "Poor Madame la Touche is, I think, to be pitied; she must suffer extremely."[14] In the event, she was soon sent back to France with an annuity of £800 from the Duke of Kingston and was received back into her family and French courtly society. But in England, to the victor went the spoils, and Elizabeth wasted no time in enjoying those spoils. By the spring of 1753, she was building a house and stables near Berkeley Square, something she could only have done with the duke's money.

The duke's riches were certainly a draw, but Elizabeth seems genuinely to have loved the duke and enjoyed his company. When she fell ill at Windsor in 1753, he sat up with her through the night. Gossips at Tunbridge Wells noted his devotion to her that summer, but Lady Mary Coke was not surprised, explaining to a correspondent: "We are so used at Windsor to them coming together there . . . that now 'tis scarce mentioned."[15] Thomas Whitehead, the duke's valet, writes of their extensive private jaunts in the country, including fishing parties that they both enjoyed.[16] Even in town, they spent time together in humble diversions like watching the proceedings of the criminal court in Bow Street, presided over by their friend, Sir John Fielding. There is every reason to believe that they were genuinely in love and faithful to each other. Had it not been for Elizabeth's foolish marriage to Hervey, she almost certainly would have been a duchess by the early 1750s.

Kingston and Elizabeth's monogamous attachment contrasts strongly with Hervey's behavior at this time. Assigned to a peacetime squadron in late 1751, he was back in the Mediterranean by the spring of 1752, where his biographer says "he was to hold for four pleasant, pleasure-seeking, exhilarating and relatively carefree years."[17] During those years, Hervey proved again to be a "gay Lothario," as Elizabeth would angrily refer to him in later years. His sexual exploits were as vigorous as on his previous tour, including a particularly memorable affair in Lisbon with the Duchess of Cadaval, who had him kidnapped at gunpoint and taken to an anonymous apartment for their first night together.

Compared to Hervey and his duchess, Elizabeth and her duke seem downright respectable, more like an old married couple than the stars of a Restoration sex comedy. Throughout their long affair, Elizabeth and the duke were so cautious that his valet—the man who traveled everywhere with him, the last person to see him in the evening, and the first to see him in the morning—claims that he never once saw the duke enter the same bedroom as Elizabeth and never saw them kiss until after they married. While Hervey had a woman in every Mediterranean port in the 1750s, Elizabeth settled in to a comfortable domesticity with the duke. But that was not enough for her.

Hervey's older brother, George, became the second Earl of Bristol upon his grandfather's death in 1750, and since George was unmarried, this put Augustus just one life away from the title. George was so prone to illness throughout his life that he became known as "the delicate earl," and those with an interest in the Bristol title watched the course of his illnesses closely. Not surprisingly, Elizabeth was one of that number, and when George's health took a serious turn for the worse in 1759, she became convinced that he was on his deathbed and did a very foolish and craven thing.

In February 1759, Elizabeth went to Lainston to visit her cousin John Merrill, the man in whose house she and Augustus had their marriage and honeymoon.[18] Early one morning, the two of them went to a public house in Winchester and sent for Judith Amis, the wife of the rector who had performed the clandestine marriage. Elizabeth introduced herself and asked Mrs. Amis if she thought her husband would provide her a register of her marriage to Hervey. Mrs. Amis went home to her husband, who was on his deathbed, and relayed the message. When she returned, she told Elizabeth that the rector wished to speak with her, so she went to Amis's bedside and the two had a conference, evidently about the best way to produce a legitimate certificate for a clandestine marriage that had occurred fifteen years earlier.

This was an important consideration because in the meantime, the Marriage Act of 1753 had become law, making clandestine marriages illegal and requiring parental consent for minors to marry. The law was passed precisely to protect the children of noble families, such as Augustus Hervey, from making foolish marriages and jeopardizing the lineal succession of land and titles. Elizabeth, confident that the Earl of Bristol would soon be dead, wanted to make sure that she would become the next Countess of Bristol, and she needed a legal marriage certificate for that to happen.

After a short conference with John Merrill, they sent for James Spearing, an attorney, to ask his opinion. Prior to his arrival, Elizabeth hid in a closet, not wanting to be seen by a third party. Merrill showed Spearing a piece of stamped paper he brought to make the register on (all legal documents of this sort required government stamps on them), but Spearing said it would not suffice: the register must be made in a book, and one of the parties must be present at the registration. At this point, Mrs. Amis went to the closet to tell Elizabeth the news. She emerged, no doubt to Spearing's surprise, and he repeated his opinion. She sent him off to buy a proper book, which he did, returning a short time later with it. Mr. Amis registered the marriage, inserting a burial that took place two days before the marriage, just to make it look legitimate. He then handed the book over to Elizabeth, who, according to Mrs. Amis, "thanked him, and said that it might be a hundred thousand pounds in her way. At the same time she added that she had had a boy, but that it was dead, and that she had borrowed a hundred pounds of her aunt Hanmer to buy baby things." The mention of these circumstantial details about young Augustus's birth and death was calculated to produce witness testimony in the event that Hervey contested her claims of marriage after the death of his brother.

Elizabeth's cold-blooded references to her dead child, like the whole sordid affair that February morning, revealed her worst qualities. Evidently, she was willing to give up her love affair with the Duke of Kingston in order to become the Countess of Bristol. And she had no compunction about demanding the complicity of a dying man. She was able to reveal painful memories of her pregnancy and her child's death because those memories might prove useful in court. Fifteen years earlier, she risked all for love in marrying Augustus Hervey; now she chose a loveless marriage to him because it would give her the barren pleasures of a noble title.

Before Merrill and Elizabeth left the house, she sealed the register and handed it to Mrs. Amis, asking her to take care of it and to deliver it to Merrill when Mr. Amis died. Not long thereafter, Mr. Amis did, in fact, die, and Mrs. Amis gave the register to Merrill. But George Hervey, the second Earl of Bristol, did not die. He defied the odds and his own delicate constitution and lived until March 1775, making his journey to the next world just as Elizabeth was making her journey from Rome to London to face the bigamy charges against her in the courts of Chancery and King's Bench. In the meantime, John Merrill died, too, and the register book traveled from the safekeeping of his library to the house of the new rector of Lainston, where it sat until 1776.

CHAPTER 5

NOBLE PROSPECTS

As news of the Earl of Bristol's recovery reached London, Elizabeth saw the prospect of becoming the Countess of Bristol diminish, but not disappear. The marriage register in Lainston might still serve its purpose: George Hervey was chronically unwell, and despite having proposed to a host of women, he had the inexplicable bad luck to be turned down by every one of them. Unless he could find a wife, the bachelor earl would die without legitimate issue and the title would then fall to Augustus. For the time being, there was nothing for Elizabeth to do but wait and see what might happen. Like Viola in *Twelfth Night*, she could only say: "O Time, thou must untangle this, not I; / It is too hard a knot for me t'untie."[1] By the end of the decade, Augustus Hervey would force her into action with the threat of a parliamentary divorce, but as the 1760s began, Elizabeth could simply enjoy being the Duke of Kingston's mistress and leave her marital quandary to fate.

Although becoming a countess had eluded her, she had the consolation of turning her sights upon another noble prospect, that of Chudleigh House, the mansion in Knightsbridge that she had begun to build in 1757. Elizabeth's is the only name to appear on the legal documents relating to the construction of this grand house, but everyone knew that it was built using the duke's money (its name was changed to Kingston House after they married). Horace Walpole said it was built on "Concubine Row."

The duke's financing of the project was not the only secret that everybody seemed to know. So common was the knowledge of Elizabeth's marriage to Hervey that a 1760 document related to the construction of Chudleigh House refers to her as "Elizabeth Hervey but commonly called Elizabeth Chudleigh."[2] But if her marriage was by this time an open secret, it was still a secret that nobody spoke too loudly of, because she enjoyed the love and protection of some very powerful people, including the duke, the Dowager Princess of Wales, who was still her employer, and King George II. And so Elizabeth remained a Maid of Honour, but lived like a duchess, and in 1760 she moved into the elegant Knightsbridge mansion that shared her maiden name.

Elizabeth was now in her fortieth year. She was still considered a very beautiful and witty woman, but the years had begun to soften her manners. As the duke's mistress, she learned to be more discreet in her public conduct. Although she still loved gambling at fashionable assemblies, she now found the company of some people to be too scandalous for her sensibilities. With no sense of irony, she would blackball such people, much to the amusement of the knowing. It was also around this time that she became one of the first women to apply to use the reading room in the newly established British Museum.

Chudleigh House became an emblem of its newly respectable owner. The very name hypocritically insisted that Elizabeth was still unmarried, which virtually everyone knew was not the case. But the house was like its owner in more than just name. From the outside, Chudleigh House presented a dignified, chaste appearance. It was a three-storey villa done in the popular Palladian style, which meant that if cut down the center, the two halves would perfectly balance each other in every detail. The symmetry made for a harmonious and rational composition that masked the house's great size.

Behind the facade, however, things were not quite so chaste and rational. The house was grand and expensive, but judging from contemporary descriptions, it was not decorated in particularly good taste. There was a luxurious extravagance to the place that typified the conspicuous consumption many people feared was undermining the health of the nation and its fledgling empire. The moralist John Brown warned that Britain had grown so rich by midcentury that the people at the top of the social pyramid, who ought to set a good example for those below, were being debilitated by the overconsumption of commercial goods. Speaking of people like Elizabeth and the duke, he said "Nothing is so Natural to effeminate Minds as *Vanity* . . . the whole Attention of the Mind is centered on *Brilliancy* and *Indulgence*."[3] Even complimentary descriptions of Chudleigh House give one pause. The German Count Kielmansegge, who had come to England in the early 1760s to see the coronation of George III, was not so much critical of Chudleigh House's brilliancy and indulgence he was dazzled by it. He claims that the interior was arranged with the "greatest of taste, so that you cannot fail to admire it greatly," yet after cataloging the knick-knacks that filled the shelves, he says: "There is hardly a place in the whole house left bare or without decoration, like a doll's house."[4]

Horace Walpole, not surprisingly, was more critical and more specific about the bad taste of Chudleigh House:

> The house is not fine nor in good taste, but loaded with finery. Execrable varnished pictures, chests, cabinets, commodes, tables, stands, boxes, riding on one another's backs and loaded with terreens [i.e., tureens], filigree, figures and everything upon earth. Every favour she has bestowed is registered by a bit of Dresden china. There is a glass case full of enamels, eggs, ambers, lapis lazuli, cameos, toothpick-cases and all kind of trinkets, things that she told me were her playthings; another cupboard full of the finest japan; and candlesticks and vases of rock crystal ready to be thrown down in every corner.[5]

Walpole's sly allusion to Elizabeth's temper is notable. She stuffed her new home with trinkets and presents she received in return for her "favours," and if Walpole is correct, she made a habit of smashing them on the floor when she wanted to show her disfavor with the duke. Years later, Walpole told a friend that one room of the house sported a hole from a pistol shot, adding "I have heard formerly that she used to terrify the Duke of Kingston in that manner, with threatening to murder him or herself."[6]

Thomas Whitehead, the duke's valet, also mentions Elizabeth's terrible temper, but like Walpole, he had a jaundiced view of her. Still, there were occasions during this generally prosperous time when Elizabeth had reason to be temperamental and jealous. When a general rumor circulated about the duke's running off to the country with the pretty young daughter of his milliner, Elizabeth left England for a tour of the Continent. Lord Chesterfield, writing to his son, puzzled about the purpose of Elizabeth's trip: "Is it to show the Duke of Kingston that he cannot live without her? A dangerous experiment! which may possibly convince him that he can."[7] A fling with a milliner's daughter was one thing, but in 1756 Elizabeth faced a more serious rival. At that time, there was talk of the duke's marrying Lady Diana Spencer, the daughter of the Duke of Marlborough. In the end, nothing came of it. As one correspondent put it, the match "ceases to be talked of and his mistress is said once more to have resumed the ascendant."[8] Had Elizabeth regained the ascendant by smashing china or by threatening murder or suicide? Perhaps. Excessive behavior was entirely characteristic of her. However she secured her position, it was obviously safe the following year when she began leasing land for the construction of Chudleigh House.

Whether one liked it or not, Chudleigh House quickly became a notable place of lavish decoration and fashionable diversions. In 1760 alone, Elizabeth hosted birthday parties for two of the royal princes. In March, Chudleigh House was the site of a concert and lunch in honor of Prince Edward's twenty-first birthday. In June came the big event: the Prince of Wales was feted for his twenty-second birthday, the last birthday he would celebrate before becoming King George III. In the not-too-distant future, Elizabeth would be held under house arrest in her grand house, partygoers and fancy dinners replaced by an army of lawyers and law books. But in the spring and summer of 1760 she gloried in her new house, her devoted duke, and her role as a society hostess.

The parties of 1760 took place in the capital of a nation at war, but that did little to dampen anyone's spirits. Britain was a confident nation with an ever-increasing empire and the global trade that came with it; the war being fought was against the French and Spanish over the North American empire. In Britain it came to be called the Seven Years' War; in America it was known as the French and Indian War. When it ended in 1763, Britain had wrested control of Florida from the Spanish and had gained the vast territory of Canada, plus everything east of the Mississippi River, from the French. As a result, the nation felt more secure than ever in its American colonies. This security was, of course, illusory: Britain's attempts to retire the debts related to the long war would ultimately lead to the American Revolution.

The year 1760 was roughly the middle point of the war, and on 25 October the nation received unpleasant news. King George II died suddenly while sitting on the toilet at St. James's Palace.

For much of his reign, George II was not the object of great affection for his subjects. The 1730s, in particular, were a rough time for him as he, his queen, and his prime minister, Sir Robert Walpole, became the objects of devastating political satires. Especially hurtful were the satiric plays that delighted audiences by making fools of the royal family and the Walpole ministry. These satires had become so audacious that the government passed the Stage Licensing Act of 1737, a repressive censorship measure that shut down troublesome theaters and muzzled playwrights. But the Jacobite Rebellion of 1745 made the nation rally around their Protestant King, even if he was a German; and in his old age, he mellowed, and the nation looked up on him with an affection born of long acquaintance. His death was an unpleasant shock to many. In a letter to a friend, the bluestocking

Catherine Talbot calls him "a gracious parent taken suddenly from a people, who had all, for some years, unitedly considered and behaved to him in that view." To her mind, his death "looked like the long suspended stroke of justice, inflicted because mercy had been abused by a profligate age."[9]

The shock of the old king's death, great as it was, was soon replaced by excitement and unprecedented optimism over the new king's reign. In the next sentence, Talbot captures this spirit of optimism as she sings the praises of George III, in whom she saw:

> Not only a steadiness of judgment, a wisdom and prudence that is seldom the lot of such early years, a mildness and benignity, an openness and sincerity that makes it equally respected and beloved; but what seems almost astonishing on so sudden a transition from the most retired life to the most important and most public post, a readiness, a presence of mind, a grace and address, a propriety of ease and dignity that every body is charmed with. And all is, as at present, peace, union, harmony, every where—all united for the public good. (2: 353)

Talbot's rosy assessment was, of course, as exaggerated as Jefferson's negative one would be sixteen years later when he said in the Declaration of Independence that George III was "a Prince whose character is . . . marked by every act which may define a Tyrant." But Talbot was not alone in predicting that the Age of George III would be the most glorious in Britain's history.

The following year was marked by three great events, all of them having to do with the new king. In June, his birthday was celebrated with a party that put the previous year's festivities at Chudleigh House to shame. Traffic ground to a halt around the palace of St. James and members of the royal family were stuck in the crowd for over an hour in the street. Once inside, the scene was not much different. The ballroom was packed so tightly that well-wishers could hardly make room for the guest of honor. Catharine Talbot's mother was there, and she summed up the experience this way: "When one has said gold, silver, and diamonds, one has said all that the subject affords."[10] The birthday ended in "illuminations" as bonfires blazed throughout the streets of London, houses glowed with candles in their windows, and fireworks lit up the evening sky.

On 8 September, Charlotte, Princess of Mecklenburg-Strelitz, arrived in London and was married to the new king that very night. Unlike Elizabeth Chudleigh, George III put honor before love when he made his choice of a spouse. Although he was known to be in love with Lady Sarah Lennox, the Duke of Richmond's sister, George prudently chose not to marry a subject; instead, he proposed by proxy to a German princess he had never met until hours before their wedding on that hot September night.

Two weeks later, the main event arrived: the coronation of George III and Queen Charlotte on 22 September. The crowds began to gather so early that day that Count Kielmansegge's party found the streets so choked with coaches at 4:00 a.m. that it took them two hours to make the mile-long journey from Pall Mall to Westminster Abbey. Walpole says that some of the peeresses had dressed the night before and slept in armchairs so as not to disturb their clothes or their hair. The coronation took place in the Abbey, but for all its importance, it was somewhat lacking in dignity. Kielmansegge records seeing vendors selling cold meat, wine, and chocolate at tables set up inside. According to one spectator, when the archbishop of Canterbury rose to deliver his coronation sermon, there was a "general clattering of knives, forks, plates, and glasses" which "produced a most ridiculous effect, and a universal burst of laughter followed."[11]

The peers and peeresses made a spectacular procession into the Abbey, shimmering with diamonds and other jewels, and dressed in their state robes. Some of the women who served with Elizabeth as Maids of Honour in the 1740s were now among the peeresses filing past her into the Abbey. The Duke of Kingston carried St. Edward's staff. As he moved past her, she must have felt a mixture of pride and self-reproach, for if she had not made her rash marriage to Hervey, she would now be the duke's wife. And as a duchess, she would be part of the spectacle, not one of the spectators. It was occasions like this that fueled Elizabeth's life-long desire for nobility.

Along with the finery there was low comedy. After the coronation, the proceedings continued nearby in Westminster Hall, where there was the business of a state feast and the King's Champion to be done. As the King's Champion, Lord Talbot had the task of entering Westminster Hall on horseback, throwing down a gauntlet, and challenging anyone who would contest the authority of King George III. To preserve decorum, he trained his horse to walk backward so that it would not turn its hind end to the king when it exited the Hall. Sadly, the poor beast was trained all too well and so Talbot made his entrance into the Hall on a horse that insisted on walking backward. After having thrown his gauntlet and made his challenge, he and his dutiful horse backed out of the Hall to the sarcastic applause of the spectators.

But these missteps aside, the day was an emotional one for the king and his subjects, and its finale was appropriately dignified. At the end of the ceremonies, the dukes and bishops filed past the king and touched his crown and kissed his left cheek, a symbolic gesture that announced their pledge to do everything in their power to keep that crown on his head. Ominously, after the ceremony was done, a large diamond fell from the crown, a sign that was later regarded as forecasting the loss of America.

At the outset of the new reign, expectations of greatness were very high, and the pious young king felt them keenly. Ever since his father's death in 1751, George had lived an especially sheltered life under the care of his mother, the Dowager Princess of Wales. To some, his seriousness and rectitude were something of a surprise given that he was bred in the scandalous air of Leicester House, which had a famously lax moral atmosphere. In fact, he had spent most of his formative years in nearby Savile House in an altogether different environment. There he was immersed in rigorous studies and largely sheltered from the world. Nevertheless, he grew up knowing his mother's Maids of Honour ("not of maids the strictest," as Elizabeth Montagu quipped), and because Elizabeth Chudleigh was a special favorite, he probably knew her better than most, as her parties for him and his brother suggest. Early in his reign, the king issued a proclamation vowing to "discountenance and punish all manner of vice, profaneness and immorality . . . particularly in such as are employed near our royal person."[12] Later in his reign, the king's reputation for moral probity was widely celebrated, and according to one historian, by the 1790s his daughters' lifestyle "exuded middle-class respectability, which newspapers of all political stances used as a stick with which to beat the aristocracy."[13] But at least initially, the royal parties at Chudleigh House did not stop after George III's ascension.

On 15 March 1762, Count Kielmansegge attended a concert at Chudleigh House held in honor of the Prince of Mecklenburg, Queen Charlotte's brother. The count confided his opinion of his hostess to his diary, "although everyone knows that she has a husband, she has kept on her appointment as Maid of Honour, and has never announced her marriage. That she has been kept all this time by the Duke of Kingston, from whom she receives all her riches, house, and garden, is just as well known."[14] From the outset, George III and Queen Charlotte were admired for their maturity and moral rectitude, but as Kielmansegge's diary shows, the new king and queen knew perfectly well that the company they kept was not living up to their good example. Royalty was back at Chudleigh House the following year for a birthday party for the dowager Princess of Wales, including an impressive fireworks display.

Perhaps the king and queen merely put up with Elizabeth because she was the king's mother's favorite. Perhaps Elizabeth's company did not cause them concern because her secret life, although common gossip among the "better sort," was still a secret from the general public. The king and queen did not have to look far to see far more obvious examples of sexual and marital impropriety; indeed, their own Prime Minister, the Duke of Grafton, had a very public personal life that made Elizabeth and the Duke of Kingston look like models of decorum.[15]

Augustus Henry Fitzroy, the third Duke of Grafton, married for love just after he turned twenty-one. Because the marriage took place in 1756, three years after the reforms of Lord Hardwicke's Marriage Act, he needed to be at least twenty-one in order to marry without parental consent. By 1756, his father was already dead, but his mother and grandfather certainly had a lot to say about his choice of a wife. In this case, love matched interest for he had chosen Anne Liddell, heiress of Lord Ravensworth, who brought £40,000 with her. One year after the wedding, the old duke died, making Augustus Henry and Anne a very rich and very young duke and duchess.

Sadly, not all the money in the world was going to save their marriage. The duchess hosted riotous parties that lasted all night long and featured gambling for high stakes. The duke took offense at these parties and consoled himself in the arms of other women. He fathered a bastard child in 1762, and shortly thereafter, became involved with Nancy Parsons, a famous high-priced courtesan. In 1764, the duke and duchess quarreled and he decided that they must separate. He ordered the duchess to leave their home, which also meant leaving her three young children, and the couple negotiated terms of alimony and child custody through intermediaries. This was, of course, not a legal agreement enforceable by the courts; rather, it was a private deal they struck in order to circumvent the courts. The church courts did allow for judicial separation in the case of adultery or life-threatening cruelty, but the duke was not physically abusive to his wife, and she became aware of his adultery only after they had finalized the terms of their private separation.

When Augustus Hervey washed his hands of Elizabeth Chudleigh in 1749, there was no deal, no elaborate negotiations, and no paperwork. He just walked (or rather, sailed) away from his marriage. For people of their class, this was an unusually lax and informal way of separating; the Graftons' separation and subsequent divorce were much closer to the norm. The Graftons' agreement stipulated a generous alimony payment of £3,000 per year and allowed the duchess to retain custody of the children. The duke was able to install Nancy Parsons in his London home, where she lived from 1764 to 1769, the period during

which he served as Prime Minister. This unseemly liaison evidently did
not cause him to blush, for he did nothing to hide his concubine from
the world.

The duchess led a less public life, but before long she was drawn
out of the shadows when her love affair with the Earl of Upper
Ossory resulted in pregnancy in 1767. The duke used this opportunity to begin the long and expensive process of obtaining a parliamentary divorce. This involved three separate legal proceedings in three
different venues. The first was to sue Ossory for damages in a "crim
con" suit in the Court of King's Bench. Any divorce needed to establish the wife's adultery, and a "crim con" suit (short for "criminal
conversation") became the standard means of doing that. These suits
were civil actions in which a cuckolded husband sued his wife's lover
for monetary damages. In the late eighteenth century, these damages
regularly amounted to thousands, and sometimes tens of thousands,
of pounds. Because Ossory and the duchess were colluding in the
process, the duke almost certainly did not collect the monetary
damages he was awarded.

Second, the duke filed a suit of separation from bed and board in
the Ecclesiastical court, the grounds being his wife's adultery. The
duchess could have ended the process here by "recriminating" his
charge with a countercharge of adultery against him. His relationship
with Nancy Parsons had been fodder for the newspapers for years,
so his adultery was obviously very well known to everyone involved,
even the sleepy judges of the church courts. That he won his suit
against the duchess proves not only that she was colluding in the
proceedings, but that the whole thing was a sham.

But it was a sham with a purpose. Now that the Prime Minister
had favorable rulings from King's Bench and the Court of Arches, he
asked parliament for a divorce on the grounds that his wife's adultery
had left him "deprived of the comforts of matrimony." This final
hurdle was cleared when the Grafton divorce bill was passed by both
houses of parliament and received the king's assent in March 1769. It
was the only time that a Prime Minister has been divorced in office,
and the brazen manipulations of common and ecclesiastical law that
paved the way for the divorce reflected glory on nobody.

But sorry as this process was, it was uncommon only for the high
public profile of the plaintiff. In a divorceless society, collusion and
legal chicanery were the understandable choices that people made in
order to escape unhappy marriages. The year 1769 also saw the collusive divorce of Lord Bolingbroke, which prompted George III to
complain to Lord Chancellor Hardwicke and urge him to take some

action "that might be likely to prevent the very bad conduct among the ladies, of which there have been so many instances lately."[16] Typically, it was the conduct of the ladies that most alarmed the king. Although he was scrupulously faithful to his marriage bed, like other men of his day, he judged sexual conduct according to the double standard, assigning more blame to women than to men.

The Grafton divorce was the subject of great public interest, prompting the publication of satirical poems, scandalous memoirs, trial reports, and stories in newspapers and magazines. In the early months of 1769, it shared newspaper space with the political firestorm that had erupted over John Wilkes, the radical politician who was winning elections to parliament despite being imprisoned on charges of blasphemy for writing a pornographic poem called "An Essay on Woman." These two stories engrossed the public's attention and overshadowed another matrimonial story: by special license of the archbishop of Canterbury, Elizabeth Chudleigh married the Duke of Kingston on the evening of 8 March. For all her love of attention and display, Elizabeth was also capable of great subtlety. The collusion and legal chicanery that she used to get her duke to the altar was even more brazen than the Grafton affair.

CHAPTER 6

JACTITATION OF MARRIAGE

If Augustus Hervey had gotten his way in 1768, Elizabeth would have been subjected to the usual three-step process that people in their position used to dissolve a marriage: a "crim. con." suit, a judicial separation by the church courts, and a parliamentary divorce. By the mid-1760s, Hervey was back in England, serving as a member of parliament from St. Edmundsbury, a seat controlled by the Hervey family. The war had ended in 1763, and Hervey, now a wealthy man in his own right, distinguished himself as a vocal advocate in Commons for the naval officers who were reduced to "half-pay" during peacetime. Because of his efforts, their peacetime pay was increased by 50 percent. He was made a groom of the bedchamber to George III, and the king is said to have liked him personally. And in 1766, when the Earl of Bristol was made lord lieutenant of Ireland, Augustus became his secretary. To the earl's dismay, he resigned this post after ten months because he was in opposition to the Grafton ministry, which the earl supported. But Augustus was always one to speak his mind, and at least in matters of politics, he seems to have been someone who stuck to his principles. When his naval patron, Admiral John Byng, was court-martialed for cowardice in 1756, Hervey stoutly defended the admiral under oath, earning him the enmity of many powerful people. (In the event, Byng was executed for failing to engage the French in the Battle of Minorca.)

In private life, Hervey was much less scrupulous. Upon his return to England from a tour in the West Indies, he began an affair with Kitty Hunter, the daughter of a lord of the admiralty and the mother of the Earl of Pembroke's bastard child. In 1764, she bore Hervey's child, another son named Augustus. But within a few years, Hervey had shed her and seems to have begun a more serious romance with Mary Moysey, the daughter of a physician at Bath. Hervey had been to Bath regularly during these years because of acute attacks of gout, which ran in the family, and he is reputed to have fallen in love with Miss Moysey during that time. Although he denied that he wished to be married, telling George Grenville that the town gossips "have already given me another person for a wife, and such a one as I am sure I should never have thought of," the desire for an heir probably motivated him to initiate the lengthy process for obtaining a divorce in the summer of 1768.[1] As Hervey's biographer reasons, the Earl of Bristol was over forty and in perennial bad health, so inheriting the title was not out of the question. And Augustus so hated his younger brother, Frederick, that he probably wanted a legitimate son in order to keep Frederick from ever becoming Earl of Bristol.

Whatever the true motivations, it is certain that in the early months of 1768, Augustus had secretly begun collecting depositions proving that Elizabeth had committed adultery. Sometime in July or early August, Hervey met Caesar Hawkins, the surgeon who attended at the birth of his and Elizabeth's child nine years earlier, in the street and asked that Hawkins come to his house for a private discussion. Hervey told Hawkins that he wanted to meet not on account of his health, but to discuss an old friend of the surgeon. They set a date and time when Hervey could receive him in secrecy, and when Hawkins arrived, Hervey apologized for the trouble he was about to put him to. He began by explaining how unhappy he had become over his "matrimonial connections with . . . Miss Chudleigh," a nicely ambiguous way to refer to his secret wife.[2] Now Hervey wanted his freedom.

Gesturing with a wave of the hand to two or three bundles of legal papers sitting on a table, he told Hawkins that he had been collecting depositions that contained "ample and abundant proofs" of Elizabeth's adultery and that he intended to pursue a parliamentary divorce "with the strictest firmness and resolution."[3]

Although Hervey had declared an informal separation from Elizabeth two decades earlier, this gave neither of them the freedom to remarry. The informal separation left them in a sort of limbo, free to lead their own lives and pursue love affairs with others, but always conscious that they remained married, and always worried about the other's intentions. We know that Hervey had good reason to worry because Elizabeth had a register made of their marriage nine years earlier. If he became the Earl of Bristol, she intended to publicize their marriage and insist on a restitution of her conjugal rights. The church courts would happily force the couple back together. But the informal separation gave Elizabeth reason to worry, too. Because husbands enjoyed total legal control over their wives, Hervey could at any moment publicize their marriage and assume ownership of all the property she had acquired with the help of the Duke of Kingston's money—including her beloved Chudleigh House. The duke was willing to take some risks, but he absolutely refused to consider marriage unless Elizabeth could prove herself a single woman in the eyes of the law.

Now that Hervey wished to marry again, he needed a parliamentary divorce. The only other legal means of dissolving a marriage was to have it nullified in the church courts, but since he and Elizabeth were both past the age of consent when they married and because there was ample proof that they had consummated the marriage, there was no hope of nullification. Divorce was the only sure way by which he could extricate himself from Elizabeth, and the only way to get a divorce was to prove that his wife was an adulteress.

If Hervey were to succeed, he needed to tread very carefully. That, more than any sense of honor or delicacy, is why he enlisted Caesar Hawkins as the intermediary between himself and Elizabeth. He hoped that having a friend bear the bad news might soften the blow. According to Hawkins, to induce her to comply, Hervey invited Elizabeth and her lawyers to review the affidavits, and "if any parts were found tending to indecent or scandalous reflections," they could be removed provided Hervey's lawyers agreed that those parts could be omitted "without weakening the case." He also assured Elizabeth (and through her, the duke) that since he "intended to act only on the principles of a gentleman and man of honour, he should hope she would not produce any unnecessary or vexatious delays to the suit, or enhance the expenses of it, as he did not intend to prosecute to gain by any demands of damages."[4] In other words, he offered a quid –pro quo: if she would consent to a divorce, he would not collect any of the damages that a jury would award him in the "crim. con." suit.

Hawkins's testimony, given at the bigamy trial, provides us a rare behind-the-scenes look at upper-class manipulation of marriage law in the Georgian era. What was meant to be an adversarial process undertaken only at the final stages of marital breakdown was frequently pursued with the adversaries colluding in advance to produce a mutually desired outcome, the legal dissolution of their marriage. Conversations like the one that Hawkins related happened scores of times in cases such as the Graftons' divorce where the husband's adultery was suppressed and the jury award in the "crim. con." suit went uncollected.

Hawkins was a man of the world, so he knew what part he was being asked to play in this minor drama. He carried Hervey's message to Elizabeth, who seems to have been prepared for it. Indeed, Hawkins may have been the second emissary sent by Hervey. During the bigamy trial, Ann Cradock (the maid servant who witnessed their marriage and who was now married to one of Hervey's servants) testified that Hervey first sent her to Elizabeth to break the news of a divorce, prompting Elizabeth to reply in horror, "Am I to make myself a whore to oblige him?"[5] News of the intended divorce soon began to spread. In a letter of 20 August, Walpole told a friend: "Augustus Hervey, thinking it the *bel air*, is going to sue for a divorce from the Chudleigh. He asked Lord Bolingbroke, 't other day, who was his proctor, as he would have asked for his tailor."[6] And two weeks earlier, Lady Mary Coke recorded a rumor that Hervey was going to prove his marriage to Elizabeth as a first step to gaining a divorce.

Obviously, word was getting around, and when Hawkins delivered his message, Elizabeth's reply was tantamount to a counteroffer. She sent Hawkins back to Hervey, extending her gratitude for the polite parts of his message, "but as to the subject of the divorce, she should cut that short by wishing him to understand that she did not acknowledge him as her legal husband."[7] She defied him to prove the marriage and vowed that she would soon institute a suit of jactitation of marriage in the ecclesiastical court.

Jactitation was a seldom-used lawsuit in which one party accuses another of boasting that they are married ("jactitation" is Latin for boasting). It was not totally unheard of; in fact Hervey had sworn a deposition in a jactitation suit involving his unstable uncle, Thomas, around this time. But it was a highly unorthodox way of dissolving their marriage by manipulating a court to declare that it did not exist in the first place.

The oddest part about this proposal was that neither Hervey nor Elizabeth had ever boasted of their marriage—far from it. The entire case would rest on the spurious claim that Hervey was going around London boasting that he was married to Elizabeth. Perhaps that is why he was struck dumb for several minutes when Hawkins relayed Elizabeth's message. He emerged from his daze by degrees, initially muttering to himself that he could not conceive how a jactitation ruling would give him the same freedom to remarry that a parliamentary divorce would. Hawkins interrupted him to say that Elizabeth desired that nothing be brought forward that "might be a subject of useless conversation or scandal."[8] Hervey replied that he had no desire to provide fodder to the gossips.

It was a risky proposal, and one that Elizabeth knew would require Hervey's collusion, just as he knew that a divorce would require hers. Acknowledging this, in her message to Hervey she said that "as he had promised before that he would act upon the line of a man of honour and a gentleman in his own intended suit, she hoped he would pursue the same line now, and that he would confine himself to proofs of legal marriage only, and not to other proofs of connections or cohabitations."[9] This was partly an inducement and partly a plea. By playing along, the process would be quick and inexpensive, especially compared to the arduous process of obtaining a parliamentary divorce.

For her part, Elizabeth hoped to be spared the scandal of having her sexual indiscretions revealed to the world. She knew that Hervey had his bundles of depositions that proved her "connections or cohabitations," and the use of the plural clearly indicates that Hervey had proof of more than just her affair with the Duke of Kingston. A public airing of multiple sexual affairs would be acutely embarrassing and it might prove so scandalous as to make the duke abandon her. She offered one final inducement: Hervey would either gain his freedom if she won the jactitation suit because the ecclesiastical court would declare them both to be unmarried, "or he would the sooner be able to institute his intended suit."[10] This was an oblique way of saying that if he would collude in the jactitation suit and it failed, she would collude in the divorce process, which would be sure to follow.

Hervey seemed to have the upper hand in this exchange, for not only did he have the bundle of depositions, but he also had control of the one surviving witness to their marriage. Four of the five people who joined them in the family chapel at Lainston twenty-four years earlier were now dead. Only the servant Ann Cradock was still alive. It was in Hervey's power to quash the jactitation proceeding at the outset by subpoenaing Cradock's testimony. That damning eyewitness testimony, along with Caesar Hawkins's, would have ended the suit swiftly. But it might also infuriate Elizabeth, and she had it in her power to deny him a divorce. A parliamentary divorce had to be preceded by a judicial separation in the church courts, and Hervey could obtain a separation only by proving Elizabeth's adultery. If she "recriminated" the charge of adultery against him (an easy thing to prove), his suit would fail. Instead of granting a separation, the court would order the couple back together, which would kill the divorce process. Recognizing this bind, Hervey reluctantly agreed to collude in the jactitation suit.

The exact dates of the exchanges mediated by Caesar Hawkins are unknown, but the first gossip about them was recorded in Lady Mary Coke's journal on 6 August 1768.[11] On 18 August, Elizabeth filed a caveat in Doctor's Commons, which meant that Hervey could not proceed in any matrimonial litigation without notifying her proctor (as lawyers in that court were called). The legal mastermind behind the jactitation suit was Arthur Collier, the same man who had sued his own lover two decades earlier for breach of contract when she refused to marry him. Collier had practiced in the ecclesiastical courts for nearly three decades and he knew the system well. In a letter written on 20 August, Elizabeth called him "my Guardian friend, the good Dr. Collier" and asked the recipient to send her regards to him. Evidently, Collier was being cautious. According to Elizabeth, she could not communicate directly with him at this date because "he order'd me silence upon [this] business, <u>and to be easy</u>."[12] She placed her fate in his hands and trusted the arcane process of a jactitation suit to rid her of Augustus Hervey once and for all.

The process began with Elizabeth filing a "libel" against Hervey, accusing him of boasting that they were married.[13] Hervey answered the charge with a "cross-libel" asserting that they were married and offering a host of circumstantial details to support his claim.[14] This cross-libel was the key document in the entire process because it was carefully crafted to mix truth and falsehood, muddying the facts and permitting Elizabeth enough justification to deny his claims. The cross-libel rehearses facts about the marriage that we know from subsequent testimony in the bigamy trial to be true. The pair met at the Winchester races; Hervey courted Elizabeth; they married secretly on 4 August 1744; and he left shortly thereafter for his tour of duty in the West Indies. But it also incorporates three inaccuracies that can only have been deliberate.

Hervey says he "did privately make his addresses of Love and Courtship to the said Elizabeth Chudleigh who was then also a minor."[15] Elizabeth was born in March 1721, making her twenty-three at the time of her marriage. It is possible that she lied to Hervey about her age, but it is more likely that this small lie was deliberately inserted in his cross-libel. More obvious lies followed.

Hervey claimed that he proposed the match to Mrs. Hanmer, who agreed that the couple should be married. This may or may not be true. Ann Cradock's later testimony seems to suggest that Mrs. Hanmer sat apart from the ceremony in the little chapel, perhaps indicating her displeasure. Ann further testified that Mrs. Hanmer angrily shooed Augustus out of Elizabeth's bed after the wedding, but that Ann had seen them in bed together on more than one occasion. This disputes Hervey's claim in the cross-libel that he and Elizabeth "consummated their Marriage at the said Mr. Merrill's House by having Carnal knowledge of each others Bodies and laying for sometime in one and the same Bed Naked and alone but without the privity or knowledge of any part of the Family and Servants of the said Mr. Merril."[16]

A more obvious false statement came next, when Hervey swore that the marriage took place in the "parish of Sparshot." It had taken place in the Parish of Lainston, not Sparshot, and there is little reason to suspect that the mistake was an innocent one. When the Meadows family brought suit against Elizabeth in the Court of Chancery in 1774, they specifically charged Hervey with colluding in the jactitation suit, pointing out that the "Sparshot" inaccuracy was a deliberate false-hood inserted so that Elizabeth could deny the validity of Hervey's cross-libel.[17]

They were right. During the bigamy trial, Caesar Hawkins told of a conversation he had with Elizabeth in the fall of 1768. When he asked her how the jactitation suit was progressing, she became grave and asked him to speak with her privately. Moving to an empty room, she told Hawkins that "she had had a great deal of concern and agita-tion of mind" since she last saw him because she had not anticipated that she would be asked to make a "positive oath" that she was not married to Hervey.[18] Evidently she expected only to have to challenge Hervey to prove the marriage without swearing herself that it did not take place. To her dismay, she learned that while the burden of proof lay with him, she would also be asked to swear to (if not prove) a negative. This put her in a panic, because making a positive false statement under oath could expose her to a perjury conviction in the future. Happily for her, that "Guardian friend, the good Dr. Collier" had found a way out. By having Hervey mix truth with falsehood, Elizabeth told Hawkins that she found that the cross-libel "had been so complicated . . . with other things that were certainly not true that she could and had taken the oath with a very safe conscience."[19]

That is exactly what she did on 3 December 1768 with Arthur Collier at Doctor's Commons. In a point-by-point response to Hervey, she says she met him at the Winchester Races "and she admits he did then privately so far as respects the knowledge of their parents of either side make his addresses of Love and Courtship" to her.[20] She even agrees that a match was arranged by Hervey and Mrs. Hanmer with-out her knowledge. But she denied that the wedding took place as he claimed. As for Hervey's claims of consummation, Elizabeth discreetly responded that "she is advised that by law she is not obliged to answer thereat."[21] And she ends by saying that although Hervey visited her once or twice in London, those visits were always in the company of others and that in 1747 she "either told him herself or caused to be intimated to him that his visits would be disagreeable."[22]

This was the heart of the case, and when Collier helped Elizabeth to circumvent the issue of taking a positive oath, the major hurdle had been cleared. Hervey's proctors may have been entirely ignorant of the machinations that produced this result, but Collier was the mastermind. Elizabeth rewarded him by inviting him to the duke's country estate, Pierrepont Lodge, for the Christmas holiday. When Elizabeth fell ill and was confined to her bed, Collier penned a mock epitaph that commented bawdily on her dubious status as an old maid: "What have we here! a Maid upon her Back! / Why that is as she should be, is it not? Good lack."[23]

But their work was not over. After the holidays, both sides had witnesses to depose and exhibits of evidence to present.

Although Hervey's inaccurate cross-libel and Elizabeth's reply were central to the case, their collusion becomes all the more evident when one turns to the witness testimony and evidence presented. On Elizabeth's part, the approach was simple. Her fourteen exhibits of evidence are an array of documents dated from 1744 onward that refer to her as "Miss Chudleigh," not Mrs. Hervey.[24] These include her mother's will, leases for property, and personal letters. Of course, presenting evidence of this sort did not induce in her the same anxiety that she felt at the prospect of lying under oath because she was merely documenting the fact that other people regarded her as a single woman. It seems on the surface to be a weak set of exhibits, but she was, in essence, trying to prove a negative. And since the law of coverture made married women legal nonentities incapable of entering into legal contracts, producing legal documents such as wills and leases that referred to her as "Miss Chudleigh" had some force. For obvious reasons, she omitted the 1760 document that called her "Elizabeth Hervey but commonly called Elizabeth Chudleigh." The witnesses Elizabeth called merely swore to the authenticity of the exhibits presented and testified that they had always known her only as Elizabeth Chudleigh, spinster.

Hervey's witnesses are another matter. There is no way to prove that any of them lied for him under oath, but since none of them was at the wedding, there was no way any of them could prove the marriage. The best they could do was report hearsay. Mary Edwards, one of John Merrill's servants, did this when she testified that there was a "Rumor among the Servants" that a marriage had taken place, but that she "never heard such Report among any of the Gentlefolks of the said Family."[25] Similarly the illiterate servant Ann Hillam, who signed her deposition by making a mark [X], swore that she heard a "general Report" that there was a marriage, but added that she "cannot mention any one particular Person she ever heard say so."[26]

The cleverest testimony was offered by William Cradock, a servant who accompanied Hervey to Winchester and Lainston in the summer of 1744. Cradock says he went to the public assembly at the Winchester races with Hervey and saw him dance with Elizabeth. He then accompanied Hervey on three or four visits to Elizabeth at John Merrill's house. And he also set sail for the West Indies with Hervey in the fall of 1744. When they returned to England at the end of 1746, Cradock says he heard a "General publick Report" that Hervey had married Elizabeth two years earlier and that many people asked him if the report was true. He claims that he "always answered as the Truth really was" that Hervey and Elizabeth were acquainted, but that he knew nothing more about the matter.[27] What Cradock failed to mention is that after 1746, he was in a position to know much more about the matter because he had married Ann, the only surviving witness to the wedding.

Where was Ann in January 1769 when all these depositions were being sworn? That is anybody's guess. Hervey's biographer suggests that Hervey sent her away to one of his family's estates in Lincolnshire for safe keeping until the jactitation suit was over, and this seems plausible.[28]

Of the twenty witnesses called, none was able to offer anything like the convincing testimony that Ann Cradock or Caesar Hawkins could have given. Hervey could easily have subpoenaed both of them and compelled their testimony. If they perversely refused to talk, he could, at the very least, have provided a hearsay version of their evidence in his cross-libel. That he did neither of these things makes his collusion in the process all too obvious. Commenting on these proceedings years later, Edward Thurloe, the attorney general, had good reason to sputter, "A grosser artifice, I believe, was never fabricated."[29]

But it worked.

On 11 February 1769, the ecclesiastical court decided in favor of Elizabeth and ordered Hervey to desist from boasting that he was married to her. Furthermore, he was liable for all the costs. There is every reason to suspect that the Duke of Kingston secretly financed the suit, so Hervey did not, in fact, have to pay for it. But the rumor that Hervey was bribed by as much as £14,000 seems to be pure invention. However unscrupulous Hervey was in his sex life, he seems to have adhered to a more-or-less respectable code of conduct in other aspects of his life. Taking a bribe seems out of character.

Elizabeth exulted in her victory, crowing to her friend the Electress of Saxony that she had won her case with "all honour" and adding "I am overwhelmed by all the congratulations that I have received these past two days that I am shaking so much I cannot write."[30] While Elizabeth celebrated, her detractors seethed with anger. As usual, Lady Mary Coke was greatly exasperated by Elizabeth. On 17 February, she wrote in her journal that Elizabeth denied that she was married to Hervey, "tho' everybody knows she is, as the witnesses to the marriage are all dead, she intends marrying the Duke of Kingston. 'Tis said she has bespoken a white gown to be presented in at Court, that is to be trimmed with point lace and pearl."[31] Three days later Horace Walpole wrote, "Next week this fair injured innocence, who is but fifty, is to be married to the Duke of Kingston, who has kept her openly for almost half that time, and who by this means will recover half his fortune which he had lavished upon her."[32]

Elizabeth and the duke wasted no time fulfilling these prophecies. After the fourteen-day period passed when Hervey could have exercised his right to appeal, they were in the clear. Just to make sure, the duke called upon Arthur Collier, who reassured him, "You may safely marry Miss Chudleigh, my Lord, for you neither offend against he laws of God or man."[33] Then, with the ecclesiastical court's ruling in hand, Arthur Collier applied to the archbishop of Canterbury for a special license for the duke and Elizabeth to be married. Although the Marriage Act of 1753 required the publication of the banns three times before a wedding could occur, those who wanted a more private and speedy ceremony could avoid this by obtaining a special license. So with the blessing of the ecclesiastical court and the head of the Church of England, Elizabeth and the duke got married on 8 March 1769.

The wedding was noted without comment in the London papers, and the duke's valet, Thomas Whitehead, offers the only firsthand account of it. In a tell-all memoir, Whitehead says that Elizabeth spent most of the day rushing around London, frantically looking for the duke. When he returned to his Arlington Street house in the early evening, she rushed into his room for a private conversation. Ten minutes later they emerged and dispatched servants to bring their lawyers to the house immediately. At 8:00 p.m., a hasty wedding took place in the duke's dressing chamber. Whitehead was the only servant to accept the open invitation to attend the ceremony.

According to Whitehead's account, this wedding was thrust on the unsuspecting duke.[34] He speculates that Elizabeth was in such a panic because Frederick Hervey, Augustus's younger brother, had arrived in London that very day to try to prevent a wedding. He wanted to keep Augustus from marrying again and producing an heir, and so he came to London to try to prove the 1744 marriage before Elizabeth took advantage of the jactitation ruling. Whitehead also says that Elizabeth got the duke to sign a bond promising to marry her if she could prove herself a single woman. If he failed to do so, he would have to pay her £10,000 per annum for the rest of her life.

After the ceremony, he says that he accompanied the couple to Chudleigh House (soon to be renamed Kingston House) and helped the duke get ready for bed. He presented the duke with a fancy lace nightcap, explaining that the duchess had given it to him as a wedding present, adding as an aside, "This was the first time I had the honour of calling her the *Duchess*: it was uttered very faintly."[35] In the morning, he says the duke was clearly suffering from buyer's remorse. He emerged from the bedroom looking glum and handed the nightcap to Whitehead, saying, "Here, Whitehead, take this; never let me see it again." Reflecting on the fate of his poor, cuckolded master, Whitehead sighed, "Alas! I thought *the cap would not fit him!*"[36]

Whitehead's version of events, colorful though it may be, is not reliable. He published his story in 1792, long after the events had taken place and after the principals were in their graves. He was catering to a public primed to believe the worst of Elizabeth, and so he represented the marriage as the product of her bullying. Other wags had a different opinion. In a 1776 double portrait print of the duke and duchess, the panel reads: "The Bishops give consent the Duke of K[ingston] said, / Then haste my love to church & be a Dutches made."[37]

In fact, there were two weddings, one in the house on Arlington Street and one in St. George's Church in fashionable Hanover Square. As a defender of Elizabeth later put it, "His Grace the Duke of Kingston, to make perfectly sure of his wife, was twice married to her."[38] Evidently the duke was eager to marry Elizabeth, but he was also eager to make the legality of the wedding perfectly clear. To do this, he arranged for Hervey's proctor from Doctor's Commons to come to his house on 8 March and read a public renunciation of Hervey's claims to be married to Elizabeth, written "in form of Laws."[39] After this was done, the first wedding took place in the duke's dressing room.

The church wedding was larger, and this was probably the one that Elizabeth claimed was witnessed by forty people, which seems like a lot to cram into the duke's dressing room. Far from trying to conduct the wedding secretly and hastily, the duke seems to have chosen St. George's because of its high profile. Ever since its construction in 1725, it had become an increasingly fashionable spot to be married. Eventually, it earned the title of "the London Temple of Hymen" and hosted the weddings of people such as Benjamin Disraeli, George Eliot, and Theodore Roosevelt. Among those who attended the Duke and Duchess of Kingston's wedding were two of the duke's good friends, Sir James LaRoche and Lord Masham, the latter having excused himself from accompanying George III to the theater that night so that he could be on hand to give the bride away. The very useful Arthur Collier was also present, no doubt happy to witness the fruits of his legal handiwork.

The church ceremony must have been immensely gratifying to Elizabeth. Now she was not only a wife, but also a duchess, married in a conspicuous church before a respectable collection of friends. For all its romance, the secrecy of her first marriage robbed her of the satisfaction of publicly passing from girlhood to womanhood (or in this instance, because of her age, from being a "spinster" to being a wife). Among those who came by the house on Arlington Street to wish Elizabeth joy on her marriage was Judith Phillips, the widow of Thomas Amis, the clergyman who had officiated at Lainston twenty-five years earlier. Elizabeth said to her, "Was it not very good-natured of the Duke to marry an old maid?" Mrs. Philips merely smiled in return.

Mrs. Philips's reticence is understandable. Elizabeth's cheeky question took them back ten years to the meeting in Winchester, when the dying Reverend Amis made out the false register of her marriage to Hervey. But Mrs. Philips could make no reply, for her husband was employed by the Duke of Kingston as a steward and a grazier. Elizabeth was making sport of her machination, safe in the knowledge that Mrs. Philips could do nothing but smile and congratulate her. But what is truly puzzling is that while Elizabeth made a sly reference to that false register, she never returned to Winchester to claim it. For whatever reason, she seems to have felt no need to destroy the one piece of material evidence that could—and would—one day prove her bigamy.

Unlike the duke and duchess, Augustus Hervey did not place much confidence in the legal chicanery that Collier had engineered. Always skeptical that this was the best way to proceed, Hervey must have been all the more troubled by the oddly conditional emphasis in the sentence the ecclesiastical court handed down. It declared that Elizabeth "was and now is a spinster, and free from all matrimonial contracts or espousals (as far as to us yet appears)."[40] In other words, new facts might someday surface to alter the ruling. Hervey let the fourteen-day appeal period pass without contesting the decision because he was happy to be rid of Elizabeth, but the conditional nature of the ruling and his own knowledge of its invalidity seem to have persuaded him not to remarry. His affair with Mary Moysey of Bath went nowhere after this.

For their part, the Duke and Duchess of Kingston felt entirely confident in the legality of their marriage and they celebrated it in style. Shortly after the wedding, they set out for their seat at Pierrepont Lodge, where the newspapers reported that they hosted a grand entertainment attended by many of the nobility and gentry. They also kept open house for a week, treating their tenants and the neighboring poor to "great quantities of meat, bread, and strong beer."[41]

When they returned to London shortly thereafter, their graces were presented at court on 19 March. They had taken care to distribute their wedding favors, rose shaped brooches of silver lace, to the king and queen and all the high officers of the court. The newspapers reported a very large crowd on hand for the presentation and said that among Elizabeth's many diamonds was "a very fine diamond necklace, a present from her Royal Highness the Princess of Wales."[42] But if the dowager princess was still happy to patronize Elizabeth, her son and daughter-in-law were not quite so pleased. The king and queen had become very adept at displaying royal disapproval in such situations by virtually ignoring someone whom they considered to be scandalous. Lady Mary Coke noted with satisfaction that the royal couple barely acknowledged the new duchess.[43] Privately, the queen was furious over the distribution of the favors because they made it look like she endorsed the marriage. As future events would show, she and the king were no friends to Elizabeth. A ducal mistress could be tolerated, even embraced, by polite society, especially when that duke was a bachelor. But a bigamous duchess was a different matter altogether. By pursuing the jactitation suit and marrying the duke, Elizabeth had created a situation that could complicate the succession of both the Bristol and Kingston titles.

Paradoxically, Elizabeth was much more socially acceptable as the duke's mistress than she was as his wife. When she obtained the rank of duchess, she found to her detriment that her social stock had fallen precipitously. The 1760s began with lavish royal parties at Chudleigh House, but when that mansion's name changed to Kingston House at the end of the decade, the society parties were a thing of the past. The valet, Whitehead, notes with relish that with few exceptions, not "a single lady of quality or fashion paid her a visit" after her wedding.[44]

Elizabeth had her title and her Knightsbridge mansion stuffed with gifts, but respectability (even by the loose standards of the eighteenth century) eluded her.

So long as the dowager Princess of Wales and the Duke of Kingston were alive, Elizabeth would enjoy their protection and the spoils that came with her elevation to the peerage. Shortly after the wedding, she noted in a letter to a friend that she was thrilled to find herself "under the protection of the most perfect gentleman in the world."[45] But if she outlived him and the princess, she would have to fend for herself—and there were already a number of people eager to prevent her from being a merry widow.

CHAPTER 7

EXIT THE DUKE

Elizabeth and the duke enjoyed a quiet married life together. Although the duke had never been much in the public eye, Elizabeth's quiet conduct as a duchess stands in strong contrast to her earlier days when she lived for attention and London's diversions. But this is not altogether surprising: upon their marriage, she was forty-eight years old and the duke was fifty-eight. Their interests now took them away from the glittering round of fashionable metropolitan life and to the more domestic comforts of home, hunting, and the company of close friends and neighbors. After their marriage, the duke sold his house in Arlington Street and the couple began to spend more and more time away from London, enjoying Thoresby, their new Nottinghamshire villa.

So quiet was their married life that most of our information about it comes not from newspapers or gossipy letters, but from the memoirs of the duke's valet, Thomas Whitehead. Whitehead made much of Elizabeth's gross habits during her years of marriage to the duke. After meals, he says, she would use the water closet adjoining the dining room, leaving the door open, which meant that her uncomfortable guests could hear her vomiting, defecating, or urinating. She would return to the table, explaining, "A fit of gout just took me in the stomach; but I am now much better."[1] After eating and drinking too much, as was her habit, she would nap on a couch, snoring loudly. On warm days, she would rise from her chair and cool herself by fanning her skirt and petticoats, then blame her body odor on the poor footmen who stood in attendance.

According to Whitehead, Elizabeth's crudity was matched only by her vanity and cruelty. Eager to assert her new privileges, Elizabeth chastised one of the maids on her wedding night for calling her "ma'am" instead of "your Grace." And the valet laments that his master "never enjoyed a week's happiness after his unfortunate marriage" (40). Once, when the duke's belongings were packed into their coach for a journey before hers were, she personally threw his things onto the ground so that hers could take precedence. Whitehead paints a vivid scene of the duke's humiliation, explaining that the duke paced back and forth during the episode, not saying a word. By the time his possessions were repacked into the coach, there were a hundred people assembled around the door, witnessing his disgrace. Then Elizabeth "turned with her usual dissimulation to the Duke, saying, 'I am ready; come, my dear Lord, shall we go?' who answered, 'My dear Ma'am, if you please,' shewing no resentment for his ill treatment" (64–66). Stories like this probably have some basis in fact, but they are almost certainly embellished by Whitehead's bias against Elizabeth. Yet even in the pages of his book, glimpses of a contented domesticity appear.

Elizabeth would join the duke for angling parties that could last three or four days at a time. These were ducal angling parties, so the rigors of wading in water all day were softened by having Whitehead along to cook stewed chicken for them in a silver pot, serving coffee and tea afterward. Elizabeth fortified herself by drinking up to two quarts of rum a day, also supplied by the valet. Thoresby became a favorite retreat for the couple: the duke enjoyed hunting and riding as well as sailing on the artificial lake where he kept a small fleet of pleasure boats, including a fifteen-foot long model of a fifty-gun frigate. While he enjoyed the outdoors, Elizabeth was happy inside, decorating the villa and holding small concerts and dinner parties. Their guest lists were much more modest compared to the royal parties of the 1760s. The Duke of Newcastle, their Nottinghamshire neighbor, was a particular friend. Isabella Chudleigh, Elizabeth's cousin, was a favorite of both of them and was frequently with them. And Sir John Fielding, whose courtroom they used to visit to see the felons examined, was also a regular guest.

Whitehead is certainly right when he says that Elizabeth and the duke did not mix with people of the first fashion, but to be fair, their quiet life was not set up to achieve that goal. Having married the duke, Elizabeth's social ambitions were satisfied. She had a noble title, enormous wealth, and a doting husband whom she rightly considered to be her "protector."

The duke took pains to be her protector even after his own death. Shortly after marrying Elizabeth, he altered his will so that she would be the sole beneficiary of his personal wealth and the income of his estates during her lifetime, provided she did not remarry. (That condition might seem like meanness on his part, but it was probably intended to keep Elizabeth from predatory suitors.) There were, of course, some small legacies left to friends, relatives, and devoted servants, but the estate went to Elizabeth alone.

Next to Elizabeth, the duke's heir at law was his sister, Lady Frances Meadows. She and her family were to be bitterly disappointed by his will. Anticipating their efforts to have the will invalidated, the duke wrote Elizabeth's name in his own hand so that his wishes concerning Elizabeth's inheritance would be perfectly clear—or as Whitehead put it, "thus putting it out of the power even of her old friend, the Devil, to set it aside"[2] Whitehead says this was all Elizabeth's idea. He writes that the will was witnessed by three of her disreputable friends, a violin player, a wine merchant, and a linen draper. The valet sniffs that these men "might have done well enough for a cobbler, not for a duke" (15–16).

The duke fell ill in the summer of 1773, just over four years after his marriage to Elizabeth. He suffered from seizures so violent that he nearly bit his tongue off during them and could hardly be restrained by even three men. Elizabeth, always prone to excessive behavior, was alternately deluded by the doctors' rosy prognoses and hysterical over the duke's imminent demise. In a letter to the Duke of Newcastle dated 3 August 1773, she says with embarrassing self-congratulation that she has developed rheumatism from kneeling for hours at the duke's sickbed, where she would pass out from sheer exhaustion, sleeping on the floor by his bed.[3] The duke was paralyzed by a stroke shortly after this letter was written and by mid-September, one of his servants wrote to Newcastle to say that everyone but Elizabeth expected the duke's death soon, noting "she does not see with the same eyes as other people."[4] But the very next day the scales fell from her eyes. Elizabeth dictated a letter to Newcastle in which she says that she is "inconsolable, not only with grief, but with surprise, for the doctors have kept her in ignorance of the Duke's danger, always telling her his Grace's pulse was good."[5] Three days later the duke was dead.

Elizabeth reacted to the duke's death with an extravagance that characterized so much of her life. Her reaction was partly the result of surprise, having learned the true state of his health only days before. It was also the product of her anxiety over losing her protector: now she was alone in the world, and the Meadows family was certain to attack her. And her grief was partly the genuine expression of pain over the loss of the man she loved. But whatever the reasons, her excessive mourning immediately became the source of contemptuous laughter.

Walpole says that Elizabeth traveled from Bath, where the duke died, to London "with the pace of an internment, and made as many halts between Bath and London as Queen Eleanor's corpse. I hope, for mercy, she will not send for me to write verses on all the crosses she shall erect where she and the horses stopped to weep."[6] Elizabeth's mourning dress for the duke gave more cause for ridicule, especially her overly long veil. And one correspondent even linked her excessive grief to her inordinate fondness for food and drink, joking that she vowed to eat only black pudding and drink only black cherry brandy, "not being able to eat or drink anything of a gayer colour."[7]

Elizabeth's much-ridiculed journey from Bath to London took her five days to complete. Upon her arrival at Kingston House, she sent a letter to Newcastle, who had possession of the duke's will, asking him to visit her that evening "not for the Opening of the Will; but to have the honor of consulting your Grace upon some points of which she is not capable of explaining upon paper."[8] One wonders what "points" she felt unable to commit to paper. Despite her disclaimer about the will, she may very well have wished to speak with him about the Meadows family's likely reaction to it.

She had good reason to worry. Before the duke married Elizabeth, his heir at law was his sister, Lady Frances Meadows, an unhappy woman whose husband, Philip, and eldest son, Evelyn, felt entitled to the duke's fortune. Years earlier, when the duke first met Elizabeth, the Meadows family moved his French mistress into their London home in hopes of keeping her in the duke's way while he was in town and thereby frustrating Elizabeth's advances. Their greatest fear was that Elizabeth and the duke would marry and produce an heir to the estate; but when their marriage was delayed until 1769, the Meadows family breathed more easily, figuring that Elizabeth was past childbearing by then. If the duke left anything like a normal will, they figured, Elizabeth would be entitled to her dowager's portion of 10 percent of the estate. But as the nearest male heir, Evelyn would inherit the rest.

So confident was Evelyn that he is reputed to have borrowed no less than £6000 in anticipation of his fortune.[9] That was a vast sum and a ruinous mistake. Not only had the duke left everything to Elizabeth during her lifetime, but he specifically cut Evelyn out of the succession to the estate after her death. All he got was a legacy of £500 in a codicil.

Nobody seems to have liked Evelyn, but the duke's hatred ran especially deep. Elizabeth explained to a correspondent that the duke was angry over his having resigned the honorable position as an aide-de-camp during the Seven Years' War in order to join a common marching regiment. Before long, he "quited the Army intirely living extravagantly, on the Hopes of Succession, which was in the Duke's Power to give to his more worthy Brothers."[10] At her trial, Elizabeth said that the duke was further enraged when Evelyn failed to marry a Miss Bishop, as he evidently had promised to do. Anna Porter, who left the detailed account of Elizabeth's trial, already knew this story so it must have been common gossip. When Elizabeth mentioned it, Anna said it "harrow'd up my soul" and called Evelyn Meadows a "vile Man, for all those on whom the name of <u>Man</u> is prostituted he is doubtless the vilest & so far is his mind from being after the Image of our Creator's—I am sure the Devil has marked him for his own."[11]

Whatever the reasons, the duke's enmity was strong enough to make him cut Evelyn out of the succession altogether. After Elizabeth's death, the estate would pass to Evelyn's four younger brothers in order of age. If they all were to die, the estate would then pass out of the family entirely and go to Lord Thomas Clinton, the Duke of Newcastle's second son. It must have occasioned Newcastle some embarrassment when he finally opened the duke's will and read it to Philip Meadows at Kingston House several weeks after the duke's death.

According to one correspondent who claims to have had first-hand knowledge of the affair, Evelyn had come with Philip but was left idling outside the gate with a cousin. When Philip emerged from the house, he "could not speak for tears."[12] Father and son left in shocked silence, already determined to wrest the estate from Elizabeth's hands.

Their determination was fired by the high stakes involved. The duke's real estate was estimated to be worth £80,000 and his personal wealth was valued at £16,000 per annum. Although far from being the richest estate in Britain (some of his peers had fortunes that dwarfed his), the duke's annual income was at least forty times what a very rich London merchant might hope to make in a year. Wealth like this was possible because in Britain the law of primogeniture ensured that noble titles and estates passed to eldest sons in their entirety, creating breathtaking concentrations of wealth among a very small social elite. At the time of Elizabeth's bigamy trial, there were fewer than two hundred peers of the realm. Spain, by contrast, had nearly half a million, and many of them were poorer than British dockworkers. Roy Porter has observed that "the English aristocracy was more of a closed circle in the eighteenth century than at any other time in history."[13] Breaking into that circle had been Elizabeth's life dream—and not hers alone.

Philip and Evelyn Meadows had been dreaming of enjoying the duke's money for some twenty years by the time he died. They had no claim to the title, which would die with the duke unless he produced an heir himself, but they were determined to have his money. Little did they know that more than three thousand miles away, a Puritan family in New Haven, Connecticut, had been vying for both the duke's money and his title for the past sixty years. In the shadows of Yale College lived another ambitious father who felt that his son, also named Evelyn, was entitled to enter the exalted circle of the British nobility.

Eighteen years before the duke's death, the *Connecticut Gazette* contained the following item:

> We are credibly informed that on the 16th of March last, the wife of Mr. James Pierrepont of New Haven, was happily delivered of a fine, well featured son, who the same day was christened by the name of Evelyn, which is the Christian name of the present Duke of Kingston; and as it is said that this child descended from the eldest branch of the Pierpont family, excepting that of the present Duke, and as the present Duke is far advanced in years and has no heirs of his body, it is possible this young Evelyn may in time succeed to the honors and estates of that ancient and honorable family of Great Britain.[14]

Behind this hopeful announcement lay a long struggle by the Pierrepont family in America to establish a claim on the Kingston estates and titles.

The Pierrepont family in Britain traces its roots back to the Norman Conquest. The family was split apart during the English Civil War, when the Puritan line moved to New England while the Cavaliers stayed home and fought vainly for Charles I. But if they lost the war, they won a significant battle, for the earldom of Kingston was created to reward their loyalty. This would eventually be elevated to a dukedom in the eighteenth century.

James Pierrepont was the eldest son of the Puritan line, born in Roxbury, Massachusetts, in 1659. He graduated from Harvard in 1681 and became the pastor of the First Church in New Haven where, to the shame of his alma mater, he also became a founder of Yale College. Despite this impeccable Yankee pedigree, it seems that the good reverend also kept an eye on opportunities across the water. At the same time that he was soliciting books from London to give Yale a library "worth six of that at Harvard College," he was making discreet inquiries about what claims he might make on the family titles and estates.[15] James believed that if the present earl of Kingston died without a male heir, the title and estates could be traced backward to the family that split during the Civil War, making a Connecticut Yankee a noble figure in Queen Ann's court. But before he could make much headway in this pursuit, he died on 22 November 1714 and was buried on New Haven Green, his Puritan rectitude unsullied by English titles.

His eldest son, James the Younger, continued his father's inquiries, and over the next fifty years he developed a nearly obsessive interest in establishing his family's claim to the title. Initially, he intended to travel to England to meet the first duke in 1724, but he never did so. However, to his great dismay, he learned from Connecticut's colonial agent, Jeremiah Dummer, that his cousin John, from Roxbury, had gotten wind of his plans and had sailed to England. Once there, John managed to obtain an introduction to the duke and attempted to pass himself off as the eldest male of the New England line. However, he was foiled by Dummer's timely intervention, the agent assuring the duke that James of New Haven, not John of Roxbury, had that distinction.

According to James Pierrepont, Dummer reported that the Duke of Kingston was very receptive to communications from the New England branch of the Pierrepont family, stating, "I am glad to see any of the name in these parts."[16] But the hospitable duke died in 1726 and the title fell to his grandson, Evelyn, the future husband of Elizabeth Chudleigh, who was to prove much less encouraging.

Undeterred, James renewed his efforts and over the next half century, he made several attempts to establish his claim to the succession in obsequious letters to the second duke. In 1749, he seemed to be on the verge of success when he sent one such letter to Richard Partridge, the new colonial agent for Connecticut. Partridge gave the letter to his son-in-law, who happened to be the duke's physician. The response, however, was disappointing. The duke, he said, "totally declines encouraging the Gentleman to come over purely to visit him, he says he has heard of the person before & tho' the name & arms may be the same with his own yet he does not much reckon there is any Relationship between them." He ended with a warning that must have broken James's heart: "As I know the Duke's Temper so very well I could wish that (if possible) thou wou'dst decline meddling with it—for I am confident no good consequences will attend it."[17]

If James was discouraged, he did not entirely give up hope. Six years later, as the *Connecticut Gazette* announced, he was still optimistic enough to name his eldest son Evelyn, in honor of his ducal namesake. He may not have been aware at that time that the second duke was involved with the notorious Miss Chudleigh, but several years later he was well aware of the connection and it became the source of his last hopes to claim the dukedom for his family. In June 1773, James wrote to Eleazer Wheelock, the president of Dartmouth College, asking him to use his connections to the Earl of Dartmouth in order to help him make a final application to the Duke of Kingston. He explains that the "Honorable Dr. Johnson, our late agent at the British Court, informs me that his Grace has two natural daughters by Miss Chudleigh before marriage and that his Grace is attempting to have them legitimized by Special act of Parliament but he thinks that the Parliament will not do it."[18] Sympathizing with the fornicating duke's predicament, the son of a New England Puritan proposes a "natural and easy way" to legitimize these supposed daughters: one of them could marry his son, Evelyn, now eighteen years old.

James was seventy-four years old when he made this final attempt, and it was all in vain. In reality, there were no bastard daughters to be married to his young Evelyn. And even if there were, he had made his move too late, for by the time he was making his appeal for the Earl of Dartmouth's intervention, the Duke of Kingston was suffering from his final illness. James followed him to the grave three years later, dying in New Haven in June 1776.

Judging from later events, young Evelyn may not have been as keen as his father to reach for British titles. When the American Revolution broke out, he became a lieutenant in the Connecticut militia and during the battle of New Haven in July 1779, as commander of Black Rock Fort he made sure that the cannons spent all their ammunition trying to repel the British and Hessian troops from landing in the harbor. Nevertheless, Elizabeth had not heard the last from the Pierreponts of New Haven, nor they from her.

It is not surprising that rumors of multiple illegitimate children were circulating in the summer of 1773. Horace Walpole, who was never scrupulous about facts when retailing gossip, also believed that Elizabeth had given birth to two children. And the duke's valet tells the story of Elizabeth Skinner, a young woman who waited on Elizabeth Chudleigh, but who was reputed to be her illegitimate daughter with the duke. She died in 1770 and was buried at Thoresby in an unmarked grave.[19] It seems that Elizabeth's reputation for audacity, begun with the masquerade costume in 1749 and cemented in the jactitation ruling twenty years later, had prepared the world to believe any rumors about her.

On 17 May 1774, Lady Frances and Philip Meadows filed a bill of complaint in the Court of Chancery to have the duke's will invalidated on the grounds that Elizabeth was not his legal wife.[20] As heir at law, the suit was ostensibly the action of Lady Frances, but Elizabeth had no doubt about who was really behind it. She explained to a correspondent that "Mr. Medows and his Eldest son" aimed to end her life by worrying her over the estate.[21] But in another letter, she had only pity for "Poor Lady Francis Medows," who, "in her intervals of sense told the Duke that her Unhappiness proceeded from the ill Treatment of this Son & her barbarous Husband."[22] Poor Lady Frances may have been in an even more miserable predicament than Elizabeth imagined. According to *The Complete Peereage*, "there is some doubt whether that lady did not marry Joseph Adey (previous to Mr. Philip Medows) and have issue by him."[23] If so, then pity Lady Frances, bullied by her husband, who was unaware of her secret bigamy, into prosecuting Elizabeth and threatening to expose herself. If that happened, then the abusive Philip and all his sons would have no claims on the estate at all.

Philip Meadows was determined to invalidate the duke's will. The Chancery case rested entirely on proving Elizabeth's marriage to Augustus Hervey; therefore, Hervey is also named as a defendant in the bill of complaint. (The Chancery suit also names the four younger Meadows boys as defendants, along with Lord Thomas Clinton, for they all stood in front of Evelyn in the line of succession.)

Between the reading of the duke's will in November 1773, and the filing of the bill of complaint six months later, Philip and Evelyn Meadows were very busy rounding up witnesses and evidence to prove the 1744 marriage. As fate would have it, Evelyn Meadows kept his horse at a stable run by John Fozard, who worked for the Duke of Kingston since his childhood and married one of Elizabeth's maids. He also happened to be the servant who accompanied Elizabeth to Lainston when she had the phony marriage register made. Fozard told Meadows that his wife had heard Ann Cradock speak of the wedding and bedding of Elizabeth and Hervey, and he offered to make contact with her on Meadows's behalf.[24] Meadows took him up on the offer and Ann deposed in June 1774, swearing that she saw Elizabeth and Augustus Hervey in bed, having consummated their marriage.[25] Her testimony gave the Meadowses such confidence that they demanded no testimony from Elizabeth and Hervey about their marriage, noting that they are "able to prove the same" and so have no need to inquire about it.[26]

In a list of questions for Elizabeth, the Meadowses asked if the duke ever suspected her marriage to Hervey. Obviously aware of her strategy in the jactitation suit, they pointedly asked her if she ever showed the duke legal documents executed in her maiden name in order to deceive him about her marital status. In an amended version of the bill of complaint, they claim that Elizabeth "imposed upon the weakness" of the duke by persuading him that she was "a Single Woman & thereby inducing him the said Duke to enter into the Sacred contract of Matrimony." So effective was she that the duke was "totally a stranger to and unacquainted with and not having the least knowledge or suspicion of" her prior marriage.[27] They clearly wanted the duke to come across as the victim of a conspiracy engineered by Elizabeth and Hervey. If they could convince the court that the duke had no idea of the prior marriage, then perhaps there would be greater pressure to invalidate the will.

One can imagine how Augustus Hervey felt when he heard that he was being sued for conspiring with Elizabeth to get the duke's money. He responded to the bill of complaint on 16 February 1775. He swore that he knew nothing specific about Elizabeth and the duke's relationship, including the ways she represented her marital status to him. But he does say that before their marriage, the duke "must have" believed she was a single woman. When mentioning the jactitation suit, however, he notes that the judgment was conditional "as far as to the said Judge then appeared."[28] This observation was probably offered to rebut the claim that he colluded in the suit for personal gain: he knew the verdict was conditional and never took advantage of the ruling to marry anybody else. The duke, by contrast, made the imprudent decision to marry on the strength of the decision, so the fault was his own. Not surprisingly, Hervey ends his statement by asking to be dismissed from the suit.

The Meadowses almost certainly did not believe that Hervey was conspiring to defraud the Duke of Kingston and his heirs. But like the rest of the world, they knew that Hervey had colluded in the jactitation suit, and the first step toward invalidating the will was proving the collusion in that case. Despite asking to be dismissed from the suit, Hervey knew that this was the beginning of a long and expensive train of litigation. At the very least, he could comfort himself with the thought that he might, at long last, be rid of Elizabeth Chudleigh.

However worried Elizabeth may have been that the Meadows family would take such a step, she was entirely ignorant that they actually had done so. She had left England in January 1774, for the Continent, and was traveling through Italy while Philip and Evelyn Meadows were beating the bushes in England for witnesses to prove her first marriage. Her lawyers had sent word of the lawsuit, but she missed the letters on her way home and only learned of the case when she arrived at Kingston House. Worried that she might be placed under arrest, she immediately left the country, explaining in a letter to the Duke of Portland: "I was obliged to submit, after twenty four hours being in my house, to be put into my Coach, once more to embark for France."[29] This was a soon-to-be infamous trip to Calais, taken in an open boat at midnight (for she could not wait for a more comfortable passage) and with just a single change of clothing.

Elizabeth would not return to England for another ten months, preferring to avoid attention by traveling on the Continent. In the meantime, Philip and Evelyn Meadows hedged their bets by initiating a second case against her. This one was different and more serious than the civil case in Chancery—they persuaded a grand jury to indict her on criminal charges of bigamy in December 1774. Elizabeth got news of this second lawsuit a few weeks later while in Rome. On the advice of her lawyers, she returned to London to answer the charges, arriving in mid-May 1775.

A few days after her return to Kingston House, *Lloyd's Evening Post* reported Elizabeth's appearance before Lord Mansfield in answer to the second lawsuit in the Court of King's Bench in West-minster Hall on 24 May. It was a dignified proceeding. She entered the courtroom discreetly, using a back door that was connected to the home of her old friend the Duke of Newcastle. When the court sat, she emerged in the company of her sureties, the Duke of Newcastle, Lord Mountstuart, James LaRoche, and Sir Thomas Clarges. The putative duchess bowed to the judges and lawyers and made some form of polite gesture to acknowledge the crowd of spectators who had packed into the courtroom to get a glimpse of her on this extraordinary occasion. The newspaper called it a "throng," but it was nothing compared to the crowd that would fill Westminster Hall the following year to witness her state trial on this same charge.

The sheriff of Middlesex, in whose nominal custody she was being held, read the indictment and she pleaded not guilty to the charge and entered her recognizance of £4,000, her sureties posting bail of £1,000 each. Upon Mansfield's advice, the opposing counsel dispensed with "some legal ceremony, which otherwise might have brought her Grace again before that Court." She took leave of the court in a "very polite" manner. The whole thing took about ten minutes.

The very same day that Elizabeth answered the criminal charges against her, *Lloyd's Evening Post* reported a bigamy case of a much different sort:

> A woman being tired of her husband, and the man weary of his wife, at Coventry, the woman consented to have a rope fastened to her neck, to

be led by it to the Market-cross in that city, and there sold to the best bidder, when she was bought by one Bland for half a crown.

Wife sales of this sort were strictly limited to the lowest levels of society, and their frequency is the subject of debate among historians.[30] But reports of them follow the same pattern: a rope or halter is fastened to the woman's neck, she is led to the market square like a cow and auctioned off, and the purchaser is usually a lover who has arranged with the husband to make the purchase for a low price. It was a cheap, brazen, and demeaning way for the lower orders to dissolve marriages that had deteriorated beyond repair. But what is most surprising about these wife sales is not that they dissolved a marriage illegally, but that they created a second, bigamous marriage in so public a manner. In this instance, circumstantial details like the purchase price, the city where the sale took place, and the buyer's name lend the report an air of credibility, yet there is no indignation expressed in the reporting, just a matter-of-fact relation of the events.

The appearance of these two bigamy stories on the same day is a striking illustration of how common that crime was in the Georgian era compared to the present day. The frequency of bigamy in eighteenth-century Britain remains uncertain. Some historians have speculated that tens of thousands of marriages were bigamous, and that bigamy was tolerated among a large portion of society.[31] But recent research by David Turner, examining the 283 bigamy trials that took place in the Old Bailey between 1700 and 1799, suggests that the number and acceptance of bigamous unions may be exaggerated.[32] The contrast between the low-class wife sale and the notice of Elizabeth's case in *Lloyd's Evening* Post illustrates how bigamy affected all levels of society, but it also shows how uncommon it was for a duchess to commit bigamy. The reasons for the difference are obvious. Mr. Bland was able to part with his half crown and take away Mrs. So-and-so because (presuming there were no children involved) there was no property at stake. That is the very point behind the humiliating spectacle of a public wife sale: the new husband has paid a fair price, and so any property disputes end when he leads the woman out of the market place. Bigamy by a noble woman, however, threatened to create endless property disputes and enormous legal headaches.

Elizabeth Chudleigh's bigamy was especially troubling because while she was en route from Rome to London that spring, George Hervey, the Earl of Bristol, finally died. On 18 March 1775, Augustus became the third Earl of Bristol, so when Elizabeth entered the courtroom and answered the charge as Duchess of Kingston, she knew in her heart that she was also the Countess of Bristol.

The Hervey family had an obvious interest in the case. Now that the charge of bigamy was out in the open, Elizabeth's marital status needed to be cleared up quickly if Augustus was to get a divorce at long last and remarry with the hopes of providing himself with an heir. This was his devout wish because he loathed his younger brother, Frederick, bishop of Derry, and wanted to do all he could to cut him and his heirs out of the succession. Now Augustus had the chance to divorce Elizabeth legally and marry his new love, Mary Nesbitt, who was still young enough to give him an heir.

Initially, the press coverage of Elizabeth's legal woes was muted. In London, the papers were dominated by the reports slowly trickling into town about Lexington, Concord, and the siege of Boston. When the front page was not dominated by the war, it was entirely devoted to the forgery trial of Mrs. Rudd, a beautiful adventurer who escaped the gallows by personally managing her defense.

Happily for Elizabeth, her legal troubles were overshadowed by these major stories. Referring to the criminal case, one newspaper reported, "To avoid the great expence attending the tryal of a Peer or Peeress in Westminster Hall, it is now supposed that a certain great Lady will be tried, if tried at all, at the bar of the House of Lords, and that under her present title."[33] This was wrong on both counts, but in the spring and early summer of 1775, Elizabeth had every reason to believe such predictions.

As for the civil case in Chancery, Elizabeth simply responded to the bill of complaint by claiming that the Court of Chancery had no business hearing this case. The legal strategy was sound. With competing and independent court systems, the English legal structure invited overlapping jurisdictions and the subsequent turf wars. Elizabeth's lawyers, probably well aware of her bigamy, decided that her strongest response was to plea the church court's ruling in the jactitation suit and the probate of the duke's will as a bar to prosecution in any other court system. And since Lord Mansfield was among her advisers, she had reason to feel confident about this strategy.

Simple as it was, the legal advice did not come cheaply. A year before she answered the bill of complaint, Elizabeth complained that she had already spent £1600 in legal fees, most of that money going to Mansfield. And that was before the Meadows family had taken any formal legal action. Now, in the spring of 1775, she faced suits in Chancery and King's Bench, respectively the highest civil and criminal courts in the kingdom. To defend herself successfully,

Elizabeth required a small army of lawyers, and she was determined to take a personal interest in her legal defense. The bookshelves at Kingston House that once displayed the trinkets she was so fond of now groaned under the weight of law books.

As Elizabeth assembled her legal team and geared up for her court cases, she also prepared to do battle in the court of public opinion. One of her lawyers introduced her to the Reverend William Jackson, the editor of the *Public Ledger*, a London newspaper that had grown very critical of the government in recent years. Jackson was a pugnacious Irishman who loved a good fight, especially in print. During his tenure at the *Public Ledger*, he had distinguished himself for his take-no-prisoners approach to public controversy, attacking his enemies (and he seemed to have a lot of them) with all the vigor that Britain's weak libel laws allowed. In some ways, Jackson seems an unlikely ally for a bigamous duchess. He was something of a political radical who opposed the policies of George III and his prime minister, Lord North, by vocally supporting the American side in the war just under way. Educated at Oxford, he became a Church of England minister (serving briefly as private chaplin to George Hervey), and although many eighteenth-century clergy were only nominal Christians, Jackson was genuinely devout. For all his pugnacity as a newspaper editor, he was a popular preacher whose style was considered to be "dignified and solemn."[34]

Jackson was a handsome man with a casually genteel air about him that women found very attractive. Not always careful about his extra-marital affairs, he often left love letters stuffed in his coat pockets, where his wife easily found them. Sometimes these letters revealed the time and place of his assignations, so his wife showed up to confront him with his adulteries. But according to a friend, he was prudent enough to avoid detection even on these occasions so his wife never caught him in the act. These affairs aside, Jackson evidently loved his wife very much. He personally cared for her when she was ill with breast cancer in 1775, "fanning her during the warmth of the season and the violence of her disorder."[35] When she died, he gave her an expensive funeral that he could ill afford.

Jackson was also popular among men. For all the political enemies his journalism earned him, his sharp wit and conviviality earned him just as many friends. Throughout his life, Jackson loved good company, good clothes, and good wine, and he was always on the lookout for ways to make enough money to enjoy his pleasures to the fullest.

In the summer of 1775 (as always) his pen was for hire, and he was more than happy to devote his services to Elizabeth Chudleigh's cause. His primary role was to provide her with flattering press coverage until her legal problems were behind her, but he quickly became a trusted adviser on legal matters as well. Feeling defensive and harassed, Elizabeth must have been attracted by Jackson's mix of pugnacity and gentility, not to mention his good looks. Having both lost spouses recently, they may also have provided a sympathetic ear to each other's sorrows. Elizabeth proved immediately receptive to his advice on a number of matters. Unfortunately for her, that advice was invariably wrongheaded. Hiring Jackson and listening to his counsel proved to be the worst of the many bad decisions she made that spring, for he guided her to every misstep she was about to make.

Initially, Elizabeth hardly needed Jackson's help. Although some newspapers, like the *Morning Chronicle*, were more likely to run unfavorable stories of her, most of the press coverage was respectfully understated throughout the spring and early summer. The clearest example of this came in *St. James's Chronicle* of 29 June 1775. The front page carries an article about a man who appeared at the Guildhall to face bigamy charges. The defendant was accused of having married no fewer than four women over the past twenty years, and when he was presented with evidence of his bigamy in court, he became abusive and threatened the opposing counsel with physical harm. The newspaper condemns the man's bigamy and courtroom demeanor in very strong terms, and the placement on the front page is surprising for such a story. On the same day, tucked away on an inside page is the following little paragraph:

> On Tuesday [the 27th] and yesterday [the 28th] came on to be argued in the Court of Chancery, a Plea put in by the Duchess of Kingston, to a Bill filed by Lady Meadows, the sister and heir at law of the late Duke of Kingston. Her Grace pleaded a sentence of the Ecclesiastical Court, by which she was declared to be a single woman before the late Duke married her, and also the Probate of the late Duke's Will; when after a long and solemn debate of the matter, the Lord Chancellor was pleased to allow her Grace's Plea.

Elizabeth had won the suit in Chancery.

For her, the news could not have been better, nor could it have been delivered in a better way. But if the newspapers underplayed it, she was not nearly so muted in her celebration. Writing to her good friend the Electress of Saxony, she exulted in her "complete victory" over her "enemies." Despite their efforts, "the Court strongly and obviously convinced of my innocence, decided in my favour. This

Decree pronounced by the Lord Chancellor is so complete and so decisive: that I find myself out of Danger from the Malice of my enemies, from now on."[36]

Brave words, but wrong on every count. Still, she cannot be blamed for feeling so confident. Lord Chancellor Bathurst had acknowledged that the ruling in the jactitation suit and the probate of the duke's will were legal decrees by the ecclesiastical courts that his court had no standing to question. This was her only legal defense, and it worked perfectly. There was no reason for Elizabeth to believe that the Court of King's Bench, presided over by her lawyer and personal friend, Lord Mansfield, would decide any differently.

As June came to a close, Elizabeth seemed to have defeated the malice of her enemies. Soon, she thought, she would have little use for her lawyers and the Reverend Jackson's newspaper. But July was to change all that.

SAMUEL FOOTE, ESQ.

Pub. Aug. 20. 1805 by, Richard Phillips, 6 New Bridge Street .

Samuel Foote, Esq. Courtesy of the University of Delaware

CHAPTER 8

ENTER THE ACTOR

Elizabeth's good humor and confidence were shaken sometime in July by a rumor that Samuel Foote, the leading comic dramatist of the day, had written a new play about her. Foote was fifty-four years old, a short, red-faced, chubby man who had only one leg. But despite his mild appearance, he was known as the most dangerous man in show business, a mimic with a mean streak who specialized in making well-known people look ridiculous on the public stage. Impersonation was Foote's stock-in-trade, and his topical satire earned him the nickname, the "modern Aristophanes."

Like Elizabeth, Foote was both famous and notorious, someone used to taking big risks and reaping bigger rewards. And like her, he rose from humble origins to occupy a prominent place in the life of fashionable London and the royal court. Foote hit the London scene in the early 1740s, the same time Elizabeth became a Maid of Honour. Ostensibly there to study law, he quickly made a name for himself as a free-spending bon vivant who spent more time at the theater and in the coffeehouses than he did at his studies.

During his early years, Foote considered himself above acting for money. His family suddenly became wealthy when one of his uncles murdered another and then was hanged for the crime, making Foote's mother the heiress to a modest fortune. This money enabled Foote to cut a dashing figure upon his arrival in London, and when he spent through it, he wrote a sensational pamphlet about his murderous uncle, further enriching himself from the family tragedy.[1] This was Foote's way all through his life: he was an opportunist who made and spent money without scruple. By the end of his first decade in London, he is reputed to have run through three inheritances with his spendthrift ways. Far from being embarrassed by this prodigality, he commemorated it by painting on the side of his carriage, "Iterum, iterum, iterumque" [again, and again, and again].[2]

Foote married sometime in the 1740s but separated from his wife and seems never to have seen her again. He was involved in various moneymaking schemes, including a bakery and a beer distributorship. He also spent time in debtor's prison, where he received a letter from his mother which read: "Dear Sam, I am in prison for debt: come and assist your loving mother." Foote replied:

> Dear Mother, So am I; which prevents his duty being paid to his mother by her affectionate son, Sam. Foote.
> P. S. I have sent my attorney to assist you; in the meantime, let us hope for better days.[3]

While this exchange may be apocryphal, one of Foote's recent biographers has proven that Foote was, in fact, imprisoned for debt in 1742 and was sued by his own mother.[4]

But despite this somewhat seedy past, Foote fancied himself a gentleman and a critic, and he turned to acting only out of necessity.[5] His first forays were unsuccessful, and throughout his long career he never was considered a good actor. It was not until he hit upon the idea of impersonating real people that his stage career really took off. In mimicry Foote had found his métier, but since he had no regular engagement at the London theaters, he spent some lean years putting up shows on his own whenever and wherever he could. For a period in the 1750s he acted in a transvestite musical revue that performed (illegally) in London taverns. This was called *Mother Midnight's Oratory*, and its creator was Christopher Smart, who is better known as one of the great Christian poets in the English language.[6]

After several years, Foote had established himself as a favorite comic performer and playwright, all thanks to his skills as a mimic. He became particularly famous (or infamous) for his impersonations of some major figures, such as George Whitefield, the charismatic Methodist minister who was largely responsible for the religious revival movement known as the Great Awakening. On Foote's stage, Whitefield, who was cross-eyed, became a hypocritical buffoon. A popular print of the day shows Foote in a parson's cassock, eyes crossed as he delivers a sermon. Foote also impersonated George Faulkner, the well-known publisher of Jonathan Swift's works. Faulkner had one leg, so Foote (when he had two legs) hopped around on stage making a cruel joke of the infirmity. When Foote lost his own leg in an accident, his detractors felt this was

God's punishment and that the ridicule of Faulkner would stop. But Foote was irrepressible. As soon as he was well, he resumed his impersonation of Faulkner, doing it all the better for missing a leg himself.

Foote's "depedidation," as Samuel Johnson called it, happened in 1766 during a riding weekend at the country house of Lord Mexborough. Foote was there with his good friend, the Duke of York, who, tired of Foote's bragging about his horsemanship, put him on a difficult horse as a practical joke. The horse threw Foote and gave him a compound fracture in one leg. This was a very grave injury in those days and Foote nearly died from having his leg removed at the knee. As Foote lay in bed at Mexborough's house, suffering incredible physical pain dulled only by heavy doses of laudanum, the contrite Duke of York begged his forgiveness and offered to do anything in his power to make things up to him. With admirable lucidity, Foote replied that a royal patent for the Little Theatre in the Haymarket might take the edge off his pain. The duke took this request to his elder brother, George III, and the king granted it.

The London stage had been under strict government regulation since the passage of the Stage Licensing Act of 1737, the most repressive censorship law in British history. One of its provisions stipulated that only theaters holding royal patents or special licenses from the Lord Chamberlain could offer plays in London. Anyone caught performing plays without permission would be jailed as a "rogue and a vagabond." Royal patents were very hard to come by and they were incredibly expensive. Having a patent meant his little theater would now be a very stable, respectable enterprise, so this was a turning point in Foote's life and career. Before 1766, he had been operating his theater by virtue of annual licenses, and every year he had to apply for renewal not knowing for sure that it would be granted. But now he enjoyed a royal patent for life.

He immediately enlarged his theater and changed its name from the colloquial "Little Theatre" to "The Theatre Royal in the Haymarket." On opening night, he delivered an address to the audience that commented on his new status and on the fall from the horse that got him there. He invited the audience to:

> Consult with care each countenance around,
> Not one malignant aspect can be found
> To check the royal hand that raised me from the ground.[7]

The point could not have been clearer: the most dangerous man in show business had become the court jester.

It was a role that suited Foote, who was never truly "danger-ous." For all his bluster about being a transgressive satirist in the tradition of Aristophanes, he was actually a good, conservative Whig and supporter of the status quo. The objects of his mimicry were never taken from the halls of power, and although his on-stage antics were audacious, they were seldom very serious. For instance, he never dared ridicule the radical politician John Wilkes (who also happened to be cross-eyed), for fear that Wilkes's partisans would riot and destroy his theater. In an important sense he enjoyed the best of both worlds: as the modern Aristophanes he had a reputation as an iconoclastic outsider, but as royal patentee he was a perfectly respectable theater impresario.

Between 1766 and 1775, Foote enjoyed his heyday. Every season he brought out and starred in a new play, and audiences flocked to see whom he would impersonate next. Edward Gibbon enjoyed unwind-ing at Foote's theater after a hard day's work of writing *The Decline and Fall of the Roman Empire*. Even those who were inclined to dislike Foote often found his wit infectious. When Gibbon's friend Samuel Johnson heard that Foote was planning to imitate him, he let the word out that he had just bought an oaken cudgel and planned to sit in the front row of Foote's theater with it. If Foote made good on his promise, Johnson would come onstage and beat him until he learned better manners. Later, Johnson personally met Foote at a dinner party held by a mutual friend. Speaking of that evening, the sometimes curmudgeonly Johnson said, "Having no good opinion of the fellow, I was resolved not to be pleased; and it is a very difficult thing to please a man against his will. I went on eating my dinner pretty sullenly, affecting not to mind him. But the dog was so very comical, that I was obliged to lay down my knife and fork, throw myself back upon my chair, and fairly laugh it out. No, Sir, he was irresistible."[8]

Johnson was far from being the only one who found Foote irresist-ible. In June 1775, Foote was at the zenith of his fame. He was rich, popular, and (as it turned out) a bit too sure of himself. He mistak-enly assumed that Elizabeth was so socially isolated after the duke's death and so damaged by the legal processes against her that she was a safe target for his satire. What he failed to realize was how confident she was feeling at the end of June, how much political power her rank still gave her, and how ready she was to employ the services of William Jackson and the *Public Ledger*.

The buzz about Foote's new play started early, sometime in May. He was going to "take off" the Duchess of Kingston in a new char-acter called Lady Barbara Blubber, an unsubtle shot at Elizabeth's excessive public grieving for the duke. But the play was not actually ready until July, when a copy of the text was submitted to the Lord Chamberlain for a license. Another aspect of the Stage Licensing Act required that the Lord Chamberlain review every new play prior to performance. Without his license, the play could not be performed; if an unlicensed play was put on the stage, the actors could be thrown in jail and the theater faced either a steep fine or closure. The review of play texts was a big job, and the Lord Chamberlain's office quickly developed a bureaucratic structure of examiners and deputy examiners of plays to handle the workload. Although there was some give-and-take between playwrights and the censors, the Lord Chamberlain's authority over the stage was absolute. There was no appealing his decisions.

Francis Seymour-Conway, the Earl of Hertford, had been Lord Chamberlain since 1766, so Foote knew him and his staff well. Unlike some of his predecessors, Hertford seems to have taken his censorial duties seriously; nevertheless, Foote had never had any troubles with him.[9] Indeed, although Foote had gotten into some scrapes with the previous Lord Chamberlain, in his three decades of playwriting he never had a play refused outright. Until now.

The trouble started as soon as he submitted the text. Lord Mountstuart, who stood bail for Elizabeth in May, went to Hertford and expressed concern over the play, by this time called *A Trip to Calais*.[10] The very title was humiliating, referring as it did to Elizabeth's panicked flight from London to Calais in 1774 when she learned that the Meadowses had filed a suit in Chancery. Lady Barbara Blubber's name was now changed to Lady Kitty Crocodile, which implied both Elizabeth's false tears over the duke's death and her treacherous nature. Hertford instructed William Chetwynd, the deputy examiner of plays, to look for passages that referred to the Duchess of Kingston's past history and present troubles. They were not hard to find.

After marking up the text, the play was returned to Foote, perhaps to give him a chance to revise it according to the censors' objections. It was not unusual for the censors to give a playwright the opportunity to "correct" a text, as they called it. Their unofficial policy was to help plays to the stage, not to suppress them outright. Despite the rigor of the law, very few plays were denied a license altogether. Most often the changes were made and the play was performed. Foote, used to gentle treatment from the censors, was not unduly upset by Chetwynd's objections, but he was not prepared to strike out all of the objectionable passages. Instead, he invited Lord Mountstuart to his home to look over the play with him. According to Foote's version of events, Mountstuart sat down with him and read the marked passages and "found them collected from general Nature, and applicable to none but those who, through Consciousness, were compelled to a Self-application."[11] This seems unlikely.

The plot is innocuous enough: a young woman has run away to Calais with her true love, rather than stay in London and marry a man chosen by her parents. But the solution to the girl's dilemma is surprising. In Calais, she meets Lady Kitty Crocodile, a hypocritical, grasping, nasty English widow who advises her simply to marry both men. The bigamy reference is, of course, a giveaway, but that alone is not what made the play objectionable. There are a number of highly specific, unmistakable similarities between Lady Kitty and Elizabeth Chudleigh. For example, Elizabeth's excessive grieving is made light of as Lady Kitty receives visitors in her "Chamber of Tears," dressed in deepest mourning.

Foote goes on to make fun of Elizabeth's sartorial excesses and her marriage to the duke. When Mrs. Clack, Lady Kitty's dressmaker, visits her, she recalls the wedding gown she made her, prompting Lady Kitty to say:

> You, I think, Mrs. Clack, decked me out like another Iphigenia, to be sacrificed at the temple of Hymen. Don't you recall the tremors, the terrors, that invaded each nerve, on that solemn, awful occasion? You must remember, with what reluctance I was dragged by Sir John to the altar.[12]

There is the obvious reference to the 1749 masquerade gown, but Foote also tucks in the nickname of St. George's, Hanover Square ("London's Temple of Hymen"), and hints at the rumors that the duke was the one dragged to the altar, reluctant to lose the £10,000 annuity he allegedly promised her if he refused to marry her if she could prove herself a single woman. Even more devastating is Lady Kitty's characterization of marriage as a "solemn, awful occasion." Spoken in the character of a well-known bigamist, this would have gotten the biggest laugh of all. And that was just one of the many passages that Foote and Mountstuart looked at. The jokes are telling enough on the page, but Elizabeth also faced the prospect of Foote onstage in drag, imitating her voice and actions. Little wonder she tried to intervene.

After going over the text, Mountstuart asked if he could take the play to Elizabeth; and perhaps surprisingly, Foote let him. It was worse than she imagined, and before long she summoned the playwright to Kingston House for a face-to-face meeting. The only explanation for why she arranged this extraordinary meeting is that the play was so thoroughly upsetting to her that she could not bear for it to be staged even if all of the marked passages were omitted. It was a risky move on her part, for Foote had the upper hand: although some passages had been marked by the censor, it seemed that the play was going to be licensed in some form, as was usually the case. And unlike Elizabeth, Foote had no incentive to keep their meeting a secret.

Exactly what passed between the two is a mystery. Foote was uncharacteristically reticent when he mentioned it in an open letter to the Lord Chamberlain, stating only that "Her Grace saw the Play, and, in consequence, I saw her Grace; with the result of that inter-view, I shall not, at this time, trouble your Lordship." He then added, "It may perhaps be necessary to observe, that her Grace could not discern, which your Lordship, I daresay, will readily believe, a single trait in the character of Lady Kitty Crocodile, that resembled herself."[13] This seems impossible. It may have been a subtle joke, Foote's way of saying that Elizabeth was so deluded that she could not recognize her own vices and follies when they were shown to her. A more believable account of the interview says that Foote invited Elizabeth to mark any passages that she felt reflected on her, but she was "too cunning to bite at this."[14] Foote could always print the piece, pointing out what passages Elizabeth applied to herself.

Foote's reticence about the interview is unfortunate because it quickly became the subject of great controversy. What seems clear is that it ended without Foote's having budged an inch, and who can blame him? He had every reason to believe that he might still be able to restore some of the marked passages by bargaining with the censors and no reason at all to voluntarily suppress the play. Far from it. His considerable income, estimated to be as much as £3,000 per annum, came solely from the theater, and the enterprise relied on the power of a new play to draw audiences with new mimicry each season.[15] If he shelved *A Trip to Calais* he would stand to lose a great deal of money.

In the event, he had to forego that money anyway, for in early August the Lord Chamberlain prohibited the play altogether. Elizabeth's allies had gone back to the Lord Chamberlain's office and prevailed on Hertford to deny it a license. Foote was stunned and upset. By returning the play with specific passages marked, the censors had made an implicit offer to license it if he omitted those lines. Now, bowing to outside pressure, they went back on that unspoken deal, and there was no appealing the decision.

Foote let his true feelings show in an angry open letter to Lord Chamberlain Hertford in which he publicized the meetings between himself, Mountstuart, and Elizabeth. Attempting to claim the high ground, Foote argued that *A Trip to Calais* was not a cheap shot at Elizabeth; rather, it was a moral satire that struck a blow for virtue against vice and folly. Excusing the specific references to Elizabeth, he explained that "if Comedy directs not her aim, her arrows are shot in the air; for by what touches no man, no man will be mended."[16] Then he complained that she had such a guilty conscience that all expressions of virtue made her feel attacked: "To such minds, my Lord, *The Whole Duty of Man*, next to the Sacred Writings, is the severest Satire that ever was wrote." But what comes through most clearly is Foote's sense of betrayal. Referring to the relationship between himself and the censors, he says that "between the Muse and the Magistrate there is a natural Confederacy; what the last cannot punish, the first often corrects; but when she not only finds herself deserted by her ancient ally, but sees him armed in the defence of her foe, she has nothing left but a speedy retreat."

This outburst was uncharacteristic of Foote, who was usually witty and urbane, unflappable in every situation. Although he claimed that the letter was published in the hopes of persuading the Lord Chamberlain to reverse his decision, he knew that was not going to happen. It is a protest letter, an angry expression of betrayal. It was risky, too, for Foote would still need Hertford's approval of any new plays he wrote. There was little to be gained from publishing it, yet it appeared in all the London papers, igniting a storm of controversy. Horace Walpole, who loved this sort of thing, told a friend all about it:

> [Foote] has already printed his letter to Lord Hertford, and not content with that, being asked why it was not licensed, replied, "Why my Lord Hertford desired me to make his youngest son a box-keeper, and because I would not, he stopped my play." Upon my word, if the stage and the press are not checked, we shall have the army, on its return from Boston, besieged in the Haymarket itself: what are we come to, if maids of honour cannot marry two husbands in quiet![17]

As Walpole's letter shows, the story was bad for both Foote and Elizabeth. To stifle the gossips and the newspaper comments, they should have let the story die. But that was not in their natures. The quarrel quickly got the better of both of them. Foote's first biographer printed the text of a handbill that Foote was planning to have publicly distributed, gratis, between Hyde Park Corner and Kingston House. It was modeled on the handbills that hawked the biographies of condemned felons at Tyburn, the public gallows in London. On the advice of friends, who told him that this would humiliate the duchess but also disgrace him, Foote never fulfilled this threat.[18]

Shortly after the publication of Foote's open letter, Elizabeth and Mountstuart invited him back to Kingston House. After the suppression of *A Trip to Calais,* Foote had been reading it at dinner tables around London (there was no law against that), and he promised to publish the play with a dedication to her grace, the Duchess of Kingston. There was also no law against that. Although the stage was tightly regulated, press censorship had expired eighty years earlier. Having caught wind of Foote's intention to publish, Elizabeth was anxious to prevent a new embarrassment.

When Foote arrived, Elizabeth said she had heard that Foote was offered £150 to publish his play; she offered to give him that sum to destroy it. Obviously she had no idea that this was a paltry sum to him, arguably one-twentieth of what the Lord Chamberlain's suppression had cost him. Foote was prepared for this and had his reply ready. He asked Elizabeth, "Are those ear-rings composed of diamonds, are those necklaces pearl? If they are, and those candlesticks silver, pray put them away, lest I should lay my hands on them. No, Madam, when my necessities reduce me to make use of dishonourable means of supplies. I will sooner go upon the Highway, than accept of an offer so much to my dishonour."[19] Elizabeth argued that there is no harm in taking the bribe because only she and Lord Mountstuart would know of it. Foote corrected her, saying, "There is a third person present, and with whom I ever wish to remain upon the best of terms, *viz.* myself." Mountstuart stepped in an assured Foote that the privacy of the bribe hides the shame of accepting it. But Foote was resolute.

Foote wasted no time in telling his friends what transpired during the meeting. According to one correspondent, Foote read the play to a friend, who called it "the most impudent thing that ever was wrote. It was Lord Mountstuart who took up the Duchess of Kingston's cause, & prevailed on Lord Chamberlain not to let it be acted. Mr. Foot has had 2 interviews with the Duchess, & told (this friend of mine) that she offered him a large sum of money not to print it."[20] David Garrick, who probably heard of the story from Foote himself, told a friend that "Cato himself tho he had one Leg more than our friend, was not more stoically virtuous than he has been."[21]

But Foote did not have long to bask in his virtuous refusal of a bribe. Failing to buy him off, Elizabeth now turned to William Jackson for help. Jackson had argued that buying the play was tantamount to succumbing to blackmail. If Foote got money from her to stop publication, other blackmailers were sure to follow. Now that the attempt had failed, she recognized the wisdom of Jackson's advice (perhaps the only good advice he ever gave her). Instead of trying to buy Foote's silence, they went on the offensive. Jackson began attacking Foote in the *Public Ledger*, which Foote might have expected; but the nature of the attack was an unpleasant surprise.

Foote was a sodomite, Jackson said. His ungentlemanly attacks on Elizabeth were proof that he had no sympathy for the fair sex, and his unnatural sexual activities were symptomatic of a perverted and diseased soul. This attack raised the dispute to a new level of seriousness. At that time, sodomy was a capital offense, and although hundreds of crimes in Georgian England were punishable by death, sodomy had a special distinction. The legal formula called it "the worst of crimes, unfit to be named by Christians." It is no exaggeration to say that calling Foote a murderer would have been less injurious to his reputation.

Things had gotten ugly, and they were about to get uglier.

Coupled with the beginning of Jackson's newspaper assault was a visit to Foote from the Duke of Newcastle on 13 August. Newcastle made a final appeal for Foote to stop publication. Alarmed by the accusations of sodomy, Foote was ready to admit defeat. He sent Elizabeth the following letter:

> Madam,
> A Member of the Privy Council, and a friend of your Grace's, (he has begged me not to mention his name, but I suppose your Grace will easily guess him) has just left me. He has explained to me, what I did not conceive, that the publication of the Scenes in the "Trip to Calais," at this juncture, with the Dedication and Preface, might be of infinite ill consequence to your affairs.
>
> I really, Madam, wish you no ill, and should be sorry to do you an injury.
>
> I therefore give up to that consideration what neither your Grace's offers, nor the threats of your Agents, could obtain; the Scenes shall not be published, nor shall any thing appear at my Theatre, or from me, that can hurt you; provided the attacks made on me in the Newspapers do not make it necessary for me to act in defence of myself.
>
> Your Grace will therefore see the necessity of giving proper directions.[22]

This was a surprising turnabout, and it showed just how effective the newspaper attacks were. Despite claiming that he was immune to "threats," the reference to the newspaper campaign shows that Foote was very alarmed by them.

Elizabeth's victory seemed complete: the play could not be staged and now Foote promised not to publish it either. That would have been the end of the story had Elizabeth been quietly content with her triumph. Unfortunately for her, she received the letter while at dinner with William Jackson and the two of them (both heavy drinkers) celebrated their victory by writing an intemperate reply to Foote and sending it to the newspapers along with Foote's letter:

Sir,
I was at dinner when I received your ill-judged letter. As there is little consideration required, I shall sacrifice a moment to answer it.

A Member of your Privy Council can never hope to be of a Lady's Cabinet.

I know too well what is due to my own dignity, to enter into a compromise with an extortionable assassin of a private reputation. If I before abhorr'd you for your slander, I now despise you for your concessions; it is a proof of the illiberality of your satire, when you can publish or suppress it as best suits the needy convenience of your purse. You first had the cowardly baseness to draw the sword, and, if I sheath it until I make you crouch like the subservient vassal as you are, then is there not spirit in an injured woman, nor meanness in a slanderous buffoon.

To a man my sex alone would have screened me from attack—but I am writing to the descendant of a Merry Andrew, and prostitute the term manhood by applying it to Mr. Foote.

Cloathed in my innocence as in a coat of mail, I am proof against an host of foes, and, conscious of never having intentionally offended a single individual, I doubt not but a brave and generous Public will protect me from the malevolence of a theatrical assassin. You shall have cause to remember, that though I would have given liberally for the relief of your necessities, I scorn to be bullied into a purchase of your silence.

There is something, however, in your pity at which my nature revolts. To make me an offer of Pity at once betrays your insolence and your vanity. I will keep the Pity you send until the morning before you are turned off, when I will return it by a Cupid with a box of lipsalve, and a choir of Choristers shall chaunt a stave to your requiem.
P.S. You would have received this sooner, but the servant has been a long time rewriting it.[23]

The overly haughty tone and the unsubtle references to Foote's sexuality made for a laughable combination of high-mindedness and gutter talk. The letter instantly became the object of public ridicule and rather than putting the last nail in Foote's coffin, it served only to reignite the controversy over *A Trip to Calais*.

Elizabeth and Jackson should have known better than to cross literary swords with Foote. He instantly realized what harm they had done to their cause and he wasted no time capitalizing on it with a devastating letter that he sent to all the newspapers:

Madam,

Though I have neither the time nor inclination to answer the illiberal attacks of your Agents, yet a public correspondence with your Grace is too great an honour for me to decline. I can't help thinking but it would have been prudent in your Grace to have answered my Letter before dinner, or at least postponed it to the cool hour of the morning; you would then have found, that I had voluntarily granted that request which you had endeavoured, by so many different ways, to obtain.

Lord Mountsuart, for whose amiable qualities I have the highest respect, and whose name your Agents first very unnecessarily produced to the public, must recollect, when I had the honour to meet him at Kingston-House, by your Grace's appointment, that instead of begging relief from your charity, I rejected your splendid offers to suppress the *Trip to Calais*, with the contempt they deserved. Indeed, Madam, the humanity of my royal and benevolent Master, and the public protection, have placed me much above the reach of your bounty.

Buy why, Madam, put on your Coat of Mail against me? I have no hostile intentions. Folly, not Vice, is the game I pursue. In those Scenes which you so unaccountably apply to yourself, you must observe, that there is not the slightest hint at the little incidents of your life. I am happy, Madam, however, to hear that your Robe of Innocence is in such perfect repair; I was afraid it might have been a little the worse for the wearing; may it hold out, to keep you warm the next winter!

The Progenitors your Grace has done me the honour to give me, are, I presume, merely metaphorical persons, and to be considered as the Authors of my Muse, and not of my Manhood: A Merry Andrew and a Prostitute are no bad poetical Parents, especially for a Writer of Plays; the first to give the Humour and Mirth, the last to furnish the Graces and Powers of Attraction.

If you mean that I really owe my birth to that pleasant Connection, your Grace is greatly deceived. My Father was, in truth; a very useful Magistrate and respectable Country Gentleman, as the whole county of Cornwall will tell you. My Mother, the Daughter of Sir Edward Goodere; Bart., who represented the country of Hereford; her Fortune was large, and her Morals irreproachable, till your Grace condescended to stain them; she was upwards of fourscore years old when she died, and, what will surprise your Grace, was never married but once in her life. I am obliged to your Grace for your intended present on the day, as you politely express it, when I am to be turned off.—But where will your Grace get the Cupid to bring me the lip-salve?—That family, I am afraid, has long quitted your service.

Pray, Madam, is not J—n the name of your Female confidential Secretary? and is not she generally clothed in black petticoats made out of your weeds?

I fancy your Grace took the hint when you last resided at Rome; you hear there, I suppose, of a certain Joan, who was once elected a Pope, and in humble imitation have converted a pious Parson into a Chambermaid. The scheme is new in this country, and has doubtless its particular pleasures. That you may never want the *Benefit of Clergy*, in every Emergence, is the sincere wish of

> Your Grace's
> Most devoted and obliged humble Servant,
> Samuel Foote[24]

Foote's letter is a masterpiece of its kind: restrained and witty, it takes both Elizabeth's pride and Jackson's dark accusations and turns them back on them. Elizabeth and Jackson went after Foote with a cudgel, while he wisely chose to respond with the rapier. Horace Walpole's friend William Mason wrote him a letter full of admiration for Foote's virtuoso performance: "Foote's answer is one of the very best things in the English language and perfect in its kind. Mr. Pope's letter to Lord Hervey is nothing to it."[25] This was high praise, indeed, for it placed Foote above Alexander Pope, who is generally considered the greatest English satirist of the century. Mason then retails an anecdote he heard from an unnamed country squire who recently had dined with Elizabeth and one of her lawyers. After dinner, Elizabeth retired and her lawyer began to sing her praises, especially her cunning in her "late manœuvres in the courts of law." The country squire bluntly replied, "Mr. Lawyer, this may be all very true. I believe the Duchess is a clever sort of woman, but by G— she never was so much out in her life as when she ventured to write a letter to Foote."[26]

As these reactions show, the exchange of public letters transformed the nature of Foote and Elizabeth's private dispute. It also permitted some to generalize Elizabeth's actions as a perfect example of aristocratic immorality and hauteur. Picking up on her metaphor about being "Cloathed in my innocence as in a coat of mail," the author of a poem called *The Devil* writes:

> When titl'd prostitution stalks,
> With crest erect, in crowded walks;
> While trulls abash'd, with modest air,

> Shrink from the bold patrician stare;
>   . . .
> But though the harsher weapons fail
> On vice, secur'd with coats of mail;
> While, spite of vanity's pretence,
> Guilt steel'd to blame is lost to sense,
> The keener sting of ridicule
> Shall pierce the strumpet through the fool.[27]

In class-based terms, this author contrasts the very proud and public "titl'd prostitution" with "modest" prostitutes who shrink from their stare. In this poem, Elizabeth's "coat of mail" is not her innocence, but her aristocratic title, which shields her from the law ("harsher weapons") but which cannot protect her from the "keener sting" of Foote's ridicule.

The same evening that Foote published his devastating letter, he starred in his own play, *The Bankrupt*. When his character spoke the lines "I have no reason to be ashamed of my family," the house echoed with thundering applause, recalling Elizabeth's attack on his parents. According to the newspapers, the theater was packed to capacity.

This was Elizabeth's worst nightmare. Even though *A Trip to Calais* did not appear on the page or the stage, Foote was making her a laughing stock in print and in performance. While she was spending thousands of pounds on her legal defense and public relations, Foote clearly had the public's sympathy and was making money from it, to boot. And she had only herself and Jackson to blame. They tried to control the damage by having her personal chaplain, the respectable old John Forester, swear an affidavit that Foote tried to blackmail her to the tune of £2000. But nobody much believed anything coming from her camp any longer. David Garrick expressed the prevailing opinion when he told a friend, "Notwithstanding Forster's Oath, Foote has thrown the Duchess on her back, & there has left her, as you and I would do. She is sick & has given up the cause, & has made herself very ridiculous & hurt herself in the struggle. Foote's letter is one of his best things, in his best manner."[28]

The scrap with Foote left Elizabeth angry, humiliated, and more vulnerable than she realized. To many people's minds, her vituperative letter betrayed her modest origins (not to mention Jackson's coauthorship). It was undignified and unladylike: no real duchess would stoop to such abusive language, especially in a letter sent to all the newspapers. The damage that letter did to her cause was immediately clear, but its full extent became evident only as the summer turned to fall and Elizabeth made the fateful misstep of moving her criminal trial out of the friendly venue of Lord Mansfield's courtroom and into the public forum of the House of Lords. She was about to learn just how much she had hurt herself by her public quarrel with Samuel Foote.

Unknown. *Representation of the Trial of the Dutchess of Kingston*. Etching and engraving, 20.8 × 12.6 cm, sheet. Courtesy of The Lewis Walpole Library, Yale University

CHAPTER 9

TRIAL FOR BIGAMY

Elizabeth had succeeded in keeping *A Trip to Calais* off the stage and out of print, but it was a Pyrrhic victory. Walking down the street in the city of London or Westminster during the summer and fall of 1775, one could not avoid the story of her argument with Samuel Foote. The windows of the print shops displayed numerous images of Elizabeth in her scandalous masquerade costume of twenty-six years earlier—hardly the image she wanted in people's minds as she faced trial. An even more barbed print showed her and Foote engaged in a duel. Elizabeth's chest is covered in chain mail, mocking the claim in her letter to Foote that she was "cloathed in my innocence as in a coat of mail."[1]

The newspapers, which were hawked at bookstalls and on street corners, kept the story before the reading public, ensuring that the dispute with Foote remained a lively topic of conversation in the coffeehouses, taverns, and private clubs. In September, two men in a tavern got into a heated argument over the dispute between Elizabeth and Foote that resulted in a challenge to duel the next day in Hyde Park. They traded pistol shots, and when both missed, they carried on the fight with swords. One man suffered three cuts before their seconds intervened and brought the duel to an end.[2]

That fall also saw the publication of *The Case of the Duchess of Kingston*, a thirty-page pamphlet that reprinted all the letters between her and Foote and provided a surprisingly detailed and evenhanded account of their quarrel. As the author points out, "It is probable that the public conversation, relative to her Grace, would have subsided till the ultimate issue of the proceedings were known" had she not entered the quarrel with Foote and made herself "once more the general topic of conversation."[3]

Confident that he had enjoyed the last laugh, Foote refrained from publishing anything more on the subject, and he made good on his pledge not to publish *A Trip to Calais*. Elizabeth's defenders, by contrast, howled in protest over the damage that Foote had done her. Led by Jackson, they published letters in the newspapers that blamed Foote for convicting her in the court of public opinion before her trial even had a chance to be heard in the Court of King's Bench. As the magnitude of Elizabeth's humiliation sunk in, Jackson's fury with Foote bordered on hysteria. Commenting on the social difference between a duchess and an actor, Jackson or another of Elizabeth's allies warned in an anonymous letter to the *St. James's Chronicle* that "All Subordination must be lost in the Kingdom if there are no Means left of protecting an English Duchess from the Insults of one whom the Laws of his Country describe as a Vagabond."[4]

At this time there were fourteen newspapers in London published on a daily or triweekly basis. Competition for readers was fierce and a story like this was just the sort of thing that sold copies. On any given day that fall, up to 20,000 papers circulated in London, and the habit of reading the news aloud and leaving copies in clubs and coffeehouses means that the stories of Elizabeth and Foote reached as many as 200,000 people a day.[5] And these numbers do not even account for the provincial newspapers, which reprinted London scandal for their gossip-hungry readers. As these numbers show, by attacking Foote through the papers, Elizabeth and Jackson only served to expose themselves to greater and greater ridicule.

In the midst of Jackson's furious campaign, one writer asked Elizabeth's defenders to consider "whether her Reputation has not suffered more, and the Publication of a certain disgraceful Charge has not been spread wider, and sunk deeper into the Minds of the Public by their Letters of Defence, than by any Attack from the most malevolent of her Enemies?"[6] Jackson seemed to follow this sensible advice and controversy began to die down at the end of September.

But the stories did not stop entirely, and Jackson and Elizabeth remained the object of common conversation and scandal. One facetious story in *St. James's Chronicle* says that modesty was in such short supply that when the libertine Earl of Sandwich threw the last parcel of it into the Thames ("in humble Imitation of" the Boston tea party) Elizabeth "immediately sent off Boats to recover it, but without Success, even though the Rev. Dr. J—ck—n took the utmost Pains to fish for it with his Cassock."[7]

It was amid all this negative publicity that Elizabeth took the fateful step of invoking her privilege as a peeress to have her case tried by the House of Lords. In November she sent a petition to Lord Chancellor Bathurst, asking him to introduce the motion to have her case tried there. By removing the indictment from the Court of King's Bench, she hoped also to remove herself from the public eye, and perhaps to avoid a trial altogether. Elizabeth gambled that Bathurst's decision to throw out the Chancery suit would prompt his peers in the House of Lords to follow his example and quash the criminal indictment as well.

Unfortunately for Elizabeth, she did not appreciate just how radically her fortunes had reversed as a result of her scrape with Foote. Before it, the lords would probably have been content to help her out by agreeing to hear the case, then quietly throwing out the indictment. But by engaging in a scurrilous newspaper war with Samuel Foote, Elizabeth had made herself a contemptible spectacle in the eyes of many, publicizing her legal predicament at the very time that she needed to maintain a low profile. To make matters worse, by asking the lords to hear her case, she politicized it, transforming it from a criminal indictment against a private person into a symbolic indictment of aristocratic sexual immorality in general. The peers may have been willing to act on the basis of class solidarity had the case largely stayed out of the newspapers. But by late fall, Elizabeth was a laughing stock, and the lords were not eager to be seen as her accomplices.

After introducing the motion to hear her case on 16 November, Bathurst led the charge to make the trial as big, public, and humiliating as possible: a state trial in Westminster Hall. On the eve of the vote to decide where the trial should be held, Elizabeth begged the Duke of Portland, who was ill at the time, to attend the House of Lords in order to oppose Bathurst's plans. She told Portland, "I have no fear from My Cause, but surely you would not have your friend and the Widow of your Relation a Publick Spectacle to Gratify the Vanity of Lord C[hancellor Bathurst]."[8] But Bathurst carried the day on nearly every point, failing only in his bid to have Elizabeth imprisoned in the Tower of London.

Faced with the prospect of an embarrassing state trial, Elizabeth did what she could to forestall the event. Just a month earlier she had asked the lords to hear her case, assuming the question would be, "Tryall or not Tryall"; now she was reduced to postponing the day of trial by pleading illness.[9] On 11 December 1775, she petitioned the lords for a two-month delay, explaining that she "finds herself under the necessity of supplicating your Lordships Indulgence, and of submitting to remain longer under the imputation of a criminal Charge."[10] It was at this time that she wrote to the king, pleading with him to stop the prosecution.

But it was all in vain. The king never replied, and although the trial was postponed, Bathurst simply took advantage of the delay to renew the question of imprisoning Elizabeth. Again turning to the Duke of Portland for help, she wrote to him with understandable bitterness that "she has heard there is to be a Motion made tomorrow to put the Dutchess into the Custody of the Constable of the Tower when she is tried, the dutchess hopes the Duke of Portland will be at the House and will do her the favour to Engage his friends if Possible as it seems to be A friendly step of the Chanc[ello]r. Towards sending the dutchess to the Tower."[11] But once again, Elizabeth's friends in the House of Lords, led by Lord Mansfield, saved her from that indignity.

Rather than being locked up in the Tower, Elizabeth would have to submit to genteel house arrest under the guard of Sir Francis Molyneux, Gentleman User of the Black Rod. Molyneux was Elizabeth's old friend and occasional card partner, so it must have been with some reluctance that he undertook this disagreeable duty.

Another old friend of Elizabeth was charged with an even more unpleasant task in anticipation of the trial. The Duke of Ancaster, who had proposed marriage to her three decades earlier, was now the Lord Great Chamberlain of the King's Household. As such, he was responsible for overseeing the monumental preparations of Westminster Hall for the trial. On 8 February 1776, Ancaster received a politely worded letter telling him, "I must desire your Lordship will be pleased to issue your orders for the furnishing and appareling [Westminster Hall] as hath been Accustomed on the like Occassions."[12] The sender was the Earl of Hertford, the Lord Chamberlain who had tried to screen Elizabeth from public shame six months earlier by banning *A Trip to Calais*. Now, under the Earl of Bathurst's direction, Hertford, Ancaster, and a host of others began setting the stage for a spectacle far worse than anything Samuel Foote could have produced at the Little Theatre in the Haymarket.

Within days of receiving the letter from Hertford, Ancaster sent ten warrants to the Board of Works to prepare the "Court and Seats in Westminster Hall for the same Number of Persons & in the same manner as at the Trial of William Lord Byron in the year 1765."[13] Byron's murder case was the most recent trial of a peer, and while it was a sensation at the time, the prospect of seeing a peeress on trial

ensured even greater public interest. Ancaster ordered the construction of private boxes for the king, the queen, the royal family, the
foreign ambassadors, Bathurst, Mansfield, and himself. He ordered
the construction of large galleries to run along the sides of the Hall,
a distance of nearly three hundred feet. One of these was to be built
especially for the Duke of Newcastle, whose house opened into the
Hall on the east side. The seating rose from the floor the rafters and
some of the seats are described as being "in the windows" that ran
the length of the Hall.

In all, these galleries and boxes would hold 3,140 people.[14] Add
to that nearly 120 lords, numerous attendants, doorkeepers, clerks,
and lawyers, and the total number of people inside the Hall reached
nearly four thousand.

Ancaster also had to consider the throngs that were sure to gather
outside the Hall. People without tickets would almost certainly
attempt to gain access to the Hall, so he issued a warrant for "fencing
every avenue leading from the several Buildings on the Leads & in the
Gutters on the East and West side of Hall" and one for "shutting
up all the Doors and Passages East and West of the Court of
Requests, and the center Door at North end of Court of Requests."[15]
Westminster Hall today enjoys a prominent place in front of the houses
of Parliament, where the public can see the nine-hundred-year-old
structure without obstruction. But in 1776, it was crowded around
with small buildings, including private residences and coffeehouses.
Ancaster received petitions from the owners of Waghorne's and the
Parliament coffeehouses, both of which had doorways leading into the
Hall. They asked to be allowed to keep their doors to the Hall open
so that they could provide refreshments to the spectators. The owner
of Waghorne's assured him that he would keep "all Idle and disorderly persons" from the area and promised to "take particular Care
not to admit any Person or Persons but such as have a Right to come
thro' his said Room into Westminster Hall."[16] It was from the upper
windows of one of these coffeehouses that the eighteen-year-old
Anna Porter marveled at the crowds outside on the first day of
the trial.

To keep those crowds from becoming "idle and disorderly,"
Ancaster deployed over 500 troops from the Horse and Grenadier
Horse Guards. They closed off the main avenue from Charing Cross
to Westminster Hall, some of these troops marching on patrol while
others towered over the crowds, mounted on their horses.

Perhaps the most difficult task was the distribution of tickets.
Given the great public interest in the trial, competition for tickets

was intense. Every lord was allotted seven tickets to each day of the trial; the special box holders were issued parcels of tickets for their boxes; the Commissioners of the Board of Works and the Duke of Newcastle got tickets to their respective galleries; and Ancaster, who had both a private box and a gallery, had nearly 400 tickets to distribute to friends and family. To prevent any chicanery, the lords had to receive their tickets in person, and the tickets were not distributed until Saturday 13 April, just two days before the start of the trial.[17] Inevitably, the peers found themselves besieged with requests for tickets. Lady Sondes asked the Duke of Newcastle if she could bring the daughter of a pregnant friend, assuring him that "it would be doing a Charitable action, as I don't think the Girl will otherwise be able to see the Sight."[18] Another correspondent begged him for a ticket for a friend who had lived in China for the last twenty years and who consequently "never was present at a Trial in England."[19] One can only imagine how many other "charity" cases Newcastle and the other peers were inundated with.

Interest in the trial was most intense in London, but it was not limited to the metropolis, or even the kingdom. Provincial newspapers reprinted accounts of preparations for the trial from the London papers, and people traveled to London from continental Europe in hopes of witnessing this remarkable event. The painter James Northcote recalled having met a young Italian who traveled to London "for the sole purpose he said, of seeing the ceremonies at the Trial of the Duchess of Kingston. He spoke English pretty well. He owned that he had been more particularly induced to undertake the journey to attend this curious Trial of a Peeress because he thought it would have ended in her being condemned and Beheaded."[20]

As the day of trial approached and London filled up with people eager to witness this spectacle, Elizabeth maintained a steady and confident public demeanor. But in private she must have been filled with self-reproach. When she first learned of the criminal charges more than a year earlier, one of her lawyers urged her to put a quick stop to the proceedings by paying off the Meadows family. Well aware of her haughty temperament, he hastened to add, "Tho' I know this Measure will be very ungrateful to your Grace, I venture to advise it; the Greatest Princes in Europe are obliged to pay for Peace, and there does not seem to me the likelihood of your Grace's enjoying any without submitting to purchase it by a Treaty."[21] At the time, Elizabeth bravely replied to his prophetic words by saying: "I will stand Tryal & you shall never blush for me tho' humanity will. Sigh for my distress, & if I am Conquer'd the victor will be ashamed."[22]

On the eve of her trial, the decision not to pay off the Meadows family must have seemed more foolhardy than brave. On 1 March, Elizabeth's old friend, Lord Hillsborough, made a last-ditch motion to stop the trial in the House of Lords by pointing out that the indictment referred to her as the wife of "Augustus John Hervey" (having been made prior to his elevation as Earl of Bristol). According to the indictment, Hillsborough argued, she was a commoner and therefore not eligible to be tried by the House of Lords. It was a pitiful attempt to quash the process on a technicality and it failed.

When Hillsborough's motion failed, William Jackson recycled the idea in a hastily published pamphlet called *A Plain State of the Case of her Grace the Duchess of Kingston*. The title page explained that the author calls upon "the Interference of the High Powers, to stop a Prosecution illegally commenced, unimportant of Example, alarming to the People, expensive to the State, and pregnant of ill Consequences." Among other things, the pamphlet claimed that since Elizabeth was referred to as "Duchess of Kingston" in the writ of certiorari that officially moved her case to the House of Lords, the lords effectively had acknowledged the legality of her marriage to the duke. Therefore, they need not hear the bigamy trial because the writ presumed her innocence. This was just one feeble argument among many that the pamphlet offered, and it had no effect other than to indicate how desperate Elizabeth had become to avoid the trial in Westminster Hall.

In the early hours of Monday, 15 April, the Horse Guards patrolled Westminster, keeping order among the thousands of people who had gathered to see the peers and peeresses arrive in their richly gilt coaches and best dress. The Earl of Bathurst, now Lord High Steward, and his twenty gentleman attendants came in a caravan of five fine coaches. Famous actors and actresses, authors, politicians, and foreign ambassadors also formed part of the spectacle that morning.

But Elizabeth, for all her brave words and all her love of attention, kept a very low profile. In the entry hall of Kingston House, she climbed into a hired chair and closed its doors. The chairmen raised her up and discreetly made their way through the throngs of curiosity seekers between Knightsbridge and Westminster. Thanks to the good graces of the Duke of Newcastle, she alighted from her chair inside his house, never having to set foot or show her face outside.

A year earlier, Newcastle had accompanied Elizabeth along the passage that led from his house into the cramped Court of King's Bench, where he stood her bail. This morning that court, along with all the others, had been cleared away. Awaiting her at the end of the passage was the giant theater of justice that Ancaster had created. Built 700 years earlier, Westminster Hall had been the site of some of the great political events in the nation's history. Edward II and Richard II were deposed in this building. Sir Thomas More was convicted of treason for refusing to acknowledge Henry VIII's authority as the head of the church. And just over a hundred years earlier, Charles I was sentenced to death as a "tyrant, traitor, and murderer, and a public and implacable enemy to the Commonwealth of England."[23]

Compared with these momentous events, the proceedings against Elizabeth Chudleigh seem frivolous. But one could not tell that by looking at the Hall that day. The boxes and galleries rose on every side to the ancient wooden rafters that were decorated with enormous angels in flight, their hue mellowed to a unique honey color. The entire structure was decorated with lamps and dark red baize. One foreign visitor was so struck by the sight that he likened it to "the pomp with which divine service is performed in *catholic countries*."[24]

The doors had opened at 5:00 a.m. as hundreds of ticketed spectators rushed in, jostling for good seats. After more than six hours of waiting, the audience finally was treated to the formal procession of the lords into the Hall, signaling the start of the trial.

As Elizabeth stood in the passageway, she heard the Clerk of the Crown call for her entrance, saying, "Oyez, oyez, oyez! Elizabeth Duchess Dowager of Kingston, come forth and save you and your bail, or else you forfeit your recognisance."[25] Flanked by three female attendants in white dresses and her apothecary, chaplain, and physician, Elizabeth entered the Hall. Dressed all in black to reinforce her widow's status, she looked resolute and dignified, yet appropriately submissive before her illustrious jury.

As part of the preliminaries, Bathurst pointedly reminded Elizabeth, "It is, madam, by your particular desire that you now stand at that bar; you were not brought there by any prosecutor" (59). Few in the audience could have known that she had made that request through Bathurst himself, confident that he would urge his peers not to try the case at all. As she entered that magnificent courtroom and felt the thousands of eyes upon her, she was fully conscious of the magnitude of his betrayal. Even so, his words were like a fresh slap in the face, adding insult to injury.

The Clerk of the Crown then read the indictment and asked Elizabeth, "Culprit, how will you be tried?" She responded, "By God and my Peers," and he said "God send Your Grace a good deliverance" (60).

Most of the spectators who crowded into the Hall that morning were eager to see good theater, and most of the lords were just as eager to provide them with a morality play featuring Elizabeth as the wicked femme fatale who had led one of their brothers astray. Unfortunately for all of them, after the exchange between the clerk and the culprit had ended the show was pretty well over for the time being. What followed was three days of highly technical legal argument that left many spectators—and judges—baffled and bored. They had come for surprise witnesses, fainting fits, and startling evidence. Eventually, they would get all they wished for, but not until a decision could be reached over whether the House of Lords had any legal standing to hear the case at all.

Elizabeth began the trial by speaking in her own defense, which was customary in eighteenth-century criminal trials. She pointed out that her "supposed marriage" to Augustus Hervey had been denied by the ecclesiastical court in the jactitation ruling, which was "still in force." She asserted that this ruling was "conclusive, and that no other evidence ought to be received or stated to your Lordships respecting such pretended marriage" (61).

This was hardly a surprising start to the trial. Just two days earlier, one of Elizabeth's lawyers had published a lengthy pamphlet entitled, *A Brief for Her Grace the Duchess of Kingston; Containing the Points of Law, and Cases Adjudged, On which her Grace's Defence will Rest.* Offering the lords and the prosecution a preview of the defense strategy, the pamphlet insisted that the jactitation sentence was the strongest possible legal proof that Elizabeth was single when she married the duke. The jactitation ruling was superior to both a legal separation and a parliamentary divorce for it "wipes out every idea of any previous contract, and deems the allegations offered to support such an idea an immoral and criminal libel."[26] The ecclesiastical court's ruling did not just dissolve a marriage, it denied its existence altogether and made it a crime even to speak of the supposed marriage.

By starting the trial this way, Elizabeth and her lawyers momentarily transformed it from a celebrity show trial into a highly theoretical discussion about the English legal system. The fundamental question was simple: Did the House of Lords, acting as a common law criminal court, have the right to try Elizabeth for bigamy when the ecclesiastical court had declared her single at the time of her marriage to the duke?

Elizabeth's lawyers claimed that the jactitation ruling created an "estoppel" or bar to a criminal prosecution. In the simplest terms, "estoppel" is a form of double jeopardy protection that is meant to ensure that people are not harassed with multiple lawsuits over the same issue. Then, as now, convictions can be appealed, but acquittals cannot be.[27]

Although this defense strategy was not a surprise, the effect it had on the proceedings was unexpected. It engrossed the lords' attention for three days of technical and sometimes personally abusive arguments between the defense and prosecution lawyers. In the end, the lords were sure to decide that they had the authority to hear the case for they had gone to great trouble and expense to stage this trial. But if that outcome was inevitable, it was not to be arrived at quickly.

The real cause of the delay was Lord Mansfield's presence on Elizabeth's defense team. Mansfield was the greatest legal mind of his age, and when questions about the law came before the House of Lords, he was the one the other peers turned to for guidance. Now they were in the uncomfortable position of seeing their point man on matters of law lined up against them. Certainly there were influential lawyers and judges on the other side, such as Attorney General Edward Thurloe and the Earl of Bathurst. But Thurloe was a sarcastic man with a reputation for immorality and meanness, and although Bathurst commanded political power, he was never respected for his legal mind. Mansfield, by contrast, commanded respect in both his private and public life, and he was generally regarded as the best orator in the kingdom. The lords might pass off his defense of Elizabeth as misguided chivalry, but when the debate turned from the specifics of her crime to the mechanics of the English legal system, Mansfield's authority was felt with full force.

When the clerk finally began to read the documents related to the jactitation suit into the record, several lords rose to complain that they could hear absolutely nothing at the far end of the Hall. Try as the clerk might, he could not speak loudly enough for them all to hear, so Lord Lyttelton proposed that these critical documents merely be placed on the table for the lords to read, should they choose to. Mansfield seconded the motion.

James Wallace then rose to speak in Elizabeth's defense. Wallace had a harsh, inelegant voice that gave an impression of vehemence, not cool reason. Even so, one observer conceded that "he seemed to make the most of a bad cause."[28] He began by offering precedents to prove that even in cases where the ecclesiastical courts had made rulings that were later found to be wrong, common law courts refused to provide any remedy because they believed that those rulings, erroneous or not, created an estoppel to a subsequent suit. This line of argument all but conceded that the jactitation sentence was a legal fiction, but insisted that the present court could not review it.

Lord Mansfield rose next, and with his usual grace, he lifted the debate out of the messy details of case precedents and elevated it to the more abstract plane of constitutional theory. Instead of protecting a perjured and bigamous woman, Mansfield suggested that he and the rest of the defense counsel were making a principled stand in defense of the English Constitution. According to the constitution, Mansfield said, only the ecclesiastical court had the constitutional authority to reconsider its own jactitation ruling.

The last to speak for Elizabeth was Dr. Wynne, who practiced in the ecclesiastical court. He was a dynamic speaker who warned that a dangerous precedent would arise from "clashing and contradictory judgments of different courts." The lords, he suggested had a simple choice: they could either respect the rule of law and the English Constitution, or they could disregard established precedents for the sole purpose of branding Elizabeth and the duke's "open and solemn marriage, confirmed by a cohabitation and reputation of so many years, with the name of a felony" (128–129).

By the time Wynne sat down, it was half past six in the evening. The defense presentation had taken seven hours, during which time most of the lords and the spectators were trapped inside the Hall. According to one diary account, some of the spectators had the foresight to bring with them "cold meat between two bits of bread, which was called Sandwichs, hard eggs, apples, oranges, &c."[29] Before the trial began, others bought coffee or tea from the coffeehouses adjoining the Hall. But pity those who did for they had no access to bathroom facilities, and the arguments had not even begun. Most of the spectators sat for ten hours or more, cheek by jowl on wooden benches without backs, enjoying no more than eighteen inches of personal space. By the end of the day, they were cramped, exhausted, and starved, so it was with a collective sigh of relief that Bathurst adjourned the house and released them all.

Mary Delany, the respectable and matronly friend of George III, had wisely decided that she was too old to suffer such conditions just to see and be seen at the trial. However, many of her younger friends attended, and she invited a group to dinner on the evening of the first day so that she could hear all about it. They arrived at seven o'clock, "starved, having been twelve hours fasting, and ate their little dinner voraciously (mutton chops and lamb-pie, lobster and apple-puffs), drank their coffee between eight and nine, and then came to my little drawing-room."[30] They described the splendid sight of the court-room and Elizabeth's dignified bearing, but said that the substance of the first day was but a "preparation for what's to come, and nobody can guess yet what time it will take."

The general impression was that the day was tedious and disap-pointing in terms of courtroom drama; nevertheless, the defense had succeeded in calling the entire enterprise into doubt. Horace Walpole grudgingly praised Elizabeth's demeanor and said that "the pleadings of her four counsel, who contended for the finality of the Ecclesiasti-cal Court's sentence against a second trial, carried her triumphantly through the first day, and turned the stream much in her favour."[31]

Elizabeth returned to Kingston House, where she was now held under house arrest. She must have felt cautiously optimistic as she, Jackson, and her legal team ran over the events of the day and looked ahead. They certainly had cause to celebrate their success in turning the focus away from Elizabeth and onto the more arcane matters of legal jurisdiction and estoppel. However, they also had cause for worry. A one-sided argument is bound to seem persuasive, but the next day the prosecution would have its say.

Despite the tedium of the first day's arguments, public interest was still great. Edward Pigott, a man who managed to get a ticket for the second day, arrived for the opening of the doors at seven in the morning. He noticed that Elizabeth seemed very self-possessed and even chatted with some of the lords who sat near her.[32]

Attorney General Thurloe began the case for the prosecution by insisting that the trial had to go on. When Elizabeth pleaded "not guilty" to the charges the previous May, she effectively submitted herself to the trial process and could not reverse that decision. As for the main claim that the jactitation sentence created an estoppel, Thurloe brushed this aside by bluntly declaring, "The sentence, being collusive, is a nullity" (133).

Thurloe was an attractive man whose "expressive eyes" caused even the proper Anna Porter to have romantic daydreams about him. He was a commanding speaker with a sharp wit that he displayed when attacking the integrity of the church court system. After expressing mock surprise that the defense put so much faith in the force of the church court's decree, he asked:

> How are Sentences given? Thus. The Court assembled, the Judges & Doctor's setting round the Table; the one who presides gives an example which the rest follow or perhaps have already given, he falls asleep—maybe grows hungry, or tired, or anything—"Come, come

(cries he) let's dispatch business; come let's give Sentence!" Everyone
is unanimous to dispatch business, to give Sentence, but how depends
on the momentary whim or resolve—however (added Thurloe looking
round most expressively) Sentence is given & that sentence you my
Lords are desired & expected to abide by.[33]

The defense had attempted to argue the case on abstract issues of
legal jurisdiction and constitutional theory, but Thurloe took those
abstractions and made them concrete—and ridiculous—by mocking
the way the church courts functioned.

Fair or unfair, Thurloe's satire rang true for many in the courtroom. The defense had asserted that the church courts were the
least likely to allow for collusive and fraudulent decisions, but every
lord sitting in judgment knew how ridiculous this claim was. They
had only to think of Lord Bolingbroke's or the Duke of Grafton's
divorces seven years earlier, each founded on collusive sentences
obtained in the church courts, to be reminded of how easily those
courts could be manipulated.

Alexander Wedderburne, the solicitor general, rose next for
the prosecution. Although not as graceful an orator as Thurloe,
Wedderburne used humor to even greater effect than the attorney
general had done. Anna Porter said of him, "I never heard more real
humour than he possesses. He makes every one laugh but himself, &
seems surprized that they laugh, whilst the surprize may be returned
that he can keep up his dry gravity."[34] She was referring to moments
in Wedderburne's speech such as when he paused to consider how
many wives "a man that had a taste for polygamy might marry with
impunity" by availing himself of jactitation rulings. After thinking for
a minute, he concluded that "a man between twenty-one and thirty-
five might, with good industry, marry seventy-five wives by sentences
of the Ecclesiastical Court" (161). Edward Pigott said Wedderburne's
satire "pleased everybody."

But Wedderburne did more than make jokes. In the most devastating moment of the day, he damned the jactitation sentence by
asking:

What is a sentence? It is not an instrument with a bit of wax and the
seal of a Court put to it; it is not an instrument with a quantity of ink
bestowed upon such a quantity of stamped paper. A sentence is a judicial determination of a cause agitated between *real* parties upon which
a *real* interest has been settled. In order to make a sentence there must
be a *real* interest, a *real* argument, a *real* prosecution, a *real* defence,
a *real* decision. (163)

Elizabeth might have a judicial ruling from the ecclesiastical court, but it was merely a legal fiction.

By the end of the day, the prosecution had knocked out the foundations upon which the defense's constitutional arguments rested. As the sky darkened outside, Lord Talbot rose to request an adjournment, explaining that "we have already heard more than we can retain; at least I honestly confess for my own part I have."[35] As they filed out of the Hall, many of the spectators were painfully fatigued by all the legal wrangling: not a single witness had testified, not a shred of evidence had been produced. As for Elizabeth, she was so ill and fatigued that Pigott says she was "half dragged away, supported by two gentlemen, two servants holding her gown, three maids in white and other attendants."[36]

There were no celebrations at Kingston House that evening. Instead, William Jackson tried to rebuild the defense argument by insisting, in the *Public Ledger,* that to hear any testimony about how the jactitation sentence was obtained is "to depart from that line of legal discussion, within which courts of judicature are rigidly bound . . . Heaven avert the day, when, in opposition to recorded innocence, suspected guilt shall bring on the trial!"[37] At least Elizabeth could enjoy the consolation of a polite letter from one of her jurors, praising her proper and judicious conduct during the proceedings. She promptly leaked the letter to the press.

The trial did not resume until three days later, which was an unfortunate delay for Elizabeth. The second day had gone badly for the defense, and now the lords had two full days to reflect on the strong prosecution rebuttal, while the thousands of fashionable spectators amused themselves with gossiping at Elizabeth's expense. The longer the trial dragged on, the worse it was for her.

When the trial reconvened on Friday morning, 19 April, the sixty-eight-year-old Lord Ravensworth rose to his feet, half mumbling to himself, half addressing the Lord High Steward. According to Anna Porter, Ravensworth "moved that the Lords should examine the Sentence given in the Ecclesiastical Court, & determine whether or not a Trial could be proceeded on.—Imagine how every one stared for what else had they been about since their meeting?" The Hall erupted in laughter, prompting repeated calls for order. Lord Mansfield rose and in the "easiest, clearest, manner, ran over the several proceedings" in order, he politely lied, "to help the general recollection of the Court."[38]

After this entertaining start, more arguments passed between the prosecution and defense until the lords finally retired to their parliamentary chamber for a private debate and vote on the issue of estoppel. During their closed-door deliberations, the lords heard the opinion of William De Grey, lord chief justice of the Court of Common Pleas. At a loss without Mansfield's disinterested opinion, the peers turned to De Grey for guidance. He wrote up a brief asserting that the jactitation ruling did not prevent a criminal trial for bigamy.[39] To this day, De Grey's opinion is cited as an important precedent on the matter of estoppel in British legal briefs. On the strength of this opinion, the undecided lords voted to proceed with the trial, giving Bathurst and his faction the majority they needed. When the lords paraded back into the Hall at midday, the real show was about to begin.

Ann Cradock was called as the first witness. She entered the great courtroom and took her place at the bar, making her oath and kissing the Bible just a few feet away from where Elizabeth sat. This was the first time the two women had seen each other in several years, and it was not a happy meeting. Before Wedderburne could begin his questions, the Duke of Richmond sprang to his feet and insisted that the witness be moved away from the prisoner so that Elizabeth could not intimidate her with whispered threats or menacing looks. After much discussion, the Deputy Usher of the Black Rod was placed between the two women and the examination began.

Cradock testified to being present at the wedding in 1744, to seeing Augustus and Elizabeth in bed together on the night of their wedding, and to having been told by Elizabeth of her baby's birth and death. These were all pertinent matters of fact that proved that the marriage was legal and had been consummated.

Under cross-examination, however, Cradock's credibility was seriously undermined. Wallace asked her repeatedly if she expected any reward from the Meadows family for her testimony, and each time she replied with evasions. First, she claimed that she knew none of the family; then she admitted to having met Evelyn two or three times in recent months; and finally, she confessed that she had received a letter from a friend "wherein I was told that a gentleman of their acquaintance would get me a sinecure, but on what account I know not." Being pressed, she insisted, "I know not who the gentleman was; it never was explained to me who the gentleman was, nor I never asked" (238). As it turns out, the friend who wrote the letter was John Fozard, the former servant of the Duke of Kingston who led Evelyn Meadows to Ann Cradock in the first place. She insisted, implausibly, "I made no answer any further, but that it was very kind in anybody that would assist me in getting me anything." And then, although she had already admitted to having met repeatedly with Evelyn Meadows, she said that she did not take the promise in the letter to be a quid pro quo from him because "I know not the person of the prosecutor, nor none of his family" (238–239).

Wallace and some of the lords sympathetic to Elizabeth did their best to get a straight answer from Cradock, but gave up in exasperation. By her evasive and contradictory replies, she made it clear that her testimony had, in fact, been bought by the Meadows family, but that did not necessarily mean that she was lying about the marriage and consummation. As night began to fall, the Earl of Derby proposed an adjournment. Noting that many lords "seem desirous of asking this witness many questions," he proposed that Cradock be called to the stand again the next morning.[40]

After a second bad day for the defense, Jackson again tried to help the cause in his newspaper. He called Ann Cradock "a menial servant in the Duchess of Kingston's family" and said that she was summoned "to prove the iniquity of that heart, which had fed, the sordidness of that hand, which had cloathed her." As for her evasive replies, Jackson sarcastically said they were characterized by "that sort of hesitation remarkable in old age."[41]

Saturday, 20 April promised to be the most interesting day of the proceedings for it would be devoted entirely to the examination of witnesses. It began with further cross-examination of Ann Cradock. Lord Hillsborough got her to admit that sometime in the early 1770s she had accepted an offer from Elizabeth of twenty guineas a year provided she would live in one of three different counties distant from London (clearly Elizabeth was interested in having her out of the way). Cradock said that she chose Yorkshire, but never actually went because she could not stand to be separated from her friends by so much distance. As a result, she never received any money from Elizabeth.

When asked why she did not testify in the jactitation suit when her husband had done so, she simply said that she was never called upon to do so. Did she know that her husband was called to testify in that case? "I know he was called upon in the Court," she said, "but what passed I am an utter stranger to, as I never asked" (242). Like many of Cradock's answers, this one strains credulity. She almost certainly perjured herself during her testimony, and was generally ridiculed for her clumsy evasions. Nevertheless, she had provided damning evidence of the marriage and it took a toll on Elizabeth, who was said to have swooned during Cradock's testimony.

Caesar Hawkins was called to the bar next. A self-possessed and respectable man of fashion, he cut a much different figure from Ann Cradock. Before he answered any questions, Hawkins wondered if his honor would permit him to divulge the contents of private conversations that had passed between Elizabeth, Augustus, and him. Lord Mansfield assured him that neither his professional ethics nor his personal honor would be sullied by answering questions in a criminal trial, so Hawkins revealed what he knew about the birth and death of Elizabeth's child and about how Elizabeth persuaded Hervey to forgo a divorce in favor of the jactitation suit.

The highlight of the day's testimony came from Lord Barrington, secretary of war and an old friend of Elizabeth and the duke. When asked if Elizabeth had ever revealed her first marriage to him, Barrington said,

> My Lords, I am come here in obedience to your Lordships' summons, ready to give testimony as to any matter that I know of my own knowledge, or that has come to me in the usual way, but if anything has been confided to my honour, or confidentially to me, I do hold, with humble submission to your Lordships, that as a man of honour, as a man regardful of the laws of society, I cannot reveal it. (254)

Bathurst told him that Hawkins had the same qualms, but overcame them. Barrington was unimpressed. Then Elizabeth rose and said, "I do release my Lord Barrington from every obligation of honour" (255). Still, he had qualms. In frustration, the prosecution decided that they could do without his testimony, but the Duke of Richmond rose to his feet and lectured Barrington about his duty and tried to make him answer some questions. Barrington was unmoved.

Ultimately, the lords were forced to adjourn to their parliamentary chamber to deal with the matter. When they returned, Bathurst said, "My Lord Viscount Barrington, I am commanded by the Lords to acquaint your lordship that it is the judgment of this House that you are bound by law to answer all such questions as shall be put to you" (258). The prosecution and defense lawyers still refused to ask any questions, but individual lords rose to do so. After more demurring, Barrington finally said that about thirty years ago Elizabeth "did entrust me with a circumstance in her life relative to an engagement of a matrimonial kind with the Earl of Bristol, then Mr. Hervey" (259).

This was a paltry admission gained at great expense, but it was an important moment in the trial. By refusing voluntarily to testify, Barrington implicitly accused the lords of conduct unbecoming of gentlemen, and by extension he shook his finger at the thousands of spectators. He made it clear that although the lords might call this trial a legal one, and although they had spent thousands of pounds from the public treasury to dress up the Hall so magnificently, this was a shameful process. They were scapegoating a defenseless widow whose marriage they had never dared to attack while her husband was living. The seriousness of Barrington's critique is why some of the lords got so angry with him, and he was roundly ridiculed for his reluctant testimony afterward.

The next witness was much more accommodating. Judith Phillips, the widow of the Reverend Thomas Amis, told the court of Elizabeth's trip to Winchester in 1759 to have the false marriage register made. When the register was produced in court and read aloud, she testified to its authenticity. The defense tried to discredit her by suggesting that her testimony was in revenge for Elizabeth's having her second husband, a servant of the Duke of Kingston, fired. But their efforts convinced nobody, and try as they might, they could not argue away the Lainston register book that sat on the table at the center of the courtroom.

The fourth day of the trial featured no salacious testimony about Elizabeth's sex life, as many hoped (or feared) it would. But Ann Cradock, Caesar Hawkins, and Judith Phillips left no doubt of the marriage between Elizabeth and Augustus Hervey. It is not surprising that all three of them were, in one way or another, employees of Elizabeth or Augustus. In trials of this nature, noble defendants were almost always convicted on the strength of their servants' testimony. Had Elizabeth taken better care of Cradock and Phillips, in particular, she might have saved herself a world of trouble. As it was, their testimony cheered the hearts of Elizabeth's enemies, such as Lady Harrington (who had served as a Maid of Honour with her) and Evelyn Meadows. When Meadows presented Lady Harrington with flowers on the fourth day of the trial, she was heard to say: "I hope in God I shall be able to present you shortly with the LAUREL."[42]

The fifth day of the trial was Monday, 22 April. Everyone knew that this would be the last day and that Elizabeth would make a speech in her own defense, so interest was especially keen. As she rose to address the court, Elizabeth began with a glance at her scrape with Samuel Foote, complaining: "I have suffered unheard-of persecutions; my honour and fame have been severely attacked; I have been loaded with reproaches; and such indignities and hardships have rendered me the less able to make my defence before this august assembly." Nevertheless, she promised, "my words will flow freely from my heart, adorned simply with innocence and truth."[43]

In fact, her defense, which she read from twelve oversized sheets of paper, was neither spontaneous nor true. She assured the lords that she would not have troubled them with her case if the issue were the saving of her life or her wealth, but explained that she must speak in defense of "the honourable titles on which I set an inestimable value, as received from my most noble and late dear husband, attempted to be torn from me." This prompted chuckles of disbelief from many in the crowd, including Anna Porter who scoffed, "Oh Oh Woman! Woman! How Could you utter such untruths!"[44]

Elizabeth's false piety fooled no one. Nor did her claim that the king approved of her marriage to the duke. Her attempt to make the lords see her case as a warning to them did not help either. She implored the peers to remember that "the orphan and the widow is your peculiar care" and to recollect "how easy it may be for a next-of-kin to prosecute the widows or the daughters, not only of every Peer, but of every subject of Great Britain." This was especially important, she suggested, if estates can be attacked by the testimony of people like Ann Cradock, a "superannuated and interested old woman, who declared seven years ago that she was incapable of giving evidence" in the jactitation suit. But having already decided to sacrifice Elizabeth for their sins, the peers were deaf to this appeal to class solidarity.

Elizabeth ended with a flourish. Although she read most of the defense from the large sheets in her hand, the last part was delivered from memory. She said, "I call upon God Almighty, the Searcher of Hearts, to witness that at the time of my marriage with the Duke of Kingston I had, myself, the most perfect conviction that it was lawful." But this grand oath did not deny the charges of collusion; it merely asserted that she considered the collusive sentence to be definitive. One observer noted, "It was astonishing how she was able to speak for three quarters of an hour . . . but it was labour in vain!"[45]

Before Elizabeth sat down, she made an unusual request of the court concerning the testimony of Arthur Collier, the lawyer who had helped her in the jactitation suit. Although she once called him "my Guardian friend," she now blamed him for misleading her, insisting, "Your Lordships in your great candour cannot think that a lady can know more of the civil law than her learned civilians could point out to her." Collier had avoided appearing because he was suffering from St. Anthony's Fire, a painful toxic infection that caused his face to swell so much that one of his eyes was nearly shut. Elizabeth told the peers that Collier was willing to be deposed and cross-examined in bed and begged them, "upon my knees, that you will hear the evidence that he will give to the justification of my honour."

A heated debate arose among the lords about the legality of accepting Collier's testimony under these conditions. There seemed to be a consensus forming in favor of the unusual step until Lord Mansfield rose to argue against it. As the head of Elizabeth's defense team, his opposition is surprising—and it certainly must have surprised her. According to one observer, Mansfield united "the eloquence of Cicero" with "the most profound knowledge of the laws of his country" in denouncing this step. He told the lords that public trials reliant on public testimony are the glories of the British legal system; therefore, admitting secret testimony under any circumstances would be a dangerous precedent. His speech "made the most lively impression on his audience" and soon "those peers who were the most zealous friends of the duchess immediately desisted from their demand."[46]

Deprived of Collier's testimony, the defense had to rely on witnesses who unintentionally undermined Elizabeth's defense. First was Mr. Berkley, an attorney of Augustus Hervey. When Mr. Berkley was called upon to discredit Ann Cradock, he explained how, when he and Hervey approached her in early 1768 to help with his divorce case, she claimed that she was old and infirm and could remember nothing of the 1744 wedding. How was it that her memory had *improved* with the passage of time? the defense wondered. But during cross-examination, Thurloe asked Berkley why Ann Cradock was never subpoenaed in the jactitation suit. All but admitting Hervey's collusion in that case, he replied: "I know nothing of that; it went out of my hands afterwards to Doctors' Commons" (283).

Ann Pritchard, an acquaintance of Ann Cradock, was called next. She said that Cradock boasted that she "was to be provided for" as a result of testifying against Elizabeth, but "in what manner she could not say till after the affair was over, lest it should be deemed bribery" (284). Pritchard, however, knew the answer. She testified that Evelyn Meadows planned to reward Cradock indirectly by getting her brother a job at the Customs House. Pritchard's husband worked there and was to secure this job, and hence, the bribe. But Pritchard was not a very credible witness. Anna Porter called her "as arrant a femme d'intrigue as ever lived. God forgive her. I am sure she was perjured every word she spoke."[47] As Pritchard's testimony began to crumple under cross-examination, the Duke of Richmond again leaped to his feet and accused Elizabeth of whispering answers to her. This caused a great stir in the Hall, and Bathurst charged the court to be more on its guard. Anna Porter's brother assured her afterward that Elizabeth said nothing to Pritchard, however, she did try to communicate answers to her using facial expressions.

Things were not going well for the defense.

The last witness to take the stand was Sir James LaRoche, one of the Duke of Kingston's dearest friends. He was a witness at both weddings of Elizabeth and the duke and had stood bail for Elizabeth when she returned to England to face the criminal charges. His testimony was meant to place any blame for wrongdoing on the shoulders of Arthur Collier. Mansfield questioned him about Collier's assurances to the duke that he could marry Elizabeth with a clear conscience. But during LaRoche's testimony, he indicated that the duke met with Collier repeatedly, suggesting that he was having a hard time believing that the marriage would be legal. Then, under cross-examination, Dunning asked LaRoche if the duke had any doubts about the legality of the marriage. He replied that the duke "certainly had a doubt upon his breast, until the suit of jactitation was over" (287–288).

LaRoche's testimony was a disaster. Unwittingly, he had all but admitted that the duke had no confidence in the truth of the jactitation case and required repeated assurances that the sentence was definitive. When Elizabeth saw the effect this testimony was having, she lost control of herself and fell into a hysterical fit that stopped the proceedings until she could be removed from the courtroom, wailing. Many published accounts of the trial politely ignore this episode, but for those in attendance, it was just the sort of theatrics they had come for. Most of the crowd merely laughed at Elizabeth's breakdown, calling her a bad actress. But to Anna Porter, it was a disturbing sight. She said, "That very wickedness that prevents most people from feeling for this miserable Woman, in my mind added to the horror of her situation.—When distress assaults, virtue is our only cordial. What a Chaos is the mind without it!"[48] Having been damned by the testimony of her own witnesses, Elizabeth broke under the strain.

When Elizabeth returned and the trial resumed, the prosecution was invited to rebut the defense case. But noting that the defense was so ineffective that no rebuttal was necessary, Solicitor General Wedderburne declined to "trouble your lordships any further on this matter" (290).

At Bathurst's command, the peers retired to their parliamentary chamber to deliberate. But this was merely a matter of form; the outcome was in no doubt. When they returned, Bathurst called upon them in turn to stand, remove their hats, and with their hand upon their breast, deliver their verdict. Starting with the youngest peer, Bathurst asked: "John Lord Sundridge, Duke of Argyll, what says your lordship? Is the Prisoner at the Bar guilty of the felony whereof she stands indicted?" Argyll replied: "Guilty, upon my honour." Every lord but one said the same. Only the Duke of Newcastle differed by saying: "Guilty erroneously, but not intentionally" (291).

Elizabeth was then called into the courtroom to hear the verdict, which she received with composure. In that instant, the proud woman was deprived of her greatest source of pride: she was no longer a duchess. One spectator said that she received the sentence without seeming to be "affected, on the contrary, [she] looked bold and angry."[49]

She was still a noblewoman, for the verdict proved her to be the wife of the Earl of Bristol, and this was more than just a psychological comfort. As Countess of Bristol she could plead benefit of clergy, an ancient loophole that exempted certain defendants, including peers, from punishment on their first felony conviction. Elizabeth said nothing in reply to the verdict, but handed a slip of paper to Bathurst on which she had written a request that she be granted benefit of clergy. Technically, the penalty for bigamy was death, but in practice that had been changed to branding on the hand. As Countess of Bristol, Elizabeth would be spared even that indignity.

However, there was one final insult in store for her. With surprising malice, Thurloe and the prosecution insisted that a woman could not claim benefit of clergy. They gave long, prepared speeches to support their claim, which caught the defense totally off guard. Wallace and Mansfield apologized for having to speak on the matter extemporaneously, explaining that they had not anticipated any objection to the request. The debate between the lawyers grew personally abusive as Thurloe accused Mansfield of trying to impress the ladies in the audience by arguing that they were eligible for benefit of clergy.

After hearing the arguments, the lords made yet another slow, formal procession out of the Hall so that they could debate and decide the matter in their parliamentary chamber. After they filed back in, Bathurst said to Elizabeth:

> Madam, the Lords have considered of the prayer you have made, to have the benefit of the statutes, and the Lords allow it you. But let me add that, although very little punishment, or none, can now be inflicted, the feelings of your own conscience will supply that defect. And let me give you this information likewise, that you can never have

the like benefit a second time, but another offence of the same kind will be capital. Madam, you are discharged, paying your fees (309).

After the sentencing, the sergeant-at-arms read the proclamation dissolving the Lord High Steward's commission. The Usher of the Black Rod delivered the white staff to Bathurst, who broke it over his knee, voluntarily relinquishing his office as Lord High Steward. And with that last bit of theatrics, the extraordinary trial was over.

It had cost an estimated £10,000 and "seemed to be a festival to the whole nation," according to a foreign observer.[50] The newspapers claimed that the audience "made a more brilliant Appearance than at any preceding" trial of a peer.[51] And one historian has noted that the trial "occasioned greater popular interest and larger aristocratic crowds in the galleries than any debates on the American war."[52]

While the trial was taking place, Hessian mercenaries were being readied for deployment to America in order to suppress the rebellion. Had Elizabeth been imprisoned in the Tower of London during the duration of her trial, she would have heard the sound of muskets being made there for the Hessians. The political goal of this armament and deployment was to force the colonies to send more tax revenues to London. But as the delegates to the Second Continental Congress gathered in Philadelphia that spring and began to hear reports about Elizabeth's trial, one cannot blame them for digging in their heels and refusing to waste their treasure on expensive and pointless shows in Westminster Hall. Elizabeth's trial was just the sort of thing to make the founders feel like virtuous farmers who had luckily escaped the contagious vices of the Old World.

Their counterparts in the House of Lords were not considering this political calculus. Increasingly the subject of hostile attacks for their sexual immorality, the British peers were eager to draw attention away from their own indiscretions by scapegoating a woman. Among the lords who took a prominent part in the proceedings against Elizabeth were the Duke of Grafton (divorced by collusive practices), the Earl of Sandwich (member of a notorious aristocratic sex club), the Duke of Richmond (whose great-grandmother was one of Charles II's mistresses), the Duke of Cumberland (convicted of "criminal conversation" with Lady Grosvenor), and Baron Lyttelton (universally regarded as the most immoral man in England).

These men believed that they would reap political benefits from making a public example of a bad woman. Although they knew that matters in America were reaching a crisis point, they clearly felt that a state trial for bigamy at this critical moment was worth the time and expense. This was an act of hypocrisy on a grand scale, but the sexual double standard was hardly the invention of the House of Lords. *The Court of Adultery*, a contemporary poem satirizing upper-class disregard for marriage, lays the blame squarely on the ladies' shoulders. Among the villains of the poem are Lady Grosvenor, the Duchess of Grafton, and Elizabeth Chudleigh, who is called "The Queen of Lust, of Sin, of Bigamy" (27). The poem is testament to the lords' political savvy for it argues that Elizabeth's bigamy trial was not a distraction from the war in America, but an important campaign in that struggle. As the poem nears its climax, it singles out Elizabeth for special condemnation, calling her a "Lascivious B[itch], vicious e'en to death," and characterizing her bigamy as a form of treason that sowed the seeds of rebellion in the far-flung empire (27). Nor was this poet alone in his view. The author of a legal text called *The Laws Respecting Women* discussed Elizabeth's case in detail and called her bigamy "an open attack upon the order of society."[53]

Ultimately, however, the trial did not produce all the benefits the lords had hoped for themselves. Rather, it had the opposite effect of fueling public anger over aristocratic sexual immorality in general. With an eye toward cases such as the Duke of Cumberland's and the Duke of Grafton's, the author of *The Honour of Marriage Opposed to all Impurities* complains that only poor morality can be expected of the lower orders "when we reflect, that most of our gentlemen of rank and figure, who can at any time declaim fluently upon the dignity of human nature, and are ready to pledge their honour upon every occasion, do yet discover very little honour in their actions."[54] For this author (and many others) the sexual immorality of upper-class men is compounded by their flagrant hypocrisy. Such publications showed that Elizabeth's bigamy trial did not effectively quell criticism of elite male behavior, nor did it bring an end to the litigation over the Duke of Kingston's estate. Almost immediately the Meadows family renewed their Chancery lawsuit to invalidate the duke's will, and the Earl of Bristol petitioned the ecclesiastical court to reconsider the jactitation ruling that had been so thoroughly discredited.

Both of these cases attracted continued public interest, but they were about to be overshadowed by a much bigger scandal, one that would engross the attention of the public and involve people at the highest levels of society—including the king and queen—for months to come. Samuel Foote was about to pay the price for crossing Elizabeth Chudleigh.

CHAPTER 10

THE PROXY WAR

At 10:00 a.m. on Monday, 6 May 1776, John Sangster walked into the crowded magistrate's court in Bow Street, Covent Garden, and swore that Samuel Foote had attempted to sodomize him on two separate occasions.[1]

This court was situated near the Covent Garden Piazza, an area teeming with taverns, brothels, and crime. Martin Battestin has described the courtroom as "among the most cheerless and despicable places in the kingdom" where, on a typical day, a plaintiff like Sangster might be surrounded by "a horrid parade of thieves and cheats, robbers and murderers, rapists and sodomites; many who reveled in cruelty, who battered women and ravished children."[2]

In an effort to combat rampant street crime a few decades earlier, the Bow Street Runners, London's first police force, was organized by the court. But their numbers were small and their effect was limited. Normally, victims like Sangster had to initiate and finance criminal prosecutions themselves.[3]

Rather than with an arrest, prosecutions of this sort began with the victim's appearance before a justice of the peace to swear the charge against the defendant. Technically, this was not a public process and so it often took place in the privacy of the justice's home since that was where many of them conducted business. However, Sir John Fielding, who presided at Bow Street, did things differently. Carrying on a tradition begun by his predecessor and half-brother, the novelist Henry Fielding, Sir John conducted pretrial hearings in a very public fashion. Although he lived upstairs, he had a public room on the ground floor with seats for spectators to watch the proceedings. Newspaper reporters, curiosity-seekers of all classes, and the merely idle could watch the administration of justice in this uniquely public courtroom. Sir John, who was blind, sat at a high desk at the front of the court, his eyes hidden behind a black blindfold, looking very much like an emblem of impartial justice. When the Duke of Kingston was alive, he and Elizabeth frequently spent time in the gallery at Bow Street, much to the distress of the duke's valet, who was embarrassed to have his master's coach parked in front of the court for the world to see. Fielding was a close friend and frequent houseguest of the duke and Elizabeth.

In general, justices of the peace had great latitude in choosing how to respond to accusations, but in cases such as attempted sodomy the law required them to follow a relatively strict procedure. Sangster told Fielding that he left his master's service after having been sexually assaulted by Foote on two consecutive days: on 1 May in an upper room at Foote's townhouse that adjoined the Theatre Royal in the Haymarket, and then on 2 May in the stables at Foote's suburban villa in Fulham. For the past seven months, Sangster had been employed by Foote, first as a coachman, then as a footman.

After Sangster announced his business that morning, Fielding interrogated him about the particulars. Fielding was a skilled interrogator, famed for his ability to detect liars simply from the tenor of their voices. When he sensed that a victim was misleading him, he subjected the person to a rigorous examination that often exposed the falsehood. He would then throw out the charge, stopping a malicious prosecution before it even got started. In this instance, however, Sangster's testimony stood up under Fielding's questioning. Fielding dictated the testimony to a clerk then issued a bench warrant for the arrest of Samuel Foote.

Evidently unaware that this was going on, Foote was on stage at the Haymarket Theatre, addressing his acting company at their initial meeting of the season. At some point in the late morning or afternoon, a constable served Foote with the arrest warrant. Foote duly appeared at Bow Street around 5:00 p.m. in the company of his trusted friend and treasurer, William Jewell, and probably William Hickey, his attorney. Fielding heard Foote's side of the story, again dictating to his clerk. Still convinced that the charges were credible, Fielding ordered that Foote be taken into custody until the case could be tried at the next quarter sessions for the County of Middlesex. As the name suggests, the quarter sessions were held just four times a year, so defendants who could not afford bail had to languish in jail until the next session. In this instance, that meant a two-month incarceration. Foote, however, was a rich man, so he posted bail, left the courtroom, and braced for the ensuing trial—and publicity.

Sangster was an able-bodied young man, probably in his early twenties, and he said that he had no trouble fending off the sexual attacks of his one-legged master. Therefore the charge he leveled was not sodomy, but *attempted* sodomy. This is a crucial distinction. The punishment for sodomy was death, whereas the penalties for attempted sodomy were lighter than those for property crimes. According to one historian, punishment on the lesser charge usually involved "any or all of the following: the pillory, prison, a fine."[4] The standards of evidence between the two charges differed as greatly as the punishments. To obtain a sodomy conviction, the plaintiff had the difficult task of proving both anal penetration and emission. But to prove attempted sodomy, one had only to level the charge and support it with circumstantial evidence or the testimony of friendly witnesses, often leaving judges and juries to make their decisions based on the character of the plaintiff and defendant.

Not surprisingly, the charge of attempted sodomy was a blackmailer's dream. In the second half of the eighteenth century, the charge of sodomy and (especially) attempted sodomy became so frequent that the courts began to require corroborating testimony. However, that testimony could be mere hearsay, making the defendant's situation a perilous one. Usually these defendants were men of means and of some standing in the community, people who would be happy to part with some money in order to keep their names free from the taint of sodomy and out of the newspapers. Just as often, their accusers were relatively indigent or were former employees. As in all cases of a sexual nature, the domestic servants of the accused frequently provided corroborating testimony. Foote's case bears all these characteristics.

By the 1770s, judges began to instruct juries to consider the "mental anguish endured by a man faced with the threat of being falsely proclaimed a homosexual."[5] At the same time, falsely accusing someone of being a sodomite became a capital offense.[6] This increased skepticism about the charge of attempted sodomy was due, in large part, to the high-profile case of Edward Walpole, brother of Horace. In the 1750s, Edward Walpole was blackmailed by a group of men who threatened to charge him with attempted sodomy. Rather than pay the hush money, Walpole took the unusual step of prosecuting the men for blackmail and conspiracy, braving the publicity that naturally followed. In doing so, he spent a great deal more money than the blackmailers would probably have extorted from him, but he cleared his name and won a significant legal victory.

After Walpole's case, the charge of attempted sodomy was never regarded in quite the same way by judges and juries, but outside the courtroom the scandal of being accused as a sodomite was still devastating. For example, in 1772 Foote's acquaintance and fellow playwright Isaac Bickerstaffe had been accused of propositioning a guardsman. When the soldier threatened to reveal Bickerstaffe's advances, the playwright fled the country never to return. The scandal was so great that he was forced to spend the rest of his life on the Continent, and even his close friends in England cut off all communication with him. When he sent a letter to David Garrick, his friend and former employer, Garrick wrote on the back: "From that poor wretch Bickerstaffe—I could not answer it."[7]

As playwright, actor, and theatrical patentee, Foote had a lot more to lose than Bickerstaffe had. Foote had to appear on stage before audiences that were not shy about demonstrating their negative opinions of an actor or actress. The rotten tomato thrown on stage is a theatrical cliché nowadays, but it was an ever-present threat in the eighteenth century, when playhouse riots broke out at the London theaters with casual regularity. How would the public greet him now that he had been charged with the "worst of crimes?" If audiences reacted negatively, would they limit their anger to Foote, or would his entire operation become anathema? Scores of people, from actors to boxkeepers to sceneshifters, relied on Foote for their livelihood, and they were all potentially jeopardized by his legal troubles.

But Foote also had more immediate worries. According to one account, he was the best-paid theater professional in English history with an annual income of £3000 a year at the time of his arraignment, more than even the great David Garrick made. He lived extravagantly, keeping two fashionable houses full of servants, gambling for high stakes on a regular basis, and frequently spending the off-season in Paris. Even so, Foote lived from paycheck to paycheck, spending as quickly as he got. After one particularly lucrative season, he went to Bath and got involved in a card game with professional sharpers. When a friend warned him that he was being fleeced, Foote assured him that he could "always draw on his talents" to supply his losses, which amounted to £2000 that evening.[8] Now, however, he faced criminal charges that might turn the public against him, preventing him from drawing on his talents for his living, and potentially sending him into exile like Bickerstaffe—and Elizabeth Chudleigh.

Several weeks earlier, on the second day after her conviction, Elizabeth ordered her servants to illuminate Kingston House as if there were to be a dinner party that evening and to drive her coach around Knightsbridge and Westminster. To all appearances, Elizabeth Chudleigh, Countess of Bristol, was carrying on with life as usual. But it was all a ruse—the coach was empty and there was no party that night. Instead, Elizabeth was secretly making her way to Calais. With the possible exception of a rumored clandestine trip back to Kingston House, Wednesday, 24 April 1776, was the last day she ever spent on English soil.

The conviction for bigamy not only left Elizabeth humiliated and stripped of her coveted title, it also exposed her to renewed legal assaults from Augustus Hervey and the Meadows family. As Earl of Bristol, Hervey was keen to protect the family estates from his once-again wife and would soon begin divorce proceedings. For their part, the Meadows family believed the criminal conviction would help finally to invalidate the duke's will. On the very day that Elizabeth fled to Calais, Philip and Evelyn Meadows had secured a writ of *ne exeat regno* against her, prohibiting her from leaving the kingdom. But as she explained to a friend a few days later, when she learned that "these good men had designs to keep me in England," she immediately fled the country.[9]

According to the newspapers, Elizabeth's entry into the harbor at Calais was characteristically grand. Cannon shots from her yacht announced her arrival, and the local dignitaries came down to the shore to welcome her "in the politest terms."[10] Here, at least, she could still command—or buy—respect and enjoy being called "Duchess of Kingston", a title she never abandoned as long as she lived. She sent letters of gratitude to the peers who had tried to support her cause and to foreign friends whom she assured that her conviction was unjust and malicious. She signed them "E. Kingston."

On the day of Elizabeth's flight, Horace Walpole wrote to a friend about her case, complaining that he was "heartily tired of this farce, having heard of nothing else this fortnight." But, he continued, "Happily in this giant town one is not long troubled with stale events."[11] For Elizabeth, however, the events of the past fortnight would rankle in her breast until her dying day. Apart from herself, she had many people to blame for her humiliation: the Meadows family, who started all this trouble; Arthur Collier, who assured her the jactitation ruling would screen her from prosecution; the House of Lords, who made her a scapegoat for their own indiscretions; the king, who refused to quash the prosecution; and so on. But from her exile in Calais, she directed her anger against the one person whom she blamed above all others: Samuel Foote.

Throughout the winter and spring of 1776, Foote had never been far from Elizabeth's thoughts or William Jackson's pen. On the eve of the bigamy trial, Jackson published an anonymous poem called *Asmodeus*. (The name Asmodeus is a reference to the title character

of one of Foote's most popular plays, *The Devil Upon Two Sticks*.)
A satire on Foote, the title page of *Asmodeus* featured a picture of
him, fat, peg legged, and leaning on crutches in front of Kingston
House, leering maliciously at the reader. And just to make things
perfectly clear, above the picture was the Latin epigraph "Stans in
Pedo" (stands on one foot). This lack of subtlety was not limited to
the title page: the entire poem was a tortured exercise in justifying
Elizabeth's bigamy and laying the blame for all her self-inflicted problems at Foote's doorstep.

In wretched verse, Jackson renames Elizabeth as Placentia (Latin
for "agreeable") and makes her into a model of virtue, generosity, and
Christian humility. Those who knew her personally and had spent any
time in Kingston House might be excused for not recognizing her in
Jackson's lines:

> Prudence in grandeur thro' her palace reigns,
> And each domestic wish of pomp restraints.
> She, like the Sisters of the sacred vow,
> Who what they take from Heav'n on Earth bestow,
> Recluse from envy, and all vulgar pride,
> Dispenses pleasures, to herself deny'd.[12]

Elizabeth had long been famous, but never for her generosity and
humility. And this is certainly the only time she was ever compared to
a nun. But she was Jackson's patron and so he was expected to exag-
gerate her virtues, if not create them from whole cloth.

But Foote is the real subject of *Asmodeus*. Reviving the charges
from the previous summer, Jackson represents Foote as a blackmailer
who threatens to destroy Elizabeth's reputation unless she buys his
silence. Motivated by a love of money and a hatred for Elizabeth's
shining virtues, Foote strikes upon a plan to hurt her:

> Quoth he, "I'll write a farce, or something clever
> Shall soil this character.—Aye.—Now or never
> A stroke at fortune. What? a thousand?—Two.
> At least a couple. Let me see.—'Twill do.
> Prudence! philosophy! and in a Duchess!
> The damn'd œconomy!—But that not much is.
> Sure as the Fates in Hell, it is decreed,
> Her character must die:—Or she must *bleed*." (7)

But unlike in real life, instead of offering Foote a modest sum to keep
silent, Elizabeth sends him a halter, which he uses to hang himself.

The poem ends with a long prose anecdote about how a party of surgeons claimed Foote's corpse for the purposes of anatomy. Extremely controversial in the eighteenth century, anatomies could only be performed on the bodies of executed murderers. According to Jackson, Foote falls under the law as a murderer of reputations. When the surgeons cut the corpse open, they discover that Foote had an addled brain and no heart at all.

This is Jackson's fantasy of poetic justice and it fulfills Elizabeth's prediction in her infamous public letter to Foote that eventually he would be "turned off" as a result of his abusive satire. If Elizabeth could not hope for vindication from the House of Lords, she might at least get it from a poem.

Foote could not have anticipated this renewed assault. There is no record of his having attended Elizabeth's trial, and his only quip on the subject is the observation that the three most remarkable women in Europe are Elizabeth, the forger, Mrs. Rudd, and Catherine the Great.[13] Coming from a man famous for his malicious wit, this is very light stuff. On 19 April, the third day of the trial, James Boswell was walking along Piccadilly when Foote came by in his coach and invited him inside. Boswell climbed in and Foote told him that he considered Mansfield's advocacy of Elizabeth to be strange. Boswell agreed, noting, "I said it was shocking to see a Lord Chief Justice so partial." Their conversation on the subject continued, but unfortunately Boswell's journal breaks off at precisely this point, so the only record of Foote's private opinion on the trial is frustratingly incomplete.[14] Judging from his public demeanor, however, it seems that he considered his spat with Elizabeth water under the bridge, so he must have been surprised by the new poem.

But the most interesting thing about *Asmodeus* is not what it says, but what it does not say. Nowhere in the poem does Jackson ever hint that Foote is a sodomite. This is the charge that brought Foote to his knees the previous summer, yet Jackson chose not to use it. Instead, he merely lambastes Foote for being a hypocrite and a blackmailer, the source of all of Elizabeth's troubles. Foote probably laughed off *Asmodeus* as the feeble attack it was. But as he left the court at Bow Street on the evening of 6 May, he knew that Jackson and Elizabeth now had much better ammunition to use against him.

Braced for the fallout from Sangster's charges, Foote was nonetheless stunned as the *Public Ledger* gleefully trumpeted the story in not one, not two, but forty detailed stories (or "paragraphs," as they were called) during the second week of May. Sangster later swore that he did not meet Jackson until two weeks after these stories appeared. If so, then

Jackson had Sir John Fielding's public courtroom to thank for the information. The Bow Street court was not far from where Jackson lived, and since he was known to be Foote's enemy, it is likely that as soon as Sangster leveled his charges, someone fetched Jackson to come and hear the proceedings. Alternatively, one of the freelance newspaper reporters who regularly attended sessions at Bow Street might have taken notes on the proceedings and then sold them to Jackson afterward. Either way, he got the information and ran with it.

James Boswell, who loved scandal and was no saint himself, was taken aback by the charges. In his private journal for 10 May, the day the first paragraphs appeared in the *Public Ledger*, Boswell indicates that Jackson's authorship was no secret and that being called a sodomite was a very grave charge. He writes that during a visit with Samuel Johnson and George Steevens, "I mentioned Jackson's shocking story of Foote. Stevens said he would rather have the character of a Sodomite than of an Infidel. I said I would not."[15] Johnson agreed with Boswell that being called a sodomite was the worst possible stain on a man's character, worse than murder, worse than not believing in God. In popular mythology, sodomites were considered to be the devil's spawn, archinfidels whose existence was an affront to the natural order of the universe.[16]

Enlightened men such as Boswell and Johnson surely did not believe this, but even so, they could not imagine a more damning accusation. It is striking that instead of discussing Foote's guilt or innocence, they talk about the effect of such charges on one's reputation. Johnson, Boswell, and Steevens were well-educated urban men. Like Foote, they were part of the literati of their age and although they were not noblemen, they enjoyed a degree of privilege and social prestige that distinguished them from the rest of society. They were, in other words, the sort of men who might be subject to blackmail, and in the charges against Foote, they saw the potential for trouble to themselves. If Foote hoped to weather this scandal he would need to rely on the public support of such friends, who were privately shocked by the charges. He was shaken by the ferocity of Jackson's newspaper attacks, but rather than flee the country like Isaac Bickerstaffe, he chose to stand his ground.

Foote began his counterattack on Monday, 13 May by sending a friend, William Law Hamilton, into the winding medieval streets of the city of London to the office of the *Public Ledger*.[17] Tucked into tiny Globe Court, Shoe Lane, the office was just ten doors away from Fleet Street. There, a man named Thomas Brewman sold him a copy of the day's paper containing eleven paragraphs against

Foote. Hamilton returned on 14 May and again purchased the day's paper, which contained seven paragraphs about Foote. The next day, Hamilton returned once more and asked Brewman if he could purchase the May 10 and 11 papers, which contained twenty-two paragraphs against Foote. Brewman apologized that they were sold out and explained that he could have sold many more copies, so great was the demand.

Foote, of course, already had copies of the paper for the days in question, as did thousands of Londoners. The purpose of Hamilton's visits was not merely to purchase the papers, but to lay the groundwork for a libel suit against William Jackson. On Friday 17 May, Foote and Hamilton went to the Court of King's Bench in Westminster Hall with Foote's lawyer, James Wallace (who, ironically, had represented Elizabeth in her bigamy trial four weeks earlier) and a friend named Thomas Hawkins. As Foote's party stood before Justice John Willes in the tiny courtroom, they were overshadowed by the scaffolding put up for Elizabeth's trial, which had still not been removed.

Hamilton presented the court with the two copies of the *Public Ledger* that he had purchased and with two copies of the paper that he was unable to purchase, but that Brewman had admitted to having sold out of. Foote told the court that although the newspaper never mentioned his name, he believed the paragraphs could only be construed to refer to him. Then Hawkins and Hamilton both testified that they "verily believe" that William Jackson was the editor of the *Public Ledger*. After their testimony, Wallace began to read the forty paragraphs against Foote. He had read only two of them before Willes interrupted him and said that he had heard enough. He immediately issued a warrant for Brewman's appearance to answer the charge of publishing the libels.[18]

Thomas Brewman was not the man Foote was after. But to get at Jackson, he needed someone to testify under oath that Jackson had written the paragraphs in question. With the help of Hamilton and Hawkins, Foote set a trap for Brewman, who suddenly found himself the object of a very serious charge in the Court of King's Bench. With enough pressure, Foote hoped Brewman would turn king's evidence against Jackson.

The following Monday, 20 May, Brewman was represented in court by his lawyer, a Mr. Morgan. Morgan produced an affidavit by Brewman in which he asked for more time from the court to respond, pleading that the joint affidavit filed by Foote, Hamilton, and Hawkins arrived too late for him to make an adequate reply. This time it was

Mansfield presiding over the court. He reprimanded Morgan for this appeal, pointing out that it would have taken Brewman no time at all to swear an affidavit that he did not publish and sell the editions of the *Public Ledger* in question. Mansfield said that Brewman's plea for time was no answer to the charges, and ruled against him, clearing the way for a trial. The *London Chronicle* reported that Mansfield also "spoke against the licentiousness of the press, which he declared was in no particular so reprehensible as in an attempt to prejudice a cause, and to prejudice the Public against the party accused previous to the trial."

That is exactly what Jackson was trying to do. As he well knew, Foote's summer season began in the middle of May, so the campaign in the *Public Ledger* was timed to coincide with opening night. Foote said as much in his deposition, complaining that the goal was to subject him to the "Detestation and Abhorrence of the Publick" and also to prevent him "from opening his Theatre and representing Theatrical pieces therein which he is presently about to do."[19] According to Foote's first biographer, Jackson almost succeeded. Foote may have been standing up to Jackson in court, but he was terrified that appearing on stage while under suspicion of sodomy would incite a riot. He even considered not opening the Haymarket theater for the season. However, his noble friends assured him of their support and encouraged him to continue with business as usual.[20]

Thus encouraged, Foote advertised a performance of his play *The Bankrupt* for the evening of Monday, 20 May. The public interest in his case was by now so great that the streets around the Haymarket were crowded with hundreds of people seeking admission. When the doors opened after six o'clock, the newspapers said that "the crowd pressed in with an eagerness that threatened the limbs of his Majesty's subjects, and afforded much employment for pick-pockets. The pit was filled in six minutes, and it was remarked that there was not a single woman in it, nor perhaps thirty in the whole house."[21] The absence of women is a strong indication that people expected a riot that evening.

At the end of the musical prelude that customarily preceded plays, the stage curtain was drawn aside and Foote faced the audience, an expression of tortured apprehension on his normally assured face. According to the *London Chronicle*, a "roar of applause ensued, which was accompanied by violent marks of disapprobation." Foote attempted to speak several times, but was constantly interrupted by the alternating cheers and boos. He bowed to the audience and was visibly trembling during these outbursts, imploring the crowd in dumb show to hear him out. Eventually, the noise subsided and Foote was able to say:

Ladies and Gentlemen,

Labouring under a charge as unjust as it is cruel, I did not intend to have made a public appearance till my innocence had been clearly established in a legal way; but the season for opening the theatre being arrived, many respectable friends advised me not to decline my usual business. I have given full security to wait the issue of the trial and I await it with patience. I have been vilely traduced and calumniated; but conscious of my own innocence and fully apprised of the nobleness of your natures, I trust you will not discard an old servant on mere suspicion. I—I—can say no more.[22]

The theater exploded in applause and a grateful Foote left the stage in tears.

It was a great gamble, and it worked: the play went off without disruption, save for thunderous applause. And *The Bankrupt* was the perfect play for the occasion. Written by Foote three years earlier, it is a satire on newspaper libels. Predictably, whenever the audience heard a line that could apply to Jackson's campaign against Foote, the applause was "astonishing." Particular approval was given to the scene in a printing office in which an unscrupulous newspaper editor boasts that he has more influence in the administration of justice than judges have, claiming, "I hold the scale."

A report the next day in the *St. James's Chronicle* complimented the audience for allowing Foote to perform, noting, "We do not remember many Events which have given us more Pleasure, as a Proof of the manly justice and Generosity of the English People." Foote, the report continued, may not be above reproach in all aspects of his life, but "the Treatment he has lately met with, while his Guilt is problematical, nay extremely improbable, is so atrociously cruel, that it would rouse Humanity in a Devil."[23]

For Jackson, this was a troubling turn of events indicating that his attacks had backfired badly. Instead of prejudicing the public against Foote, his attacks had created an opportunity for Foote to appear the victim, not the victimizer. In the process, Jackson had made the *Public Ledger* vulnerable to an expensive libel prosecution that could potentially undermine Sangster's case. And lest anyone should forget that Elizabeth Chudleigh was behind all of this, the *St. James's Chronicle* archly noted that after the performance of *The Bankrupt*, "an Express went off from the Little Theatre in the Haymarket for

Calais, with an Account that the House is still standing, and the Manager has been able to keep his Legs by the Favour of his Friends and the Justice of the Public."

After reading the reviews of Foote's opening night, Jackson and Elizabeth realized that their only hope lay in Sangster's success in the courtroom. If the servant could prove his charges, then the libel case against the *Public Ledger* would be rendered moot because Jackson had merely printed Sangster's accusations. For her part, Elizabeth finally would have the satisfaction of seeing her enemy ruined. Accordingly, on Thursday, 23 May, Jackson contacted Sangster through an intermediary and promised to "support the prosecution" against Foote with the help of his pen and Elizabeth's money.[24]

Just days after making contact with Sangster, Jackson renewed his attacks in the *Public Ledger*. Attempting to counteract the good publicity Foote received from his opening night, Jackson praised the audience's behavior in ironic terms: "If Aristophanes of Athens was raised from the dead, and, living amongst us, was to conceive a passion for one of his own sex, he ought nevertheless to be publicly encouraged."[25] Foote, he continued, was so famous that he should not be held to the same rules of morality as the rest of society: "We should pass over the crimes, for the sake of the wit of the man. Forgetful of his impudence, we should encourage his hypocrisy. If he smiled at infamy, we should applaud his mirth. If he wept—we should admire his skillfulness in the mechanism of tears."

For all of Jackson's malice this renewed attack was really an acknowledgment that Foote was the recipient of extraordinary indulgence and public support. The strength of that support became clear a few weeks later when, on 12 June, King George III and Queen Charlotte did something they had never done before: they commanded a performance at Foote's theater. Although Foote had operated the Little Haymarket throughout George's sixteen-year reign, the king, who loved comic plays, had never graced Foote with his presence. Foote had a royal box fitted up for the occasion, hung with a blue-and-white silk canopy. He met the king and queen at the door and personally escorted them to their box, joking all the way. One of the plays that evening was *The Contract*, written by Thomas Francklin, chaplain to George III. With his usual impudence, Foote told the royal couple that although the play was written by their chaplain, it was dull enough to have been the work of a bishop.

But all joking aside, this was an important public demonstration that the king and queen took a personal interest in Foote's case and that they considered him to be an innocent man. A contributor to the *St. James's Chronicle* implies as much when he says: "The King, who is also a Friend to Merit, and ever shows it with due Distinction and Prudence, honoured our English Aristophanes with a Command on the second Opening of his Theatre last Night."[26] As this notice insinuates, the royal presence at the theater that evening indicated to Jackson that he might be in for trouble. Sangster's charges had been implicitly rebuked and the libel suit vastly strengthened by the king and queen's actions. For Elizabeth, the king's personal intervention in the case must have been like a slap in the face. Six months earlier she had sent a letter, begging him for such a demonstration of favor, only to be met with stony silence. Once again, she was being shown up by Samuel Foote.

In response to the worsening situation, Jackson did what he could: he took up his pen and began to write. On 17 June, he published a new version of *Asmodeus,* this time altering the poem so that it delivered a stronger attack on Foote. In the new version, Jackson refers to Foote's participation in a cross-dressing musical revue in his younger days. He also changed the end of the poem, when the surgeons anatomize Foote's corpse. This time, they discover that Foote is a hermaphrodite. His mixture of male and female genitalia, Jackson suggests, is the result of his theatrical cross-dressing. The *Monthly Review* dismissed the work with one line: "Asmodeus is Samuel Foote, Esq.; concerning whose affair with the Dutchess of Kingston the Author has taken most scurvy pains,—for a dinner."[27]

On the same day, Jackson also earned his dinner by publishing a pamphlet called *The Whole of the Evidence upon the Duchess of Kingston's Trial,* noting that it contains "an authentic copy of her grace's defence, as spoken by herself."[28] This is a highly partisan exercise in damage control. Simultaneously, Jackson was using the *Public Ledger* to warn Augustus Hervey against initiating divorce proceedings against Elizabeth, whom he continued to call Duchess of Kingston.

But this flurry of publication was merely the prelude to Jackson's major work, a 540-line satiric poem about Foote's case called *Sodom and Onan.* Published on 22 June the poem is an exceptionally audacious diatribe against Foote, Lord Mansfield, Justice Willes, and King George III, among many others. Jackson begins by telling the story of Foote's sexual attacks on Sangster, but most of the poem looks forward, not backward, predicting that the legal system, the aristocracy, and the king himself will conspire to violate the laws of man and God in order to protect Foote from conviction.

Pulling out all the stops, Jackson names names, finding "powerful Sodomites" and their protectors at the highest levels of society. When he sets his sights on Mansfield, Jackson had to negotiate between his anger over Mansfield's ruling in the libel case and Elizabeth's continued support for the man who stood by her. Instead of damning Mansfield, Jackson cautions: "Mansfield beware, a cause like this is nice; / No tongue has dar'd to taint your name with vice / Like this." Instead of bending the law to protect Foote, Mansfield is warned to "weigh in equal scale / The pros and cons, and let the truth prevail."[29]

Lines like these dominate the poem, betraying Jackson's anxiety that Foote is going to be acquitted thanks to his powerful friends. This anxiety leads Jackson to warn George III that he may be inviting God's wrath by taking Foote's side. And he comes very close to sedition when he writes:

> As heaven's Viceregents Kings on Earth are plac'd,
> But G[eorge]e the seal majestic hath disgrac'd;
> Inveigled by Scotch Insinuation
> To pardon Sodomites and damn the Nation. (17)

One might expect that with a claim like this, Jackson had spent his fury, but in fact the poem goes on for more than a hundred lines, singling out one alleged sodomite after another, from the printer Samuel Drybutter to the Duke of Ancaster.

The poem concludes with a complaint that by ravaging only heterosexual bodies with venereal diseases Nature has emboldened sodomites like Foote who "Conclude that she is partial to their flame / Urging as argument for their desires, / That they're exempted from venereal Fires" (22). In order to correct this injustice, Jackson calls upon Nature to "Transfer the curse" of sexual disease from heterosexuals to homosexuals so that their bodies might serve as signs of their sinful natures. In a grisly passage, he calls upon Pandora to open her box and unleash hideous torments on Foote's body:

> Let his whole mass with poison be condens'd,
> And for each pang of his, one Whore be cleans'd;
> Let rank corruption, mining all within,
> Consume his vitals, e'er the cause is seen.

The doctors will be so revolted by Foote's diseased and stinking body that they will not dare approach him. For his part, Foote will not even be able to cry out for help because, sores will "perforate his mouth and nose, / That not a single want he may disclose."[30]

The violence of this passage is especially shocking from our historical perspective for the way it anticipates modern interpretations of AIDS as God's judgment against homosexuals.

Sodom and Onan has the distinction of being one of the most violent satires of the eighteenth century, no small achievement in an era famous for satire. And yet for all its malice, the poem betrays Jackson's anxiety that Foote will escape punishment. Although the quarter sessions for the county of Middlesex were still two weeks away, Sangster's case might have been undermined by the strong showing of public support for Foote. *Sodom and Onan* was Jackson's attempt to undermine that support. Typically, he did too much, lashing out with an indiscriminate fury that did a disservice to the very cause he hoped to promote.

It was under these circumstances that Sangster's charges were brought before a grand jury during the quarter sessions on 9 July. Although important legal business would be heard during the few days of each quarter session, these events typically took on the air of a festival. The judges, lawyers, and grand jurymen brought their wives and daughters along for the socializing, dining, and dancing that took place. From 1612 until 1778, the Middlesex sessions occurred in Hicks Hall, a building specifically constructed as a sessions house in the heart of London near the Smithfield meat market and just a short walk from the office of the *Public Ledger*. The sessions began with the chairman delivering a "charge" to the grand jury, a brief homily enjoining them to do their duty to uphold public morality. Then the lawyers, judges, and juries got down to work, often plowing through hundreds of cases in a single day.

John Sangster was represented by a lawyer named Luke Naylor. The very presence of legal counsel is proof that Elizabeth's money was funding the prosecution at this point. Most victims prosecuted cases themselves at this time, and as an unemployed menial servant, Sangster is the last person one might expect to have retained counsel. Naylor presented Sangster's evidence about the alleged assault on 1 May to the grand jury, who heard only the prosecution's side. Finding that evidence credible, the jury returned the indictment as a "true bill," the last step before the trial itself. Sangster's testimony proved stronger than the outpouring of royal and aristocratic support for Foote. He was going to stand trial after all.

At this point, Naylor rose again and took the unusual step of asking the court to issue a warrant for Foote's immediate arrest. This was a gratuitous move. Foote would have to appear before the court to enter his plea in a day or two and since he had posted bail in this matter at Bow Street, he was not, logically, a flight risk. The goal of requesting the warrant was to catch Foote unawares and have the pleasure of seeing him jailed. Nevertheless, the request was granted and the warrant was issued.

Naylor left the session house with a constable and headed to Foote's house in Suffolk Street, where they were told that Foote was not at home. The pair waited outside for an hour and a half when they finally saw Foote approaching in a coach, accompanied by his attorney, William Hickey. As Naylor approached the coach, Hickey burst out, "By Jasus, you are Mr. Jackson's brother in law." Naylor snidely responded, "By Jasus, Hickey, if you was not old enough to be Foote's grandmother, I should suspect you to be his mistress."[31]

Jackson reported the details of the grand jury's actions and his brother-in-law's witticism in the *Public Ledger* the following day. Unfortunately for him, however, Foote had been tipped off. By the time Naylor approached him with the arrest warrant, Foote and Hickey had been to Hicks Hall with three sureties who stood bail for Foote. Hickey also entered a writ of certiorari, removing the case from the Middlesex sessions to the Court of King's Bench. This raised the stakes considerably. Not only would the case be delayed, it would be much more expensive, and it would be heard by the likes of Mansfield or Willes, judges whom Jackson already mistrusted.[32]

Frustrated in their attempt to have Foote jailed, Jackson and Sangster had one more card to play. The next day, Naylor presented Sangster's second charge against Foote, for the assault on 2 May in Fulham. The grand jury returned a second true bill, and so Foote faced the prospect of a second trial, another arrest warrant, and the need to post bail yet again. This was merely an attempt to make the defense more expensive and complicated for Foote. Hickey protested the move and asked the court to unite the second indictment with the first one, removing them both to the Court of King's Bench under the writ of certiorari he obtained the previous day. Naylor objected that the second indictment was returned after the writ had been made out; therefore, the writ could not extend to the second charge. But once again he was bested by Foote's counsel. Hickey replied that while this was true, the writ was not delivered to the clerk of the peace until the second indictment had been returned. The court agreed with Hickey, sparing Foote the expense of two trials and ensuring that his case would now be heard in a court that was known to be favorably disposed to him.

According to Jackson's account of the proceedings in the *Public Ledger*, this was but one more instance of how the justice system was manipulated in order to protect a privileged sodomite like Foote. He then claims that after "Mr. Foote had escaped from the Bench of Justices, he threw off the masque of gravity, and—forced a laugh." But it was not a sincere laugh; rather, it was the forced "grin of guilt," which, "like Milton's ghastly smile, is most horrible—The features of Mr. Foote have always been deemed expressive."[33]

Jackson's sense of disappointment, already obvious from his report on the day's proceedings, was made even clearer by a notice printed directly below that report: "THIS EVENING THEIR MAJESTIES WILL BE AT THE THEATRE ROYAL IN THE HAYMARKET."[34] The capital letters scream Jackson's incredulity. After having twice been indicted for attempting to commit the worst of crimes, Foote was being rewarded with yet another royal command. Even worse, that evening, Foote performed the role of Lady Pentweazel in his play *The Orators*. As the *Gentleman's Magazine* observed, Foote appeared before their majesties "with a head-dress stuck full of feathers in the utmost extravagance of the present mode, being at least a yard wide. Their Majesties laughed immoderately; and to heighten the ridicule, the whole fabric of feathers, hair, and wool, dropped off as Foote waddled off the stage, which continued the roar for some time."[35]

Jackson's incredulity is understandable. It is remarkable to think of Foote's having appeared in court two days running, responding to the legal assaults of people who were clearly intent on his ruin, and still summoning the energy to appear on stage each night. It is all the more surprising that he did so in an extravagant drag costume before the king and queen. Foote was performing more than just the role of Lady Pentweazel that evening; he was suggesting to the world that the charges against him were a matter of no concern, not to him, not to his king and queen. The idea of his guilt was so absurd that he could appear dressed as a woman before their majesties and everyone would take it for what it was—a joke.

It was, of course, more than a joke: it was also a performance of Foote's power and privilege, which were considerable. And yet despite the extraordinary public support of his noble and royal friends, the grand jury had listened to Sangster's accusations and found them credible. If Foote was winning in the court of public opinion, his accuser, financed by Elizabeth Chudleigh, seemed to be winning in the courts of law. Foote had mounted an unprecedented counterattack to the charges, but his success was far from assured, and failure would mean his ruin.

CHAPTER 11

TRIAL FOR ATTEMPTED SODOMY

Ever since John Sangster's first appearance before Sir John Fielding, many leading aristocrats had rallied to Foote's defense. The grand jury's double indictment did nothing to diminish their support. According to an early biographer, the more dire Foote's situation seemed, the more his noble friends consoled and encouraged him:

> Our hero was so far from being abandoned, that his house, from the first moment of the charge being preferred against him, to the close of the trial, exhibited a continual assemblage of rank, learning, fashion, and friendship. Among the two former classes particularly, are to be numbered two royal Dukes, the late Duke of Roxburgh, the Marquis of Townshend, Mr. Dunning (afterwards Lord Ashburton), Mr. [Edmund] Burke, Sir Joshua Reynolds, Mr. [William] Fitzherbert, beside several foreign noblemen, and a group of other persons of the very first respectability.[1]

Jackson was beginning to learn what some of Foote's other detractors had learned earlier. Nine years earlier, when Foote was denounced in a satirical poem called *Momus*, one writer explained to the poem's author: "Here you only betray the most consummate assurance, but an absolute ignorance of your subject. I say *ignorance*, for it is known to all who do not breathe in total obscurity, that Mr. F—te is actually caressed by the brightest geniuses, and persons of the most exalted stations in the kingdom."[2] And now that included the king and queen.

The royal couple's appearance at the Little Haymarket on 10 July, the night that the second grand jury indictment was handed down, drove Jackson to a fury of denunciation. The next day he published a

notice assuring "young gentlemen of a florid appearance, and a promising aspect" that they could join Foote's acting company without
any fear of anal rape by the manager because "for their further safety,
Mr. Jewell has orders to supply them with—CORKS."[3]

On 12 July, Jackson denied a charge published in the *Morning
Chronicle* that he was at the Middlesex sessions with Sangster and was
responsible for the bench warrants to arrest Foote. Those warrants
were necessary, he claimed, to prevent Foote from paying a "visit to
his old friend, my Lord Pierre Goa, at Paris . . . If this fact is mis-
stated, let Mr. Foote, or his abettors, deny it if they dare. Let them
deny that he wanted to decamp; and the persuasive means used for his
retention shall be displayed to the public."[4] This is a veiled threat to
start publishing the names of Foote's supposed homosexual lovers. If
Foote's friends continued to attack Jackson, he would take measures
to defend himself. He warns that "they will be suspected of rancour.
If they attempt to explain away facts, they will be charged with duplic-
ity. Silence is prudential, when nothing can be said to the purpose."

By this point, however, Jackson was unable or unwilling to hold
back. The next day he published an extraordinary paragraph, leveling
charges of sodomy that extended well beyond John Sangster's testimony. He asks Foote:

> Do you know Monsieur. Perduccat of Paris? 2. Have you not been
> intimately well acquainted with the Prince d'Elbouef? 3. Hath not that
> Prince been long remarkable for the excellence of his taste? 4. Have you
> not passed the most agreeable hours of your life with the Prince and
> his agent, Monsieur Perduccat? Have you not lived in the same house
> with them? There is no harm in this: it is only proof of a similarity of
> manners. 5. Do you imagine that Lord Piere Goa knows any thing
> of your conduct? Do you not think that he can give an excellent account
> of your amours? Prepare yourself. Who knows what the Beau-Monde of
> Paris may be entertained with the secret history of your intrigues? The
> Prince d'Elboeuf is a most pleasing companion. 6. Pray, Mr. Foote, what
> is become of Charles Fryer, the Westminster barber? Has he retired for
> a continuance, or, for the season only? He is a fellow of humour. I wish
> he would deign to be forth-coming. 7. Is it, or is it not true, that, when
> you was first taken on the information, your friends found it necessary
> to PREVAIL on you to stay in England? This last Query it is necessary
> that you should answer.[5]

This is a significant but puzzling paragraph. By publishing new
names, Jackson was implicitly leveling new charges of sodomy against
Foote. Phrases such as "intimately well acquainted" and "a similarity

of manners" are oblique, but since Foote had already begun a suit for libel against the paper, he could easily make the case that this paragraph libeled him as a sodomite. The risk for Jackson is that by going beyond Sangster's case he left the paper open to prosecution for libel even if Sangster were to win his case.

Odder still is that Jackson lays the most emphasis on the final question: Did Foote's friends have to persuade him to stay in England and face the charges? This seems to be a minor matter compared with the outing of four new homosexual lovers, yet Jackson says it is the only question that Foote *must* answer.

Foote is the obvious target of Jackson's campaign, but Jackson was also aiming at bigger game. His goal seems to have been to tar Foote and his aristocratic friends with the same brush. By doing so, he hoped to intimidate Foote's allies into withdrawing their support, lest he drag them into the newspaper by name (as he had already done in *Sodom and Onan*). It was also a way of furthering his defense of Elizabeth. Not only were the leading aristocrats unfaithful to their marriage beds, and not only had they victimized the Duchess of Kingston, they were also using their rank to protect a notorious sodomite. In a society like Georgian England, where power was based on close bonds between men of rank, it was an easy thing for a political outsider like Jackson to suggest that those privileged male bonds had become a little too close.

Jackson was not alone in noticing the outpouring of aristocratic and royal support for Foote during the summer of 1776. One magazine commented that "Mr. Foote entertains the town in the Hay-Market, and although he has, as yet, produced nothing new . . . he has had great success, playing generally to crowded houses. This may, in some measure, be ascribed to their majesties frequently honouring him with their presence."[6]

According to Horace Walpole, the conspicuous presence of royalty and nobility inside the theater was not Foote's only means of fighting back against Jackson and Sangster. Foote also "exhibited a whore that he kept. Lord Townshend, seeing her in a box at Foote's theater during the Prosecution, said, 'There is Foote's Alibi.'"[7] It is not surprising that Townshend would recognize Foote's "whore" at the theater. The actor had two illegitimate sons (then at boarding school) and his frequent visits to London's brothels figure prominently in *Nocturnal Revels*, a mildly pornographic book that was published a few years later.[8]

But asserting his virility was not enough. In the face of Jackson's continuing attacks, Foote decided that he needed to do even more to defend himself in the court of public opinion, so sometime in July he dusted off the banned copy of *A Trip to Calais* and began to revise it. He removed Lady Kitty Crocodile (i.e., Elizabeth Chudleigh) and replaced her with a new main character: Dr. Viper, editor of the *Scandalous Chronicle*.

The plot remained largely the same: a standard comic tale of two young lovers who flee to Calais in order to escape their tyrannical parents so that they can remain together. But then, Foote's plays were never really about their plots; rather, they were about his daring impersonations. Instead of Elizabeth Chudleigh, audiences were going to be treated to a strong dose of the Reverend William Jackson.

Foote renamed the work *The Capuchin* and submitted it to the Lord Chamberlain's office on 6 August, where it was licensed without objection. The very appearance of the play was a further sign that the government held Jackson in contempt. The previous year, *A Trip to Calais* had been banned on the grounds that its appearance might prejudice Elizabeth's forthcoming trial. But even though the *Public Ledger* was now facing trial for libel, the Lord Chamberlain allowed Foote to portray its editor on stage as a vicious scandalmonger.

John Palmer, an actor in Foote's company, studied Jackson's voice and demeanor so that he could impersonate him on stage to the greatest effect, and Foote had a copy of Jackson's favorite jacket, covered in black embroidered frogs, made up for Palmer to wear. The satire against Jackson is blatant. In the play, a Frenchman describes Dr. Viper as an English newspaperman who "lay about him like *le diable*! Poff, poff, poff! he make all de my lors, ay, and my ladies too, shake in dere two shoe."[9] Like Jackson, Dr. Viper is a Protestant minister, a newspaper editor, and the self-appointed scourge of the British aristocracy. Also like Jackson, he makes one exception to his universal scorn for aristocrats: a noblewoman who resides in Calais. Her name is Lady Deborah Dripping, and although she never appears on stage, the reference to her constitutes Foote's sole jab at Elizabeth Chudleigh.

It is surprising that Foote did not personally mimic Jackson, but he was saving the best role for himself. Foote played an Irish charlatan named O'Flam, a former writer of false obituaries for the *Scandalous Chronicle*, now turned Capuchin monk and living in Calais. O'Flam has no love of his old employer and denounces Dr. Viper's "poison pen" for doing "more mischief than me: My dead men walk'd about afterwards, and did their business as if nothing had happen'd; whilst the stabs made on peoples' good names, by your rancour and malice, will admit of no consolation" (113). In lines such as these, Foote had the satisfaction of damning Jackson on stage in front of packed houses. One review noted that in this speech, O'Flam describes Dr. Viper "in the very Words which we suppose Foote to have often delineated his supposed Enemy in a Daily Paper."[10]

But the role of O'Flam allowed Foote to do more than vent his anger against Jackson; it also gave him the opportunity to retaliate against John Sangster by enacting a ridiculous version of attempted sodomy on the public stage.

In the third act, Dr. Viper and O'Flam plan to lure the heroine, Jenny, away from the convent in which she has been hiding from her parents on the pretense of leading her to her true love, Dick. Instead, they will take her to Sir Harry Hamper, a rich old Englishman of their acquaintance who plans to rape her and then return her to the custody of her parents. Sir Harry awaits Jenny's arrival in a darkened bedroom, hoping that she will assume he is Dick and yield to his sexual advances.

The plan goes awry almost immediately. After some comic confusion, Viper takes Jenny away so that he may rape her himself; in her place, he sends O'Flam to keep Sir Harry busy while he attacks Jenny in a nearby room.

Foote, playing O'Flam, enters Sir Harry's darkened room, pretending to be Jenny. He gives Sir Harry his hand, prompting the old man to remark, "Egad, Miss has a good thumping fist of her own!" When Sir Harry tries to steal a kiss, he feels O'Flam's beard and shouts, "Zounds, Miss, what the Devil's this?" Thinking quickly, O'Flam says in a falsetto, "A fur Tippet, that I just threw round my Neck." Sir Harry, now very aroused, swallows these lies eagerly, pawing at O'Flam and trying to haul him off to bed, prompting the latter to say in an aside, "What the Devil will I do? if Doctor Viper does not speedily come, I shall be ravish'd here in spight of my teeth!"[11]

On paper, the scene is rather silly, but given Foote's legal situation, it is incredibly daring. And the joke does not end there. When Jenny's cries from a nearby room bring her parents onto the stage, Sir Harry is discovered with O'Flam and realizes the trick played on him. Still, he must not reveal who he thought was in the room with him, so when asked what he was doing in the room with O'Flam, Sir Harry mumbles out an excuse about questioning "the Monk about his Religion a little." This prompts O'Flam to say, "Upon my Soul, and some very home questions he put me; I could not have conceiv'd Sir Harry had been so warm and able a Disputant. You may say that; he would have puzzled me, if you had not come in just in the nick."

O'Flam's reference to the "home questions" Sir Harry put to him echoes the *Public Ledger*'s claim that Sangster gave Foote a "home thrust" in May. And O'Flam's characterization of Sir Harry as a "warm and able" disputant who "would have puzzled" him function as sexual double entendre. Ultimately, Jenny is rescued from the clutches of Dr. Viper with her virtue intact, but not before Foote has drawn out the comic potential of Sir Harry's unintentional attempt to sodomize O'Flam.

In the context of Foote's legal situation, this scene illustrates the absurdity of Sangster's charges. Sir Harry's near-assault turns the charge of attempted sodomy into farce, using mistaken identity and the darkened-bedroom trick to suggest that only under such improbable conditions could one imagine the sexual assault of one man by another.

According to one review, the scene was not well received and "it was with Difficulty that the Play went on."[12] This review says that the audience objected to the "absurdity" of passing off O'Flam as Jenny, but that may just be a way of saying that it was too daring for the audience's taste (although the censor had no objections). Foote may have cut it from subsequent performances, but this is impossible to tell from the existing reviews. The play was never published during Foote's lifetime. Perhaps because of the scene's indecency, when George Colman the Elder published the play in 1778, he omitted the scene. It survives only in the Lord Chamberlain's manuscript copy.

The Capuchin dominated the repertory, playing on nine of the sixteen nights left in the season. On one of those nights, 4 September, the play was performed at the command of King George and Queen Charlotte. It is impossible to overstate the symbolic importance of this performance. The four previous visits of the king and queen were implicit gestures of support for Foote, but by commanding *The Capuchin*, that support became explicit. It meant that the royal couple came not only to patronize Foote during his legal troubles, but also to scorn his enemies.

During this period, George III was consumed with the American crisis, holding a series of emergency meetings of the Privy Council to decide how to respond to the worsening colonial situation. The Declaration of Independence had just made its way across the Atlantic and gave the king and his ministers serious cause for worry. Under these circumstances, it must have been extremely gratifying to Foote to know that the king cared enough about his fate to make time to visit the Haymarket.

After the season ended in mid-September, Foote was exhausted. It had been a triumphant summer, but a draining one. He seemed older than his fifty-five years, his energy sapped by hard living, the exertions of performing nearly every night for three months (on one leg, no less), and the sheer anxiety that Sangster's and Jackson's charges had induced. Foote had thoughts of retirement before 1776, but had never acted on them. Now he decided that it was time to quit.

Aware that announcing his retirement before his trial might prejudice the case, Foote instructed his lawyers to get the word out secretly that he was interested in leasing his patent on the Haymarket Theatre. Before long, and without any publicity, Foote's lawyers struck a deal in mid-October with George Colman the Elder, a prominent playwright and former copatentee of Covent Garden Theatre. Colman agreed to lease Foote's patent for £1600 a year, and he paid Foote £500 for the right to perform his unpublished plays, including *The Capuchin*. It was a good deal for both parties: Foote got paid for doing nothing and Colman got a valuable theatrical patent for a bargain. A decade earlier, Colman and his partners had paid £60,000 to purchase the Covent Garden patent outright.

Most significantly, Colman agreed to keep the deal quiet until after Foote's trial, which was slated for early December. At the end of October, the *London Chronicle* reported that Colman had "absolutely engaged with Mr. Foote," but Foote denied everything.[13] In a letter to Colman on 4 November, David Garrick says that Foote "damns himself, that there is no bargain yet struck . . . I suppose HE would not proclaim his Abdication, till the tryal is Over—that will soon be & then you will come forth."[14] To Foote's relief, his denials worked and the news of his deal with Colman remained secret in the weeks leading up to his trial.

Foote's trial took place in the Court of King's Bench at 9:00 a.m. on Monday 9 December 1776. At the front of the court on a raised bench sat the Earl of Mansfield. To his right sat a "special jury" of twelve men. Members of a special jury were "persons of higher social and economic status than those on panels for ordinary juries."[15] They were not nobility or even gentry, but they were more respectable than "common" jurors, and in the Crown Roll summary of Foote's case, they are all given the honorific "Esquire."[16] Theoretically, such juries were more deferential to the authority of judges. At least that is what Foote and his lawyers were hoping for since they knew that Mansfield was personally fond of Foote and had, like other judges, a skeptical view of attempted sodomy prosecutions.

The venue, to put it mildly, was favorable for the defense.

John Sangster was there with no fewer than four lawyers: Mr. Davenport, Mr. Cooper, Henry Howarth, and William Jackson's brother-in-law, Luke Naylor. Foote was represented by Francis Buller, William Hickey, Arthur Murphy (Foote's old friend and fellow playwright), and James Wallace. Also on hand were a host of witnesses, four for the prosecution, the rest for the defense; several newspaper reporters; and (presumably) as many curiosity-seekers as the court could accommodate. Jackson, exercising uncharacteristic prudence, stayed out of sight.

Also notably absent was Foote himself, whose presence was not required by the court, not desired by the prosecution, and not necessary to his own defense. At the beginning of the century, criminal defendants were prohibited from being represented by counsel at all because, according to one legal commentator, "It requires no manner of skill to make a plain and honest defence."[17] But by the 1770s, defense lawyers had become a fact of life, and in some cases, like Foote's, the defendant did not even need to appear. Vestiges of the old rules prohibited defense lawyers from addressing the jury and the court directly, but this was often ignored in practice. Their main function was to question friendly witnesses, and especially to cross-examine those for the prosecution. This is particularly important in Foote's trial because the entire case rested on witness testimony. To Sangster, the sight of four lawyers eager to cross-examine him must have been unsettling.

The process began with a statement by lead prosecutor, Henry Howarth, who explained the nature of the case to the jury, but begged them to spare him the embarrassment of describing the attacks in detail. They would hear more than enough from Sangster himself. According to one newspaper account, Sangster then took his oath and, refusing to "evince the least appearance of shame for the infamous falsehoods he was declaring," began his testimony.[18]

Sangster said that he accompanied Foote from Fulham to London on 1 May 1776, arriving at Foote's house in Suffolk Street at 10:45. Foote then "went on stage and continued there about an hour and a half," after which he returned to the house and summoned Sangster to the dining room on an upper floor.[19] After Sangster entered, Foote turned to him and asked, "John, are you quite well of the measles?" grinning oddly in Sangster's face. Foote then turned and gestured to a looking glass on a shelf and said, "John, reach me this." When the servant rose to fetch the mirror, Foote shut and locked the door, laughing and grinning with his back to the door. Again Foote asked:

"Have not all my servants been good to you, while ill of the measles?"
"They have," said Sangster.
"Have I not taken a great deal of care of you, giving physic and things?"

"I thank you for it, sir."

"The best recompense you can make is to let me have a fuck at you."

Staggered, Sangster asked "What do you mean by that?"

"Don't you know?" asked Foote.

"Yes, and I had sooner be hanged. I am very much surprized a man like you would offer such a thing to a servant. I did not know you was such a person before I came. Had I known you was such a person I would not have lived with you for a hundred guineas a year!"

"Why, John, what is your reason?" asked Foote.

"Sin and a shame worse than a brute beast," rejoined Sangster.

"Damn the sin, it is no sin at all," Foote assured him. "And the shame: who knows it? Louis [Vallet, another servant] would let me fuck him every day, but I cannot get into him. I have frigged him five hundred times and he has buggered me, but his damned little nasty prick gives me no pleasure."

"Louis Bally and you may do as you please, sir," said Sangster, who was standing in the middle of the room.

Throughout the conversation, Foote stood with his back to the door and "had his prick in his hand." Not realizing the door was locked, Sangster tried to flee. As he struggled with the door, Foote embraced him and began to rub his penis on Sangster's thigh, repeatedly declaring, "Damn you, I'll be in you!" Foote then tore the button from Sangster's breeches, reached his hand inside and clutched his testicles so tightly that Sangster said they remained swollen for days. "Damn your blood if you don't let me fuck you," Foote hissed, "I insist upon frigging you!"

Sangster said that as he struggled, Foote gripped his testicles harder with one hand and began "shaking my prick" with the other. Roaring in pain and nearly ready to faint, Sangster yelled, "Damn you dirty dog, I'll call out at the window!" and threw Foote to the side.

Panting from the struggle, Foote buttoned up his breeches and ruefully said, "By God, John, there is no fellow I should like better to have to do with."

Sangster shot back, "If I do not make you suffer for this, never believe me more."

"Damn you," replied Foote, "what will you do? If you say I wanted to fuck you, I have not fucked you. And if I had, nobody will believe you."

"You shall see whether they do or not!" Sangster cried as he passed out of the room and down the stairs. He was met at the foot of the stairs by a maid, who asked, "Jack, what have you been doing above stairs?" Pulling on his hat and stepping out onto the street, he told her, "You shall hear that very soon."

Then Foote emerged from the doorway and called down, "John, where are you going? Damn you, I suppose you are going to tell Sir John Fielding I wanted to fuck you. By God, if you do it shall be your ruin. You shall never get a place. I am acquainted with all the nobility and gentry!"

"I don't care a farthing," said Sangster. "I will not stay with you another minute. I'll expose you and all such rascals."

By this time Foote had descended the staircase and stood in the parlor, where he coaxed Sangster inside, saying, "Damn you, what are you afraid of? I don't want to fuck you now. Damn me if ever I touch you more." Placated, Sangster went into the parlor with Foote, who shut the door and said to him, "John, you are a lad. I wish you very well. For your sake, don't say anything about it, for by God it will be your ruin. I have all the nobility on my side. Your character will be gone, you will never get a place. Consider. Stay with me till tomorrow. I'll pay your wages, give you character, and then you may get a place. Sir John Fielding will not take your oath; my oath will be taken before yours."

Fearful of his master's power to ruin his good name and chances for future employment, Sangster agreed.

The next day he accompanied Foote to his villa at Fulham. As Sangster was bridling a horse, Foote entered the stable and locked the door. But rather than give Sangster his wages and a letter of recommendation, Foote once again thrust his hand into Sangster's breeches and said, "Now, John, as this is the last day of your service, ten or twenty guineas shall be at your service if you'll let me have a do at you."

Sangster turned about and shouted, "You damned old buggering rascal!" and struck Foote with his fist. Backing off to a safe distance, Foote threw down the key. Sangster unlocked the door, walked into the yard and shouted back at his master, "You old sodomitical rascal, see how I shall serve you!"

John Williams, Foote's coachman, drove Sangster to town the next day, Friday, 3 May. Unsure how to proceed, Sangster went to the home of Dr. William Fordyce, his previous master, and told him what had happened. Fordyce advised him to take his story to Sir John Fielding.

After delivering this riveting account of the attacks to the jury, Sangster then offered more details of Foote's homosexual tendencies. Five months before the attacks Sangster accompanied Foote on a trip to Ireland. One day, Foote summoned him and asked for a massage as he reclined on a settee. As Sangster complied, Foote asked him,

"Well, John, have you ever had a whore? Does your prick never stand? I daresay you have a large prick?"

The following day Foote called for him again and said, "John, come and undo my leg. It pains me." While Sangster was removing the prosthetic limb, Foote slipped his hands into the servant's breeches, explaining, "I only want to see what sort of a prick you have got." And then a few days later, as Sangster was arranging Foote's clothes, his master stood with his breeches at his ankles, penis in hand, and said, "Don't you think I have got a fine one?"

Suspicious that Foote was sodomizing another servant, Louis Vallet, Sangster said, "I am convinced you are a sodomite and so I should not choose to live with you." But Foote convinced him to remain in his service and say nothing of what had passed, so Sangster returned with him to England at the end of February.

At a time when homosexual sex was so taboo that it was conventional to call it "a sin not to be named among Christians," the effect of Sangster's graphic testimony was profound. His attorney refused to repeat the details, and none of the London papers or magazines would publish them, either out of deference to Foote or out of fear of an obscenity prosecution. Indeed, right down to the twentieth century, Foote's biographers continued this tradition by referring to sodomy euphemistically as a "crime of the blackest dye" or an "unnatural crime." Were it not for Lord Mansfield's manuscript notes on the case, we would know none of the details at all. Eighteenth-century England was anything but squeamish, and pamphlets reporting the details of sodomy trials were published throughout the century.[20] But the total suppression of Sangster's testimony from print suggests that Foote was afforded special consideration.

Unfortunately for the prosecution, as soon as Sangster finished his testimony, the case began to unravel. Under cross-examination, he admitted that the prosecution was being funded by a third party. Sangster said that on 23 May he was approached by a man calling himself Mr. Harvey who offered to "stand my friend and support the prosecution." He also admitted that he had placed a bet that Foote would not appear on the stage after his indictment by the grand jury, explaining, "I thought people would not suffer him." Both of these admissions were damning because they suggested a malicious prosecution by a third party and a desire to profit from the case.

But the most critical moment of the cross-examination seemed the most innocuous. Sangster was asked to give the date he appeared before Sir John Fielding: "Monday, 6 May," he replied. Then he was asked when Foote had called together his acting company for their initial meeting of the season: "The first of May was the general meeting of his players," he stated. Unaware that he was digging himself into a hole, Sangster went on: "I said at Sir John Fielding's that [the first attack took place on] Monday the first of May, when [Foote] came down to look over his players." However, Mr. Bond, Fielding's clerk, had failed to include the date when he wrote down Sangster's testimony. When that testimony was read to Foote on the evening of 6 May, the actor objected to the lack of a date. According to Sangster, Bond then recalled that Sangster had specified 1 May, but Fielding did not require him to alter the record.

Bond was then called to the stand by Sangster's lawyers to corroborate his claims. However, he told the court that when Sangster's testimony was taken, the servant said the first attack occurred "on Monday last," which was 29 April, not 1 May. "Sir John dictated from the mouth of the man, and I wrote. I do not remember a syllable about the 1st of May being mentioned in the morning."

At this point, Sangster and his lawyers realized that something was up, but they did not know what. It seemed that Foote's lawyers were trying to undermine the credibility of Sangster's claim that the attack at Suffolk Street took place on 1 May. Because "Monday last" was not 1 May, Sangster was eager to set the record straight back on 6 May at Bow Street, and his lawyers were all the more eager to do so now before Lord Mansfield. To help clear this issue up, they sent for Sir John Fielding. While he was being summoned, the trial continued.

The prosecution called three more witnesses, Dr. Fordyce, a Mr. Campbell, and John Williams, who served as Foote's coachman at the time of the alleged attacks and who was fired shortly after. Fordyce testified that Sangster had come to him in tears, alleging, "My master wanted to commit an unnatural crime."[21] Campbell said that Sangster told him he was leaving Foote's service because "for reasons he was ashamed to express."

For his part, Williams said that Sangster had asked him if he had heard that Foote was a buggerer. "He said he was pretty sure he was." Under cross-examination, he admitted that he had gone to Foote's house on 6 December to speak to Mrs. Jewell, wife of William Jewell, Foote's treasurer and friend. Williams told her that he had been subpoenaed on behalf of Sangster. "I thought it would be a great hurt to me. I told her I hoped the defendant would give me a character, and if he pleased, I would go out of the way. I had rather not have been a witness." Perhaps sensing a trap, Foote did not come to terms with the seemingly reluctant Williams.

James Wallace then began his defense of Foote and was well into his speech when Sir John Fielding arrived. Wallace stopped so that

Fielding could be sworn in and provide his testimony. Like Bond, he remembered nothing of a specific date, but he did confirm that Sangster claimed the first attack took place on the day when Foote came to the Haymarket to meet with his actors.

Fielding's recollection that the first attack allegedly took place on the day Foote met with his acting company supported Sangster's version of events. But if this corroboration pleased the prosecution, it did not please them for long.

After Fielding gave his testimony and the prosecution reiterated that the first attack took place on 1 May, Wallace sprang his trap. He presented to the court the single piece of material evidence in the case. It was a copy of the *Morning Chronicle*, dated Friday, 3 May 1776. From it, Wallace read a notice published by Foote, calling his acting company together for their first meeting of the year on Monday, 6 May. Wallace then repeated Sangster's testimony that Foote attacked him on 1 May after Foote returned from meeting with his acting company.

Even more damning, at the very time that Sangster was leveling his charges before Sir John Fielding, Foote was on stage at the Little Haymarket conducting the meeting that Sangster claimed took place five days earlier. Having been so adamant about linking the first attack to the day that Foote came to town to meet with his company, Sangster was now caught in a terrible bind.

Wallace called to the stand Jeffrey Pearce, a member of Foote's theatrical company. Pearce said that because it was customary for Foote to meet with the company on 1 May, he and many other performers were in the theater that day, waiting for Foote's arrival. After several hours, many of the performers left, and at 2:00 p.m. Pearce received an order to tell the company that Foote would call them together next week. Thomas "Dibble" Davis, another actor, corroborated Pearce's story. Wallace had many others on hand, but Lord Mansfield assured him that the testimony of Pearce and Davis was sufficient to prove the point.

Sangster and his lawyers might have responded by cross-examining these witnesses and using that as an opportunity to suggest a conspiracy to protect Foote. After all, it was odd that Foote broke with his long-established custom of meeting with the company on the first of May. But because the prosecution had taken such pains to establish that the attack took place immediately following Foote's return from meeting with his players, they left themselves with no room to maneuver. Sangster and his lawyers sat in miserable silence as Wallace destroyed their case.

William Jewell was called to the stand next. His job was to represent the prosecution as the consequence of Sangster's anger over having been fired by Foote. Jewell said that on 3 May he noticed that Sangster and the coachman, John Williams, were carousing at a London tavern in the early morning hours, their presence betrayed by Foote's horses and carriage, which they had left on the street outside. When Jewell showed up at Foote's home in Fulham later that evening, Sangster approached him and said: "You are come to tell my Master you saw me drunk." Jewell replied, "I did not know it, but I see you are drunk now."

According to Jewell's version of events, he told Foote of the encounters, and Foote summarily fired Sangster. The next day, 4 May, Sangster came weeping to Jewell, saying: "I have parted with the best of Masters." They next saw each other two days later, at 5:00 p.m., in the court at Bow Street.

Jewell's wife corroborated his testimony. Then two of Foote's servants, a Mrs. Barker and Louis Vallet, the servant whom Sangster suspected of having a homosexual relationship with Foote, testified that Foote remained in Fulham during the entire week of 1 May. Vallet added that Sangster never complained to him of any "indecent liberties" on the part of their master. With that, the defense concluded.

In a feeble effort to undo the damage of Wallace's presentation, the prosecution recalled John Williams to the stand. The coachman swore that he drove Foote to London on 1 May, but under cross-examination he could not recall when they came, how long Foote stayed, or whether Foote dined in town. Foote's lawyer, James Hickey, then told the court, "Williams told me Sangster never complained to him. This is a bad accusation."

Mansfield agreed. In his instructions to the jury, he ruminated on the nature of the charge of attempted sodomy and on the consequences of a guilty verdict. As was customary at the time, he then reviewed the evidence for the jury, pointing out the inconsistencies in Sangster's testimony and questioning why the prosecution did not produce more witnesses to corroborate his story. He also cast doubt on Williams' testimony. He summed up with a speech that pointedly referred to William Jackson's involvement in the case. Referring to Samuel Clay Harvey, the friend whom Jackson used to initiate contact with Sangster, Mansfield said, "And here a man takes up the Prosecution, who is a stranger to the Prosecutor, does not know him, and never meddled with the affair till the 23rd of May. Who is that man? Is he a friend to Justice, or an enemy to Mr. Foote?" Then, alluding either to Jackson's efforts or to Elizabeth Chudleigh's funding, Mansfield said, "I expected to have heard of the real person who acts behind the curtain."[22]

Mansfield concluded his instructions in a manner that was heavy-handed even by the standards of the day:

> It must here be observed that there are two Indictments, two Special Juries, in order to aggravate the cost and prepossess the minds of the people with the guilt of the Defendant, when the circumstances were all connected in one fact. It was expensive, it was cruel. The Indictments appear founded on conspiracy, and a prosecution supported by perjury. . . . The Providence of God interposes for the Prosecutor to fix on such a day as Mr. Foote did not go to town, though he had done it for many years back, and in such cases it can only be by providential means, or the Prosecutor's contradicting himself in evidence, that the innocent escape the ruin of their reputation and welfare. Gentlemen, I say this more for the sake of the audience than for you; you are in possession of the Evidence, you are masters of the whole matter and will, I do not doubt, do your duty.[23]

Without leaving the box, the jury deliberated for a mere two minutes before declaring Foote "not guilty."

Arthur Murphy rushed from the courtroom to bring the good news to his friend. When he ran up to Foote's house on Suffolk Street, he waved his hat and beamed victoriously at Foote, who was watching from an upper window—perhaps from the very room where the attack was alleged to have taken place. By the time Murphy reached the top of the stairs, Foote had collapsed in a fainting spell. He awoke, delirious, and it was an hour before he was able to acknowledge the welcome news.

In the days that followed, press accounts of the trial trumpeted Foote's innocence while heaping abuse on Sangster. These accounts invariably cast the story in terms of class difference: far from being a "rogue and vagabond" (as actors were once called) Foote was described as a gentleman cruelly victimized by a disgruntled servant. One correspondent to the *St. James's Chronicle* said that Foote's case "was the common Cause of every Master and Mistress in the Kingdom," and asked, "The Life, the Property, and good Fame of the Master claim the Protection of the Servant; and if the Guardian turns Thief, who can be safe?"[24]

Had Foote been interested in revenge, he could have had Sangster hanged for malicious prosecution. But evidently he was happy to let the story die, and so John Sangster fades from the historical record. Disgraced and unemployable, he was now a ruined man for having gotten caught up in a bitter feud between his social superiors.

In retrospect, Foote's acquittal might seem unsurprising. Mansfield was, after all, a friend, and the king and queen had made repeated public demonstrations of their support. But Foote's hysterical reaction to the good news shows how heavily the matter weighed on his mind right up to the day of trial. He had won his case, but that did not mean that his reputation would not suffer simply from having been accused. Sodomy remained anathema to the public, and Foote knew that from this point forward his name would forever be associated with "the worst of crimes."

If Foote needed any reminding, the danger he had been in was made clear in a story reported in the *St. James's Chronicle* a week after his conviction. On Sunday night, 15 December, a well-dressed man propositioned a sentinel in St. James's Park. When the sentinel threatened to detain him, the man pulled a pistol from his coat pocket and shot the soldier in the hand. As he fled up the long gravel walk toward the Queen's Palace (now Buckingham Palace), the wounded soldier called out to one of the grenadier guards on duty. The guard fired on the man, wounding him, but still the man eluded his pursuers. The next day the man was found in a grove of trees, dead from the guard's gunshot. "He appeared to be a Gentleman," the newspaper said, "and had Fifty Guineas and a Gold repeating watch about him."[25]

The penalty for attempted sodomy was not death, but to some it was nearly as bad. Simply being charged with this crime was so shameful that it led Isaac Bickerstaffe into permanent exile. Fear of such a charge led the gentleman in St. James's Park to attempted murder and death.

Foote was much luckier. He fought the charges and won. Equally important, apart from Jackson's *Public Ledger* and *Sodom and Onan*, no newspaper, pamphlet, or poem ever dared to print the embarrassing details of his case. And just weeks after his acquittal, he was invited to attend the queen's drawing room, a critical first step in his social rehabilitation.

For Elizabeth, news of the royal family's continuing efforts to support Foote must have been galling. Once again, the actor was succeeding where the self-styled duchess had failed. Worse still, her conviction in the bigamy trial presented the prospect of renewed lawsuits from the Meadows family and a divorce suit from the Earl of Bristol. Both her wealth and her noble title of Countess of Bristol were in peril. For Jackson, Foote's acquittal was very bad news because he had staked everything on Sangster's success. Foote might have been content to let Sangster slink away, but his libel suit against the *Public Ledger* had just been given new life.

CHAPTER 12

EXILES

Samuel Foote wasted no time in turning the victory over Sangster to his advantage in the libel suit against the *Public Ledger*. On 6 February 1777, Foote's lawyers persuaded Thomas Brewman, the manager of the paper, to provide evidence proving that William Jackson had written the libelous paragraphs about Foote. Brewman had good reason for his decision to turn King's evidence: Foote's acquittal made a conviction in the libel case all but certain—especially since it was going to be heard in the Court of King's Bench, where Lord Mansfield and Justice Willes were both known to be sympathetic to Foote and hostile to the paper.

The spring of 1777 must have been a very strange time for Foote. For the past seventeen years, he had spent the winter and early spring away from London, frequently dispensing with the previous season's profits in Paris. He would return to London in late spring to assemble his company and begin rehearsing his newest play. This year, by contrast, he was forced to remain in London to attend to his lawsuits, and because he leased his patent to George Colman, he had no theater work to keep him occupied.

But he was not entirely idle: he was busy trying to repair the damage done to his reputation. Being invited to the queen's drawing room in January was helpful for it gave him an opportunity to show-case his unique blend of social privilege and irreverent humor. When George Warren had a diamond-studded decoration worth £700 stolen from his coat, Foote facetiously accused the Anglican priests in attendance. One observer recalled, "Foote was there, and lays it upon the parsons; having secured, as he says, his gold snuff-box in his waistcoat pocket upon seeing so many black gowns in the room."[1]

Foote's friend and attorney, Arthur Murphy, also helped to repair his reputation by including a fond depiction of him in the character of Dashwould in Murphy's last play, *Know Your Own Mind*, which premiered at Covent Garden Theatre on 22 February. In that play, Dashwould is described as a man who "has a quick sense of the ridiculous, and draws a character with a lucky hit." Like Foote, he is accused of occasionally ridiculing his own friends on stage for a laugh. When warned, "Don't lose your friend for your joke," Dashwould replies, "By no means, . . . Except now and then, when the friend is the worse of the two."[2] This is a fitting tribute to Foote, written by a man who knew him well, who loved him despite his malicious wit, and who wanted to help him move beyond the scandal of the past year.

Not everyone wished him so well. Hester Lynch Piozzi, confidante of Samuel Johnson and others in Foote's circle, believed that Foote was a sodomite, noting in private manuscript that he "broke his heart because of a hideous detection."[3] Charles Macklin, Foote's old acquaintance and acting coach, continued to have doubts about his innocence. In a private journal recalling Foote's appeal to the audience at the beginning of the 1776 season, Macklin wrote that Foote "said not a word of his Innocence, nor any thing Specific in his defence."[4] Macklin is wrong; Foote did assert his innocence that evening, and he announced the commencement of his libel suit against the *Public Ledger*. Nevertheless, it is significant that Macklin's suspicions led him to remember the event differently. For his part, Foote was conscious of the lingering effects of Sangster's accusations, lamenting afterward, "My friends all come in pairs."[5]

On Saturday 19 April, the Court of King's Bench ordered a subpoena to be served on Jackson, summoning him to show cause why Foote's suit should not go forward. But when the messenger arrived at Jackson's lodging in Lyon's Inn between 6:00 and 7:00 p.m., Mary Tempelman, his laundress, announced that he was not in.[6] The subpoena was left with her, but because Jackson returned home very late, she did not give it to him that evening. Tempelman claims that she mislaid the subpoena the next day, and fearful that Jackson would be "angry and enraged at her," she told him nothing of it. She spent the next two days in search of the document, finally discovering it late in the evening on Monday. Unfortunately, by that time Jackson had left for Paris "upon some particular Business." The hapless servant had not had "an opportunity of delivering the said paper to the said Mr. Jackson," but she added helpfully that as she believes that "Mr. Jackson will return home again in about a month," she "intends and will then deliver him the said Paper."

The story is suspicious. Foote's lawyers and the judges suspected that Jackson's trip to France was more impromptu than his servant let on, and their doubts were not put to rest by another affidavit filed in that case. On 23 April, Jackson's friend Samuel Clay Harvey swore that a week before the subpoena was served, Jackson announced his intention to travel to Paris on business. Like Mary Tempelman, he said that he expected Jackson back in three or four weeks. But Harvey was hardly a credible witness. In his affidavit he said that he was "intimately acquainted" with Jackson. The Court of King's Bench already knew as much: Harvey is the man who approached John Sangster the previous year on behalf of Jackson and Elizabeth Chudleigh, offering to support his prosecution against Foote.

It seems that Jackson was following Elizabeth's example. He took one look at the subpoena and made his own hasty trip to Calais in order to avoid prosecution.

Despite Jackson's flight, Foote pressed forward with the libel suit. On 12 May the court received Foote's information against Jackson, formally changing the case from "The King against Thomas Brewman" to "The King against The Reverend William Jackson."[7] Two months later, on 12 July, Foote and Brewman filed a joint affidavit accusing Jackson of writing the libelous paragraphs. Brewman's testimony was particularly damning. He said that on 12 May 1776, a messenger brought several anti-Foote paragraphs to him for inclusion in the *Public Ledger*. Brewman recognized Jackson's handwriting immediately, having "for a long time past known and been well acquainted with the manner and Character of his hand Writing."[8] Later that same day, Brewman said, Jackson came to the office and proofread the copy in his presence.

With the support of Brewman's evidence, Foote was virtually certain to win his case; however, it seems never to have come to judgment. There is no record of a ruling in the King's Bench archives. This means that either a settlement was reached out of court (which is unlikely) or that Jackson succeeded in staying out of the country and stalling the process in the hopes that Foote would either give up on the case or die.

He did not have to wait long.

Foote's health declined rapidly in the spring and summer of 1777. Although relieved of managerial duties, he continued to act on occasion at the Little Haymarket, where his failing health became more and more noticeable with each appearance on stage. Describing Foote during a performance of his popular play *The Nabob*, an early biographer says, "His cheeks were lank and withered, his eyes had lost all their wonted intelligence, and his whole person appeared sunk and emaciated."[9] Foote's appearance must have come as a shock to an audience well acquainted with his former girth and his comic, leering eyes. On 6 June, a performance of *The Devil Upon Two Sticks* had to be halted because Foote fell into a fit of convulsions on stage. Three days later, the convulsions returned and Foote fainted. Fearful for his life, he advised Colman to apply for a special license from the Lord Chamberlain. If Foote died midseason, the patent would expire with him, leaving the theater with no legal basis for operation.

As if to prove to the world that he had not leased his patent out of shame over his attempted sodomy trial, Foote stubbornly continued to appear on stage despite his ill health and scattered hissing from the audience. He managed to act a few more times in late July, but when he collapsed during a rehearsal in early August, he finally accepted the advice of his doctors and stayed off the stage.

Foote traveled to Brighthelmstone to bathe in the curative waters there, returning to London sometime in September. He seems to have been suffering from a series of small strokes, and his doctors advised him to winter in the south of France, hoping that a warmer climate would be good for him. He was sociable up until the end, hosting his final dinner party at his villa in Fulham on 12 October, a week before he left for Dover to await passage across the Channel.[10]

Foote spent the night of 20 October in Dover at the Ship Inn, where he amused the company and servants with banter and bad puns. When the cook boasted of never having been out of England, Foote replied:

"Why, cookey, that's extraordinary, as they tell me upstairs that you have been several times *all over grease*."

"They may tell you what they please, above stairs, but I was never ten miles from Dover in my life," said the cook.

"Nay," replied Foote, "now that *must* be a fib, for I have myself seen you at *Spit-head*."[11]

This was Foote's last joke. In the morning of the following day, he took a chill and began to tremble so violently that he was put to bed, where he died at 2:00 p.m. In all likelihood, William Jackson was just over the water in Paris or Calais, devoutly praying for this very event. Since one cannot libel a dead man, he was now able to return to England in safety.

On the day of Foote's death, Elizabeth Chudleigh was far away in St. Petersburg. She had arrived there on her magnificent new yacht three months earlier and had been basking in the flattering attention of Catherine the Great and her courtiers. The rococo flamboyance of Catherine's court was very much to Elizabeth's taste, and she would have stayed in St. Petersburg longer had it not been for the entreaties of her lawyers, begging her to leave for Calais to attend to legal business. Her husband, the third Earl of Bristol, was appealing the jactitation ruling of 1769. After much delay, she was now forced to respond.

Elizabeth first learned of Hervey's intentions a year and a half earlier, with a knock on the kitchen door of her Calais home on the afternoon of 26 June 1776, two months after the bigamy trial. Three men came bearing the unwelcome news that Hervey was moving against her in the ecclesiastical court in London. Two French royal notaries accompanied the Sieur Lazare Claude Morlet as he attempted to deliver a letter from Hervey's lawyers explaining that he was appealing the ruling of 1769.

Morlet and the notaries were greeted by two liveried servants who informed them that "the Duchess," as they still called her, was indisposed. However, her valet would soon return, so they invited the three men into the house, where they waited in the dining room. When news of their arrival was passed on to Elizabeth via her chambermaid, she exclaimed, "I receive letters from nobody, and the letters coming from London give me so much uneasiness, that I am resolved to live in peace!"[12] When a servant returned to the dining room with this account of Elizabeth's refusal to accept the letter, Morlet assured him that it would be "interesting" to her. But the servant, no doubt fearing his mistress's famous temper, "gave a Thousand Reasons why he declined going back."

So the three men continued to wait in the dining room, hoping at least to serve the letter to Elizabeth's valet when he returned. According to Morlet, before long, "Another Servant appearing at the Window called out him who was with us and told him that my Lady Dutchess was very much surprised at our being suffered to come into her House." This was spoken "in a very harsh Manner," prompting Morlet and the notaries to slink off to the kitchen. Morlet appealed again to the servant who was with them, but he refused to listen, so Morlet opened the letter, spread it out in the middle of the kitchen table, and commanded the servant to deliver it to Elizabeth. As Morlet and the notaries stepped out of the kitchen door, they "perceived at the Window of an upper Apartment my Lady the Countess of Bristol calling herself Dutchess of Kingston dressed all in black." Aware that she had been spotted, Elizabeth stepped away from the window before Morlet could say a word.

For all of the farcical elements of this scene, Elizabeth's situation was, in fact, a dangerous one. Hervey was appealing the jactitation ruling as a first step to obtaining a parliamentary divorce. To make matters worse, the Meadowses were renewing their Chancery suit to have the Duke of Kingston's will invalidated. The legal furies, it seemed, were not quite through with Elizabeth yet.

Reversing the jactitation ruling would clear the way for Hervey to obtain a legal separation from Elizabeth, a necessary prelude to a divorce. (Normally a prosecution against a lover for "criminal conversation" was also required, but since the Duke of Kingston was dead, this was unnecessary.) However, the ecclesiastical court could not grant the separation until it formally reversed the jactitation ruling for, despite what the House of Lords had just decided, in the eyes of the ecclesiastical court, Hervey and Elizabeth were not married to each other. In other words, Hervey first had to prove the marriage in order to dissolve it.

In order to do so, he had the difficult task of persuading the ecclesiastical court that Elizabeth was solely responsible for the fraudulent jactitation ruling. As the bigamy trial showed, this was patently untrue. Hervey had suppressed the testimony of Ann Cradock, had directed her husband and others to deliver misleading testimony, and had supplied bad information himself so that Elizabeth could deny his claims under oath. The court was not going to make it easy for him.

The ecclesiastical court was suffering as greatly from Elizabeth's bigamy trial as she was. She acknowledged as much in a letter to a friend immediately after her flight to Calais. The lords, she said with some self-serving exaggeration, "have disgraced the Ecclesiastical Court whose dogmas have been inviolable for 1475 years."[13] The institutional damage done to the court was immeasurable, and Elizabeth's trial is one of the key moments in the court's decline (it was ultimately abolished in the 1850s). From her exile in Calais, she escaped the wrath of the court, but her husband was not so fortunate.

When Hervey first appeared before the court on 7 June, the judge, John Bettesworth, was not welcoming. He had presided over the jactitation suit, and consequently had been made to look like a venal fool before thousands in Westminster Hall when his ruling was shredded to bits by Attorney General Thurloe and the other prosecution lawyers. As a result, Bettesworth was in no mood to let Hervey cavalierly undo the ruling the court had delivered as a result of his manipulation. He implied that Hervey might be deceiving the court again and refused to let the case be reopened until Elizabeth was apprised of his intentions, hence the visit of Morlet and the notaries to Calais three weeks later.

Hervey appeared before Bettesworth again on 3 July, presenting the letter that Morlet had tried to deliver, along with his account of Morlet's reception by Elizabeth. Still, Bettesworth was reluctant to reopen the case. According to an account of the proceedings, he first "threw out some expressions that were rather severe," pointing out that Hervey "had not used the Court well, and must expect no favour from it."[14] Hervey's counsel feebly insisted that he took no part in the deception of the court, but Bettesworth was unwilling to accept this, insisting that "it was plain now that somebody had colluded" in obtaining the jactitation verdict and that allowing the case to proceed without Elizabeth's presence would be "like beating the air."

What really bothered Bettesworth was that he felt personally implicated in the collusion. He hotly denied having anything to do with the fraud perpetrated in the 1769 ruling, saying that "a whole profession, were most unjustly involved in the charge of collusion." He said that he was glad of having an occasion to say publicly that the court's decision was an upright and defensible one—the only one that could be delivered given the evidence presented. But as an interested party to the suit, Hervey was within his rights to appeal, so after this bit of self-justification, Bettesworth granted the request.

Bettesworth's ruling was yet another defeat for Elizabeth, and Hervey obtained it despite William Jackson's menacing paragraphs in the *Public Ledger*. On 15 June, for example, Jackson wrote: "Lord Bristol has been a little premature in moving to have the sentence in [Doctors'] Commons annulled. If that should happen, his Lordship may find that he will be premature in praying a divorce by the Lords." Hervey could only have a divorce after first obtaining a legal separation from the ecclesiastical court based on Elizabeth's adultery. Jackson warns that Elizabeth could deny him a separation "by recriminating the charge" of adultery against him, which would kill the separation suit. In cases where both spouses could prove adultery, the court denied them a separation, forcing them to remain married. This being the case, Jackson snarled, "Lord Bristol . . . had better sit down unhappy and contented."

But these threats proved fruitless. As Jackson himself reported in the *Public Ledger*, when Bettesworth granted Hervey's appeal he also ordered that a decree informing Elizabeth of the decision "be executed on one of the pillars of the Royal Exchange, after the manner of citing Peers and Peeresses resident out of the kingdom."[15] In yet another case of poor judgment, Elizabeth had exposed herself to further public humiliation. By not receiving the letter privately in Calais, she caused it to be publicly displayed in the heart of London. Posting such notices on the pillars of the Royal Exchange, a popular shopping arcade near the Bank of England, was not unusual; Dickens refers to the practice in *A Tale of Two Cities*. But in the wake of Elizabeth's conviction and flight from England, one can only imagine the crowds of shoppers, bankers, and passersby that gathered to read this particular notice with relish.

And as Elizabeth well knew, even worse publicity was possibly in store. Because Hervey's divorce suit would have to be based on her adultery, she feared that now he would finally expose her sexual secrets to the world. Her mind inevitably went back to the summer of 1768 when Caesar Hawkins came to her with a bundle of depositions that Hervey had collected to prove her multiple infidelities. At the Duke of Kingston's insistence, she had foolishly returned them. Hervey was certainly too smart to have destroyed them.

But Elizabeth had more to fear than just the revelation of old love affairs. On 6 November 1776, Philip and Frances Meadows filed an amended bill of complaint in Chancery. In it, they asserted that the bigamy conviction in Westminster Hall was based on proof that Elizabeth and Hervey had conspired to defraud the Duke of Kingston by obtaining the jactitation ruling and luring him into a bigamous marriage. If Hervey succeeded in reversing the jactitation ruling, Elizabeth would be all the more exposed to the Meadowses' suit in Chancery.

In this delicate situation, Elizabeth's best option was to delay the progress of both lawsuits. When Dr. Bettesworth ruled on 24 January 1777 that Elizabeth's counsel had to appear in court to respond to Bristol's suit, she responded by filing an "inhibition" that would reverse Bettesworth's decision.[16] Elizabeth's counsel also presented a list of tough questions for Hervey's witnesses, especially Ann Cradock. The intent of these questions was clearly to show that Hervey and these witnesses had colluded with Elizabeth to obtain the earlier decision. But the court seems to have decided that the best way out of this mess was to side with Hervey, let the case move forward, and formally reverse the embarrassing ruling. Ignoring Elizabeth's "inhibition," on 5 May Bettesworth allowed Hervey to file his formal allegation against Elizabeth.[17]

Two days later, Elizabeth wrote to the Court of Chancery, begging for more time to prepare her reply to the Meadowses' amended bill of complaint.[18] Unlike Hervey, the Meadows family seems to have been in no rush, believing that their case would only be strengthened if they waited until the ecclesiastical court reversed the jactitation ruling.[19]

And wait they did. Elizabeth and her lawyers succeeded in deferring a judgment in the ecclesiastical court for nearly a year.

Throughout the intervening months, she carried on a secret negotiation with Hervey over the divorce he was hoping to obtain. On 7 August 1777, the day she left Calais for St. Petersburg, Elizabeth wrote to her old friend Lord Barrington from her yacht, asking that he serve as an intermediary between her and Hervey. Revealing the depth of her distrust for Hervey, she writes: "Lord Bristol I understand would offer terms of Accomodation, but you and all mankind can tell how little he is to be trusted, and when he desires to converse with my friends on that subject, it is with a design only to defame me for he has ever with a double Tongue stung me to the Heart."[20] However, she had no choice but to deal with Hervey, so she tells Barrington: "I must trespass once more on your Lordship to solicit you in case it should become necessary to receive Lord Bristol's proposals, but always to excuse yourself from coming to a conclusion until I return which will be as soon as possible." If Hervey chooses to pursue his appeal in the ecclesiastical court in her absence, she declares, "I never will accommodate with him" in the divorce.

Near the end of September, after having spent just a few weeks in St. Petersburg, Elizabeth realized that she had to be closer to England in order to negotiate with Hervey and deal with her lawsuits. On 19 September, she wrote to Barrington telling him that she would be leaving for Calais shortly and adding, the Baltic Sea "has not treated me so Unkindly as have the Cruel Lords my Countrymen, my relations, my Companions, and many that call themselves my friends."[21] However, two days later, even the Baltic Sea turned against her. A violent storm damaged her yacht so badly that she had to delay her departure until November, when the winter ice forced her to abandon a sea journey and race to Calais over land.

Meanwhile, Hervey was losing patience. On 22 October, the day after Foote's death, Hervey wrote to tell Barrington that immediately after Elizabeth's conviction for bigamy, he informed her that he would seek a divorce. At the time, he "received Assurances in return of her being willing to assist me in my Divorce as far as was honourable in every thing."[22] But now she was prevaricating and he was receiving anonymous letters in the mail, "many with threats & sometimes soothings," urging him to delay legal action against Elizabeth until she could reach an accommodation with Evelyn Meadows and put an end to the Chancery suit.

At the end of this letter, Hervey assures Barrington that he has no interest in humiliating Elizabeth by revealing her sexual secrets.

The only grounds for judicial separation and divorce will be her marriage to the duke. He does, however, make a subtle allusion to the depositions he collected in 1768: "I neither mean nor wish anything but a Divorce, obtained in the least offensive way to her, which is her Marriage with the Duke, tho' I have still wherewithal left for other Matters."

In the event, Elizabeth was unable to travel from St. Petersburg to Calais in time to stop Hervey's moving against her in the ecclesiastical court. On 20 February 1778, while she was in Brussels, Dr. Bettesworth reversed the jactitation ruling. At last, she and Hervey were married in the eyes of the court and a judicial separation was possible.[23]

Upon her return to Calais in March, she became even more distraught over the prospect of a divorce. In a letter to Barrington she told him of the depositions Hervey possessed: "I fear he has me now at a great disadvantage at his Solicitation and with the Dukes Consent I returned him all his Iniquitory papers that I could find, after the Jactitation Cause was determined, the Duke Imagining all that business at an end saw it was not Generous to detain those Papers he Solicited particularly as he Appeared so thoroughly to repent; his ill behaviour to me."[24]

In a startling attempt to prevent Hervey from using those depositions, Elizabeth asked Barrington to "Consult Lord Hillsborough privately if the Lords could not be moved, to reverse their Sentence. They have been Generous Enough to do it when they have found themselves wrong, and I could Cite many Instances to that Effect." And if the lords reversed her bigamy conviction, she added, then "it is highly probable that the Ecclesiastical Court, to whom I have Appealed, would follow the Judgment of the Lords and reject Lord B's Cause in their Courts, and he would be as much at liberty as by Divorce."

This was a truly desperate and unrealistic proposal, yet the extent of Elizabeth's delusion becomes clear only in the postscript to this letter. In an effort to persuade Barrington that the lords might be amenable to reconsidering her case, she reminds him that Lord Bathurst "said in his Court that my case was the Hardest that Ever Appeared before the Lords." That may be so, but Bathurst was also the man who engineered her public humiliation and sat in judgment over it—he was, therefore, the last person who had any interest in reversing her conviction.

A week later Elizabeth came to her senses and accepted the fact that her only options were either to cooperate in the divorce process or to suffer the shame of Hervey's publishing his depositions. She wrote to Barrington that she would cooperate in the divorce, grousing that if Hervey hoped to seize her inheritance from the duke, he was welcome to it since the riches had only brought her grief. But as Hervey had repeatedly assured her, he had no interest in her money. Nor had he any desire to expose her sexual affairs to the world. So long as she cooperated in the divorce, she was welcome to her secrets and her riches.

Throughout the months and years following her conviction in Westminster Hall, Elizabeth's correspondence reveals nothing so much as her lack of judgment and candor. In the days following the trial, she agreed to give Hervey a divorce, but then sought to frustrate the process every step of the way. After she finally agreed not to oppose the judicial separation, she continued to deceive her lawyers and family, insisting to them that she would never consent to a divorce. While she flattered the duke's heir, Charles Meadows, with attention and even helped him obtain a parliamentary seat from Nottinghamshire, she was also secretly courting his brother, Evelyn, who eventually joined her in exile. And when the opportunity presented itself, she betrayed both Charles and Evelyn by making secret overtures to Evelyn Pierrepont of New Haven, Connecticut, the American revolutionary soldier whose father had spent his life trying to prove his claim to the Kingston titles and estates. When Elizabeth met one of the American Evelyn's cousins on the Continent, she passed word on to New Haven that she would be receptive to his claims. But evidently he was not as hungry for a title and riches as his father had been and he never replied.[25]

The result of all Elizabeth's scheming was, inevitably, more trouble for herself. And yet she is the one person who escapes any blame in her letters; instead, they are laced with invective and elaborate ruses to avoid blame. In a typical passage she tells Barrington:

> My Enemys have treated me so Ill that I am Contented to remain in a Voluntary Banishment, and living by the Industry of my Own Hands would not be so painfull as what I have felt at that persecuting trial in the year 1776. As a Subject of England and a free born English woman. I have lived too long, that lived to see the Laws of my Country so Straind, if not perverted, by prejudice, Envy, & Interest. They bartered for my life, my fortune, & liberty. All that regards myself I could bear; but where is the liberty of the English Subject, when the Law is so perverted as to Indite me as a Commoner for Bigamy, try me as a Peeress, Convict me of a Collusion <u>for which I was not Indicted</u>—they might as well have tryd me for murder.[26]

In a real way, her conviction in the bigamy trial was far from the end of her legal troubles. And yet contrary to all good judgment, Elizabeth did everything in her power to aggravate the situation for years to come.

On 15 April 1778, two years to the day after the bigamy trial began, Hervey informed Lord Barrington that if he finds Elizabeth "still determin'd to give further trouble, as her Agents have hitherto done in the Course of two Years contrary to all her and their professions," he will "take every legal step in his power to distress the Lady." Specifically, he threatens to notify all her tenants, agents, and bankers that as her husband, he is laying claim to all of her income and assets, "as well as such other Actions in the Ecclesiastical Court, as he is informed he will be Authorised in doing, & which may go very great lengths."[27] These were his legal rights, and many other men would have exercised them long ago. But Hervey seems always to have been patient with Elizabeth to a fault. He never carried out his threats, and so the tortured negotiations over the divorce continued.

Finally, on 20 February 1779, Hervey began his divorce from Elizabeth by filing a suit in the ecclesiastical court for "Separation or Divorce from Bed Board and mutual Cohabitation by reason of adultery by her committed."[28] But it was the beginning of a divorce process he never lived to see finished. At the time of his death on 23 December 1779, he left behind him a noble estate, a beloved mistress, Mary Nesbitt, and a dry-eyed widow, Elizabeth Chudleigh, Dowager Countess of Bristol.

Now that Elizabeth was free from the threat of divorce all that remained was the Chancery suit, which had long since stalled, and a challenge in King's Bench to the validity of the duke's will. On the eve of the fourth anniversary of her bigamy trial, Elizabeth at last extricated herself from the Meadows family's lawsuits. On 14 April 1780, Lord Mansfield ruled that the duke's will was valid despite the illegality of his marriage to Elizabeth. Because the duke had personally written Elizabeth's name in the will, Mansfield reasoned that there could be no second-guessing his intentions.

On the first day of Elizabeth's bigamy trial, Evelyn Meadows menaced her with the promise that she "should have no rest while on the face of the Earth."[29] But after the King's Bench decision, he was reduced to begging from her. Surprisingly, she was magnanimous, quietly granting him an annual allowance of £400 beginning in December 1781 then later raising the amount to £600.[30] The reconciliation with Meadows came as an understandable surprise once it became public in the summer of 1787. As usual, Horace Walpole captured the general sentiment best when he observed, "Methinks this is robbing Peter to pay *Peter*."[31]

When Elizabeth died on the morning of 26 August 1788 at her home near Fontainebleau, Evelyn Meadows was there with her. After her death was pronounced, the still disgruntled and disinherited heir helped himself to whatever parts of the Kingston estate he could carry away with him, including most of Elizabeth's silverware and some jewelry.

William Jackson evidently still worked for Elizabeth at this point, but in what capacity she retained his services after Foote's acquittal is unclear. She is rumored to have rewarded him handsomely for his persecution of Foote, and he was receiving money from her as late as October 1779, and he is said to have traveled to France on her business in the late 1780s.[32] Jackson evidently lived off his earnings from Elizabeth until 1784, when William Pitt, the new prime minister, hired him to give his fledgling ministry favorable press treatment as the secret editor of the *Morning Post*. In that capacity, Jackson attacked his former political allies with his usual vigor. Once his apostasy became known, however, the entire venture was ridiculed and Jackson was sacked.[33]

In one of the odder chapters in Jackson's very odd life, his next venture was to build a new theater in the City of London. He was the secret partner of John Palmer, the actor who, eleven years earlier, had mimicked him as Dr. Viper in Foote's *The Capuchin*. Although one needed a royal patent or special license from the Lord Chamberlain to offer spoken-word plays in London, Jackson succeeded in deceiving Palmer and a host of investors into believing that he had found a way around the law. Evidently he was a persuasive man for Palmer and the others sunk £18,000 into the construction of the Royalty Theatre in Goodman's Fields, near the Tower of London. The theater opened with a charity performance of Shakespeare's *As You Like It* on 21 June 1787. It was the first and last spoken-word play performed there. The government promised to arrest Palmer and his entire company if they dared to offer another play.[34] Soon after, Jackson wisely decamped for France, where he evidently joined Elizabeth and served as a foreign correspondent to the *Oracle*, a London newspaper.

After Elizabeth's death, Jackson joined in the unseemly melee over her will and estate, vying with several others for a share of her riches. He was supposed to be among the three people who filed a "caveat" in the ecclesiastical court to stop the probate of her will so that would-be beneficiaries could assert their claims. However, his characteristic pugnacity was too much for his lawyer. In a letter to one of Elizabeth's lawyers, a correspondent tells him that the third caveat "was entered by Parson Jackson—and has since been struck out by his own Proctor, on some Offence given him by his Client."[35]

Throughout his life, Jackson seems to have had the reverse of the Midas touch: everything he put his hands to came to ruin. His greatest folly was his last. After Elizabeth's death, he remained in Paris through-out the early revolutionary period and he became involved with a group of Irish expatriates working with the Jacobins.[36] In the spring of 1794, he accepted a fool's errand and was sent on a spy mission to England and Ireland to ascertain whether the common people would support a French invasion of either country. Jackson, an indiscreet drunk, was not cut out for spying. Once across the Channel, he imprudently revealed his secret mission to his friend and lawyer, John Cockayne. Cockayne immediately took the news to the prime minister. Pitt hired him as a government spy, and in that capacity Cockayne accompanied Jackson to Dublin.

Meanwhile, Pitt's secret service was intercepting Jackson's reports back to Paris, which he was sending through the open mails. The government waited to pounce until Jackson had met several of the leaders of the United Irishmen, a reform society that advocated eman-cipation from English rule. Although most of the United Irishmen were highly suspicious of the heavy-drinking Jackson and his oddly quiet companion, a few key figures embraced the idea of French assis-tance. When the government finally raided Jackson's Dublin lodging in April 1794, they found all kinds of incriminating papers lying out in the open. Those documents, along with Cockayne's testimony and the intercepted mail, were more than enough to convict Jackson of high treason.

Archibald Hamilton Rowan, the leader of the United Irishmen, fled to France. Theobald Wolfe Tone, chief spokesman for the group, accepted a government deal to leave for exile in Philadelphia. But Pitt wanted Jackson's head, so Jackson languished in jail for a year before his trial was held in May 1795. During that time, he wrote a spirited Christian reply to Thomas Paine's *Age of Reason* to help pay for his legal defense and he published a collection of his sermons. The latter was, however, published posthumously.

Jackson was convicted of high treason on 23 May 1795. On the day he was to be sentenced to death, he stood in the prisoner's dock, evidently unwell. As his lawyers argued that the case had to be thrown out because of a technical mistake on the indictment papers, Jackson's physical condition became a matter of great concern to the court. The windows were ordered to be opened to let in fresh air. Then a chair was provided. Then a doctor was called to examine him in the dock. Then Jackson dropped dead. An autopsy later revealed that he died from drinking a large quantity of arsenic, which his pregnant wife had smuggled into his jail cell in his tea that morning.[37]

EPILOGUE

I, Libertine

On an April day in 1956, an all-night disc jockey, Jean Shepherd, went in search of a book containing the old radio plays of Vic and Sade. At the Doubleday Book Shop on Fifth Avenue in Manhattan, Shepherd asked a clerk to help him locate the title, leading to a fruitless search that ended in an unpleasant exchange as the clerk produced one publisher's list after another to prove that the book Shepherd sought did not exist. If it did, he insisted, then it would be on one of his lists. Annoyed by the officious clerk who gloried in lists and the certainties they seemed to offer, Shepherd stepped back out onto Fifth Avenue, vowing to shake the clerk's faith in his lists. He began to conceive of one of the greatest literary hoaxes of all time—one he would pull off with the help of Elizabeth Chudleigh.

At twenty-nine, Shepherd was already a celebrated cultural critic.[1] The self-appointed leader of the "Night People," as he called his listeners, he hosted a show on WOR in New York City from 1:30 until 5:00 a.m., during which he played jazz records occasionally and spoke almost continuously about the cultural and intellectual wasteland he saw all around him in Eisenhower's America.[2] Among his fans were J. D. Salinger, Steve Allen, and James Thurber. In 1955 *Metronome* named Shepherd "Jazz Artist of the Year," noting that "his instruments are his words."[3]

For Shepherd, the exchange in the bookstore was a classic confrontation between a Day Person and a Night Person. He summed up the differences between the two types this way:

> Night people are aware of the real world. They wonder vaguely or specifically where it's going. People who live in the day are interested in things; people who live at night deal with ideas . . . Day people love red

tape, switchboards, best-seller lists, offices, the routine of a busy, active life. Night people aren't eggheads, but they wouldn't mind spending a year in Maine doing nothing.[4]

This was a theme he expounded on regularly as he spoke to the Night People, and on that April evening, he had a new example for them. And a mission.

After relating his encounter in the bookstore, Shepherd challenged his listeners to send him fictitious book titles and author names. Once he had settled on the winners, he would then send the Night People out to the daytime world to ask for the book, and they would all enjoy the resulting confusion as bookstore clerks searched their publisher's lists and made frantic phone calls in an effort to find the book and fill the orders. "What better way to restore the status quo," Shepherd asked, "than to shake the Day People's faith in their organization? And what better place to start than with the bookshop clerks whose lists make them the most organized of all?"[5]

The Night People responded with scores of titles and author names, and Shepherd finally settled on Frederick R. Ewing as the fictitious author. An Oxford graduate, Ewing was best known for his prewar BBC radio series on "Erotica of the Eighteenth Century." He served on several minesweepers in the North Atlantic during World War II and was said to be currently filling a civil service post in Rhodesia, where he finished his first novel, *I, Libertine*. The book, first volume of a projected trilogy, is the "turbulent, turgid, tempestuous" story of an eighteenth-century adventurer named Captain Lance Courtenay, secret son of the notorious Elizabeth Chudleigh, Duchess of Kingston.[6]

Armed with an author and title, the Night People began to demand the book from libraries and bookstores. The Doubleday Book Shop got twenty-seven requests for the book in a single morning. A pilot for Pan American Airlines encouraged colleagues to request the book in Chicago, San Francisco, Miami, Paris, and Finland. The book somehow made its way onto the "to-be-published" list in the Sunday *New York Times*, onto the League of Decency's list of books banned in Boston, and into the card catalog of the Philadelphia Public Library. And according to an article in *The Village Voice*, people at Manhattan cocktail parties were claiming to have read it.[7]

The success of the hoax took even Shepherd by surprise. "My God!" he said, "Maybe there was no Chaucer! It could've been some guy 400 years ago, putting on the whole world!"[8]

Eventually, the hoax was reported in the *New York Times*, the *Wall Street Journal*, *Life* magazine, the *Times* of London, and *Publisher's*

Weekly. It also attracted the attention of Ian Ballantine, head of Ballantine Books and a fan of Shepherd's show. Aware that there was no such book, but impressed by the demand the Night People were creating, Ballantine approached Shepherd with a proposal: fill the demand with an actual book written by the science-fiction writer Theodore Sturgeon, a Ballantine author. It would be published under the pseudonym Frederick R. Ewing.

Shepherd agreed, upholding his end of the deal by providing Sturgeon with Elizabeth Chudleigh's story as the centerpiece of the novel. Shepherd had learned of Elizabeth's life and bigamy trial from T. H. White's *The Age of Scandal*, a popular history of the racier bits of eighteenth-century English life published in 1950. Sturgeon did the rest, spinning a picaresque yarn of the fortunes and misfortunes of Lance Courtenay, a professed libertine whose life becomes hopelessly mixed up with Elizabeth's marital affairs.

Elizabeth's story appealed to Shepherd for a couple of reasons. It seemed appropriate that the subject of his fraudulent book should be the story of a famously fraudulent marriage. The trickster in Elizabeth appealed to the trickster in Shepherd, who had a penchant for hoaxes. (One night he hosted "Operation Down-Fall," a parody of charity telethons in which he solicited money for one lucky listener to spend in a life of "feckless dissipation.") Elizabeth's story also attracted him because it confirmed his belief that the good old days were just as corrupt and venal as the present day.

In Sturgeon's retelling, Elizabeth is a femme fatale with an evil genius for manipulating the men in her life. For instance, instead of personally overseeing the fabrication of the Lainston marriage register in 1759, as she did in real life, Sturgeon has her hire a lawyer to do the work for her. In return, he demands that she have sex with him in a stable, which she does. But she denies him pleasure by being completely unresponsive during intercourse. Afterward, the enraged lawyer tries to strike her, but she avoids his blow, horsewhips him, and leaves him moaning in the stable. He vows to revenge this humiliation by riding to London and making her marriage to Hervey public. However, by the time he arrives, he learns that she has preceded him to town and has foiled his plans by preemptively circulating the rumors herself.

Whereas in real life the son Elizabeth conceived with Hervey died months after birth; in *I, Libertine*, the boy, Lance, lives and grows up in the household of a lowly hostler, totally unaware of his true parents. Eventually, Lance becomes a member of the demi monde and takes for his lover a young confidante of Elizabeth. In return for sex, the young woman makes Lance promise to help Elizabeth to marry the duke, which he does, first by advising her to initiate a jactitation of marriage suit against Augustus Hervey, then by having Evelyn Meadows (a homosexual eccentric in love with Lance) shipped off to Boston to serve as the colony's tax collector.

Eventually, however, Elizabeth is tried for bigamy by the House of Lords. But in the novel, she remains in control of the entire process and emerges with her title and riches intact. As she says to Lance afterward, "You can push Parliament to do a thing, you see, but you can't stop them from doing it in their way."[9] The lords were forced to try her, but they did so in the privacy of their parliamentary chamber, away from the prying eyes of the common people. "Under no circumstances," she explains, "were they going to make a House performance of this matter, partly on my behalf, bless them all, and partly because they really like Augie." During the trial, she cuts a deal with the lords: they will let her remain Duchess of Kingston so long as she leaves England. At the end of the sham trial, the Earl of Bath, her old flame, takes a hot brand and flourishes it at her; but instead of branding her on the hand (the actual punishment for bigamy), he sinks it into a pint of ale and then asks her to drink it. She does that, kisses the lords all around, and leaves in triumph.

No doubt this is how the real Elizabeth had hoped the lords would deal with her case when she made the fateful step of removing it from the Court of King's Bench. The last thing she expected was a humiliating trial in Westminster Hall.

I, Libertine includes all the main events of Elizabeth's remarkable story, but it also takes great liberties, for which Shepherd and Sturgeon were unapologetic. In an afterword, they invite "historically minded sharpshooters to draw their beads on this narrative. . . . When they are done, let them proceed to Aesop and delete everything they find there about talking animals."[10] Nevertheless, given Shepherd's cynicism about the virtues of the good old days, it is disappointing that instead of indicting the lords for hypocrisy, the church courts for venality, and the broader society for its voyeuristic delight in the sex crimes of the better sort, *I, Libertine* boils Elizabeth's story down to the wild adventures of an eccentric vixen. The real story is much more damning.

I, Libertine is not alone in reducing the story of Elizabeth Chudleigh's secret life and trials down to a surprising tale of a quixotic eighteenth-century character. Willful, reckless, cunning, and excessive, Elizabeth is a powerfully attractive figure who has commanded the attention of every generation, and increasingly the biographies of her tend to be admiring. Charles Pearce's two-volume *The Amazing Duchess* (1911) praises Elizabeth's "indomitable courage" and "superabundant energy and spirits."[11] In *The Virgin Mistress* (1964), Elizabeth Mavor's sympathy for her subject leads her to regard Elizabeth's exploits as an inspiring study in survival. And most recently, Claire Gervat's *Elizabeth: The Scandalous Life of the Duchess of Kingston* (2003) downplays the importance of the bigamy trial in Elizabeth's long life, which Gervat sums up this way: "It had not always been a strictly virtuous life, but it had always been a full one."[12]

Although it is easy to see why biographers have been seduced by the life and persona of Elizabeth, there is a danger of focusing too narrowly on her. In doing so, her remarkable legal history becomes merely the effect of one woman's machinations. But in reality, her story was made possible—even encouraged—by a social and legal system that was thoroughly corrupt in regard to marriage law. Elizabeth did not pioneer the manipulations of the ecclesiastical court in order to get out of an unhappy marriage, nor was she the only bigamist in eighteenth-century England. She became notorious not for her legal chicanery, but for how clumsily she tried to do what so many of her peers had been doing all along: dissolving bad marriages in a divorce-less society.

If she had followed Hervey's lead and colluded in a divorce process in 1768, she might have ended up as just another footnote in a legal history book. But by listening to the bad advice of Arthur Collier, she chose a novel form of legal manipulation and ended up the subject of sensational biographies for more than two centuries after her death. It would be little comfort to her to know that those biographies have grown kinder with the passage of time. Sympathetic or not, her marital history is invariably presented as the work of one designing woman, not the product of a bad system.

The other danger in focusing too narrowly on Elizabeth is that the other key players have faded away from the story. Gervat's biography, for all its scrupulous research, takes scant notice of Samuel Foote, fails to connect her to his attempted sodomy trial, and never once mentions the Reverend William Jackson.

The dispute with Foote was one of the defining moments of Elizabeth's life, and as she recognized at the time, it had an enormous impact on her legal affairs. She moved the trial to the House of Lords largely in response to the bad publicity she and Jackson brought upon her by their furious assaults on Foote. Elizabeth hoped that the lords would close rank around her and spare her a trial altogether. But that move merely gave the Earl of Bathurst an opportunity to betray her and engineer the state trial in Westminster Hall. To tell Elizabeth's story without full attention to the roles played by Foote and Jackson is to tell only half the story.

This is not merely a story about one woman's bigamy. Elizabeth's trial is directly related to Foote's trial for attempted sodomy, which she encouraged with her money and Jackson's pen. And that, in turn, led to the libel case against the *Public Ledger*. The roles that Foote, Jackson, and Elizabeth played in this legal drama reflected glory on none of them, but their actions are mitigated when we remember that they were caught up in legal and social systems that were bad in many respects. The absence of divorce invited lawbreaking, but so did the criminalization of sodomy. Despite the manifest harm that these laws did to people, Enlightenment England refused to be enlightened about some matters of sexuality.

Middle-class English men and women, did, however, want to learn all about the sexual misbehavior of the "better sort." And there were plenty of theaters, newspapers, and print shops to retail salacious stories to a greedy public. It is no coincidence that Richard Brinsley Sheridan's famous play *The School for Scandal* became a smash hit in 1777. Spreading scandal became a national pastime during the 1770s. Stella Tillyard attributes this phenomenon to the lapsing of the (print) Licensing Act, the weakness of the law of personal libel, and the proliferation of print in the third quarter of the eighteenth century, concluding, "So it was that a free press and a weak libel law created a climate of speculation and gossip far freer, more direct, personal, and scurrilous than we have today."[13] Foote initially came to London to study law, Jackson to preach, but they both left those callings for the more lucrative trade of scandal mongering. In *The Capuchin*, Foote renamed the *Public Ledger* as the *Scandalous Chronicle*. The play was performed in Foote's theater, sometimes called the "Scandal Shop in the Haymarket."

Although Foote's role has been diminished by Elizabeth's biographers, his posthumous reputation has been defined by his dispute with Elizabeth and the resulting trial for attempted sodomy. For nearly two hundred years, his biographers have recognized the importance of the events of 1775 and 1776, yet they have refused to name the crime he was accused of. Nor would they entertain the notion that he might have been a sodomite. Foote, they say, was the "English Aristophanes," a daring satirist who heroically exposed vice and folly to corrective ridicule on the public stage. According to this biographical tradition, the charge of attempted sodomy was merely a fiction cooked up by his most vicious satiric targets.

Recently, historians of homosexuality have taken the charges against Foote more seriously, but they have tended to err in the opposite direction, reinterpreting the case as an important episode in the historical oppression of homosexuals. For them, Foote is an eighteenth-century Oscar Wilde, a brilliant wit whose career was ended because of the exposure of his secret sexuality.[14]

Both sides have it wrong. Foote was not a daring satirist; rather, he was a surprisingly conservative comic playwright who took few risks and who enjoyed a downright chummy relationship with the key figures of the government, including the censor of the stage and the king. His reputation as being the most dangerous man in show business was mostly hype. Nor was he the Georgian equivalent of Oscar Wilde. The true nature of Foote's sexuality is a mystery, and will probably always remain one. But when we understand more about the source of Foote's prosecution, especially William Jackson's role, and Foote's vigorous—and successful—defense, his candidacy for gay martyrdom fails, or at least falters.

It is a great irony that Jackson has been largely erased from both Foote's and Elizabeth's biographies. Without his bad advice, Elizabeth might have been persuaded to reach a settlement with Evelyn Meadows and avoid a criminal trial. And without his encouragement, she might never have escalated the newspaper war with Foote, thereby avoiding the negative publicity that lost her crucial support in the House of Lords. Without Jackson's assistance (and Elizabeth's money), John Sangster might not have carried his case against Foote as far as he did. Certainly the details of the case would never have been made public were it not for Jackson's willingness to use the pages of the *Public Ledger* to settle the score between Foote and Elizabeth. History, for the most part, has forgotten all about the Reverend William Jackson, yet in many ways he is the central figure in this story.

Elizabeth, Foote, and Jackson are all eccentric characters, to be sure, but it would be a mistake to regard their story merely as a costume drama that does nothing so much as illustrate the alien pastness of the past. It is not at all surprising that the British government elevated Elizabeth's trial to a state occasion at the very moment when the colonial revolt in America became a full-blown war. The anxieties produced by external threats can often lead a nation to "put its own house in order." At a time when a wife's murder of her husband was known as "petty treason," it is understandable that Elizabeth's peers would see a moral equivalency between rebellious colonials and a bigamous duchess.

Elizabeth, whose life goal was to be a member of the aristocracy, was deeply offended by the representation of her as an enemy to the established order and to holy matrimony. The fact that these charges were coming from the pen of a mere actor was all the more aggravating. In order to realign herself with the angels, she and Jackson cleverly hit upon the idea of maligning Foote as a woman-hating sodomite. If you want to see a true enemy to God, marriage, and the church, they suggested, look no further than the sodomite Samuel Foote.

The very public nature of their dispute was entirely characteristic of a new media culture that exploited the private lives of public figures, sometimes for the purpose of voyeuristic titillation, sometimes for moral denunciation—and frequently for both at the same time. The mere fact that Elizabeth felt the need to hire Jackson to provide her with good press is proof that one could not ignore the power of the newspapers. Foote, it must be remembered, controlled a major media outlet, and it was his threat to ridicule Elizabeth's legal troubles on the stage of the Little Haymarket that started the feud that eventually consumed them both. In a sense, Jackson's shocking attacks against Foote were different in degree, but not in kind, from the sort of thing that Foote did on the stage.

Most of all, however, it was riches and fame that made Elizabeth and Foote vulnerable. The fact that divorce and sodomy were illegal in Georgian England is not solely to blame for their misfortunes: plenty of bigamists and sodomites went unpunished either because neighbors were unwilling to expose them or because judges and juries were unwilling to subject them to the excessive rigors of the law. But such leniency was mainly the privilege of the anonymous. Celebrity was a double-edged sword, and Foote and Elizabeth suffered not for their crimes, but for their success and visibility. Apart from Elizabeth's loss of rank, neither of them suffered any legal penalty for the crimes they were accused of; nevertheless, both were forever changed for the worse by their very public legal troubles. (Lacking riches and fame, Jackson survived them both and enjoyed the luxury of ruining his life on his own terms.)

There may not be any heroes in this story, but there are victims enough to go around. With the legalization of divorce and the decriminalization of sodomy, this is now a story that cannot be repeated in quite the same way. But some of the destructive attitudes have survived despite the changing legal code, and the intrusive nature of the media has been magnified incalculably. In these important ways, our world is not altogether different from the one inhabited by Foote, Jackson, and Elizabeth.

Jean Shepherd was attracted to Elizabeth's story because it proved a point he enjoyed making about nostalgia for the good old days. "Thinking that the old days were the best days," he said, "is a terrible sickness. Everything was just as bad then as it is now—maybe worse."[15]

And he only knew the half of it.

Sources

I. Manuscripts

Barrington Papers, British Library.

Blandford, Anne, "Commonplace Book, 1791 and later," Beinecke Library, Yale University.

Chudleigh, Elizabeth, Correspondence, Beinecke Library, Yale University.

Court of Chancery Records, National Archives, Kew.

Court of King's Bench Records, National Archives, Kew.

Diocese of London Records, London Metropolitan Archives.

Doran, Dr., *Their Majesties Servants* (London: J. C. Nimmo, 1888). Extra-illustrated.

Foote, Samuel, *The Capuchin*, Larpent Collection, Henry E. Huntington Library, San Marino, CA.

Hardwicke Papers, British Library.

Macklin, Charles, "Memoranda and Anecdotes," The Folger Shakespeare Library, Washington, DC.

Manvers Collection, The University of Nottingham Library Special Collections.

Newcastle Papers, The University of Nottingham Library Special Collections.

Northcote, James, "Northcote's Life," British Library.

Pigott, Edward, Diary, Osborn Collection fc80, 1770–1783, Beinecke Library, Yale University.

Portland Papers, The University of Nottingham Library Special Collections.

Thoresby Park Papers, British Library.

"Trials of Peers," House of Lords Record Office, London.

Walpole, Horace, *Book of Materials*, Lewis Walpole Library, Yale University.

Wilkinson, John Wells, "The Life and Works of Samuel Foote. Part One. The Dineley-Goodere-Foote Family," Henry E. Huntington Library, San Marino, CA.

Whitefoord Papers, British Library.

II. Primary Printed Material

Anonymous, *Aristophanes, Being a Classic Collection of True Attic Wit, Containing the Jests, Gibes, Bon-Mots, Witticisms, and most Extraordinary Anecdotes of Samuel Foote, Esq.* (London, 1778).

———, *Atys: Or, a Letter to Momus* (London: C. Moran and Richardson & Urquhart, 1767).

————, *An Authentic Detail of Particulars Relative to the Late Duchess of Kingston. The Third Edition, With Considerable Additions* (London, 1790).

————, *Les Avantures Trop Amoureuses ou Elisabeth Chudleigh Ex-Duchesse Douairiere de Kingston* (A Londres aux Depens des Interessez, 1776).

————, *A Brief for Her Grace the Duchess of Kingston* (London, 1776).

————, *The Case of the Duchess of Kingston* (London, 1775).

————, *Ceremonial for the Trial of a Peer* (London, 1776).

————, *Characters, Containing an Impartial Review of the Public Conduct and Abilities of the Most Eminent Personages in the Parliament of Great Britain* (London, 1777).

————, *The Ciceroniad* (London, 1777).

————, *The Court of Adultery. A New Edition, with Additions* (London: M. Smith, 1778).

————, *The Devil: A Poetical Essay* (London: J. Dodsley, 1776).

————, *An Epistle from Mrs. B—y to his R—l H—ss the D— of C—d, or, Beauty Scourging Rank* (London: W. Batteson, 1772).

————, *The Intriguing Courtiers; or, The Modish Gallants . . . in which is introduced an Interlude called The Promised Marriage; or, the Disappointed Lady . . . Inscrib'd to Lord O**** (London, 1733).

————, *The Laws Respecting Women, as they Regard their Natural Rights, or their Connections and Conduct* (London, 1777).

————, *The Mock-Marriage: or, A Lady and no Lady* (London, 1733).

————, *Nocturnal Revels: Or, The History of King's-Place*, 2 vols. (London, 1779).

————, *Sketches from Nature, in High Preservation, by the Most Noble Masters*, 5th ed. (London, 1779).

————, *Sodomy Trials, Seven Documents*, ed. Trumbach, Randolph, (New York and London: Garland Publishing, Inc., 1986).

————, *The Trial of Elizabeth, Late Duchess of Kingston* (Dublin, 1776).

————, *The Trial of His R. H. the D. of C. July 5th, 1770, for Criminal Conversation with Lady Harriet G—r.* (London, 1770).

————, *True and Genuine Account of the Proceedings and Trial of the Duchess of Kingston* (London, 1776).

The Book of Common Prayer (Oxford, 1743).

Boswell, James, *Life of Johnson*, ed. George Birkbeck Hill and L. F. Powell, 6 vols. (Oxford: Oxford University Press, 1934).

————, *Boswell's London Journal, 1762–63*, ed. Frederick A. Pottle (New York: McGraw Hill, 1950).

————, *Private Papers of James Boswell*, ed. Geoffrey Scott and Frederick A. Pottle, 18 vols. (New York, 1928–1934).

Brown, John, *An Estimate of the Manners and Principles of the Times*, 2 vols. (London, 1757).

Burney, Frances, *The Early Journals and Letters of Fanny Burney*, vol. 1, *1768–1773*, ed. Lars E. Troide (Oxford, Clarendon Press, 1988).

Burr, Thomas Benge, *The History of Tunbridge-Wells* (London, 1766).

Carter, Elizabeth, *A Series of Letters between Mrs. Elizabeth Carter and Miss Catherine Talbot*, 4 vols. (London: F. C. and J. Rivington, 1809).

———, *Letters from Mrs. Elizabeth Carter to Mrs. Montagu*, 3 vols. (London, 1817).

Combe, William, *The Diaboliad* (London, 1777).

Cother, E., *Serious Proposal for Promoting Lawful and Honourable Marriage*, 2nd ed. (London, 1751).

Covent Garden Magazine; or, Amorous Repository: Calculated Solely for the Entertainment of the Polite World (1774).

D'Archenholz, M., *A Picture of England*, 2 vols. (London, 1789).

Delany, Mary, *Autobiography and Correspondence of Mrs. Delany*, ed. Chauncey Woolsey, 2 vols. (Boston: Roberts Bros., 1880).

Dryden, John, *The Works of John Dryden*, ed. Edward Niles Hooker and J. T. Swedenberg, Jr., 17 vols. (Berkeley: University of California Press, 1956–).

Etherege, Sir George, *The Plays of Sir George Etherege*, ed. Michael Cordner (Cambridge: Cambridge University Press, 1982).

Foote, Samuel, *A Trip to Calais* and *The Capuchin*, ed. George Colman (London, 1778).

Gally, Henry, *Some Considerations upon Clandestine Marriages* (London, 1750).

Garrick, David, *Letters of David Garrick*, ed. George M. Kahrl and David M. Little, 3 vols. (Cambridge, MA: Belknap Press of Harvard University Press, 1961).

———, *The Private Correspondence of David Garrick*, ed. James Boaden, 2 vols. (London: H. Colburn and R. Bentley, 1831–1832).

Gentleman's Magazine

Grosley, Pierre, *A Tour to London; or, New Observations on England and its Inhabitants,* trans. Thomas Nugent, 2 vols. (London, 1772).

Hervey, Augustus, *Augustus Hervey's Journal*, ed. David Erskine (London: William Kimber, 1953).

Hervey, John, Baron Hervey, *Lord Hervey and His Friends, 1726–38*, ed. Ilchester, Earl of (London: John Murray, 1950).

Jackson, William, *Asmodeus* (London, 1776).

———, *A Plain State of the Case of her Grace the Duchess of Kingston* (London, 1776).

———, *Sodom and Onan, A Satire* (London, 1776).

———, *The Whole of the Evidence upon the Duchess of Kingston's Trial* (London, 1776).

Kielmansegge, Count Frederick, *Diary of a Journey to England in the Years 1761–1762* (London: Longmans, Green, and Co., 1902).

Le Blanc, Jean-Bernard, *Letters on the English and French Nations* (London, 1747).

Leman, Sir Tanfield, Baronet *Matrimony Analysed* (London, 1755).

Lloyd's Evening Post

London Chronicle

Mandeville, Bernard, *Pretty Doings in a Protestant Nation* (London, 1734).

Montagu, Elizabeth, *The Letters of Mrs. Elizabeth Montagu, part the second*, 4 vols. (London, 1813).

Monthly Review

More, Hannah, *Letters of Hannah More*, ed. R. Brimley Johnson (London: John Lane and the Bodley Head Ltd., 1925).

Morning Chronicle

Murphy, Arthur, *Plays by Samuel Foote and Arthur Murphy*, ed. George Taylor (Cambridge: Cambridge University Press, 1984).

Onslow, Thomas, Baron Onslow, *The L—d's Protest against the Marriage Contract* (London, 1733).

Piozzi, Hester Lynch, *Autobiography, Letters, and Literary Remains of Mrs. Piozzi (Thrale)*, ed. A Hayward, 2 vols. (London: Longman, Green, Longman, and Roberts, 1861).

Pope, Alexander, "Epistle to Dr. Arbuthnot" (London, 1734).

Public Ledger

Sampson, William, *The Trial of the Rev. William Jackson at the Bar of the King's Bench in Ireland for High Treason* (Dublin, 1795).

Sandeman, Robert, *The Honour of Marriage Opposed to all Impurities: An Essay* (London, 1777).

Shakespeare, William, *The Complete Works of Shakespeare*, ed. David Bevington, 5th ed. (New York: Pearson Longman, 2004).

Stanhope, Philip Dormer, Earl of Chesterfield, *Letters Written by the Late Right Honourable Philip Dormer Stanhope, Earl of Chesterfield, to his Son*, 7th ed. (London, 1776).

St. James's Chronicle

Town and Country Magazine

Walpole, Horace, *The Correspondence of Horace Walpole*, 47 vols., ed. W. S. Lewis (New Haven, CT: Yale University Press, 1937–1983).

Westminster Magazine

Whitehead, Thomas, *Original Anecdotes of the Late Duke of Kingston* (Bath, 1792).

III. Secondary Sources (books)

Andrew, Donna T. and McGowen, Randall, *The Perreaus and Mrs. Rudd: Forgery and Betrayal in Eighteenth-Century* London (Berkeley: University of California Press, 2001).

Bailey, Joanne, *Unquiet Lives: Marriage and Marriage Breakdown in England, 1660–1800* (Cambridge: Cambridge University Press, 2003).

Barton, Margaret, *Tunbridge Wells* (London: Faber and Faber, 1937).

Battestin, Martin, *Henry Fielding, A Life* (London and New York: Routledge, 1989).

Baylen, Jospeh O. and Gossman, Norbert J., eds., *Biographical Dictionary of Modern British Radicals*, vol. 1, 1770–1830 (Sussex: Harvester Press, 1979).

Beattie, J. M., *Crime and the Courts in England, 1660–1800* (Princeton, NJ: Princeton University Press, 1986).

Burling, William J., *Summer Theatre in London, 1661–1820, and the Rise of the Haymarket Theatre* (Madison and Teaneck: Fairleigh Dickinson University Press, 2000).

Clark, Anna, *The Sexual Politics of the British Constitution* (Princeton, NJ: Princeton University Press, 2004).

Cockayne, George E., *The Complete Peerage*, 13 vols. (London: St. Catherine Press, 1929).

Cockburn, J. S. and Green, Thomas A., *Twelve Good Men and True: The Criminal Trial Jury in England, 1200–1800* (Princeton, NJ: Princeton University Press, 1988).

Coke, Lady Jane, *Letters from Lady Jane Coke to Her Friend Mrs. Eyre at Derby 1747–1758*, ed. Mrs. Ambrose Rathbone (London: S. Sonnenschein, 1899).

Coke, Lady Mary, *The Letters and Journals of Lady Mary Coke*, ed. James Archibald Home, 4 vols. (Edinburgh, 1889–1896; rpt. Bath, 1970).

Conolly, L. W., *The Censorship of English Drama 1737–1824* (San Marino, CA: Huntington Library Press, 1976).

Cooke, William, *Memoirs of Samuel Foote, Esq.*, 3 vols. (London: R. Phillips, 1805).

Elliott, Marianne, *Partners in Revolution: The United Irishmen and France* (New Haven, CT: Yale University Press, 1982).

Ewing, Frederick R. [pseud.], *I, Libertine* (New York: Ballantine Books, 1956).

Fitzgerald, Percival, *Samuel Foote: A Biography* (London: Chatto & Windus, 1910).

Forster, John, *Biographical Essays*, 3rd ed. (London: J. Murray, 1860).

Gerhold, Dorian, *Westminster Hall: Nine Hundred Years of History* (London: James & James, 1999).

Gervat, Claire, *Elizabeth: The Scandalous Life of the Duchess of Kingston* (London: Century, 2003).

Gillis, John R., *For Better, For Worse: British Marriages 1600 to the Present* (New York and Oxford: Oxford University Press, 1985).

Goldsmith, Netta Murray, *The Worst of Crimes: Homosexuality and the Law in Eighteenth-Century London* (Aldershot: Ashgate Publishing, 1998).

Hibbert, Christopher, *George III, A Personal History* (London: Viking, 1998).

Hicks, Carola, *Improper Pursuits: The Scandalous Life of Lady Di Beauclerk* (London: Macmillan, 2001).

Highfill, Philip, Kalman Burnim, and Edward Langhans, *Biographical Dictionary of Actors, Actresses, Musicians, Dancers, Managers, and Other Stage Personnel in London, 1660–1800*, 17 vols. (Carbondale and Edwardsville: Southern Illinois University Press, 1973–1993).

Holmes, M. R. J., *Augustus Hervey: A Naval Casanova* (Edinburgh: Pentland Press, 1996).

Ingram, Martin, *Church Courts, Sex and Marriage in England, 1570–1640* (Cambridge: Cambridge University Press, 1987).

Kinservik, Matthew J., *Disciplining Satire: The Censorship of Satiric Comedy on the Eighteenth-Century London Stage* (Lewisburg, PA: Bucknell University Press, 2002).

———, ed., *"The Production of a Female Pen": Anna Larpent's Account of the Duchess of Kingston's Bigamy Trial of 1776*, Miscellaneous Antiquities, no. 17 (New Haven, CT: The Lewis Walpole Library, Yale University, 2004).

Lewis, Judity Schneid, *In the Family Way: Childbearing in the British Aristocracy, 1760–1860* (New Brunswick, NJ: Rutgers University Press, 1986).

Mavor, Elizabeth, *The Virgin Mistress: A Study in Survival* (Garden City, NY: Doubleday & Co., 1964).

McFarlane, Cameron, *The Sodomite in Fiction and Satire, 1660–1750* (New York: Columbia University Press, 1997).

Melville, Lewis [pseud.], *Society at Tunbridge Wells in the Eighteenth Century— and after* (London: Eveleigh Nash, 1912).

———, *Trial of the Duchess of Kingston* (Edinburgh and London: William Hodge & Company, Ltd., 1927).

Mounsey, Christopher, *Christopher Smart, Clown of God* (Lewisburg, PA: Bucknell University Press, 2001).

Nicholson, Watson, *The Struggle for a Free Stage in London* (1906; New York: Benjamin Blom, 1966).

Nigh, Douglas Julian, "Lesser Luminaries: Samuel Foote and the Little Theatre in the Haymarket, from 1766 through 1777" (PhD. diss., UCLA, 1971).

Norton, Rictor, *Mother Clap's Molly House: The Gay Subculture in England, 1700–1830* (London: Gay Men's Press, 1992).

Oldham, James, *The Mansfield Manuscripts and the Growth of English Law in the Eighteenth Century*, 2 vols. (Chapel Hill: University of North Carolina Press, 1992).

———, *English Common Law in the Age of Mansfield* (Chapel Hill and London: University of North Carolina Press, 2004).

Outhwaite, R. B., *Clandestine Marriage in England, 1500–1850* (London: Hambledon Press, 1995).

Peake, Richard Brinsley, *Memoirs of the Colman Family*, 2 vols. (London: R. Bentley, 1841).

Pearce, Charles E., *The Amazing Duchess*, 2 vols., 2nd ed. (London: Stanley Paul & Co., 1911).

Porter, Roy, *English Society in the Eighteenth Century* (London: Allen Lane, 1982).

Ribeiro, Aileen, *The Dress Worn at Masquerades in England, 1730–1790, and its Relation to Fancy Dress Portraiture* (New York: Garland, 1994).

Richardson, Samuel, *The Correspondence of Samuel Richardson*, ed Anna Laetitia Barbauld, 6 vols. (London: Richard Phillips, 1804).

Roberts, Richard Arthur, ed., *Calendar of Home Office Papers of the Reign of George III, 1773–1775* (London: Public Record Office, 1881).

Stone, George Winchester, ed., *The London Stage 1660–1800, Part 4: 1747–1776*, 4 vols. (Carbondale and Edwardsville: Southern Illinois University Press, 1962).

Stone, Lawrence, *Broken Lives: Separation and Divorce in England, 1660–1857* (Oxford: Oxford University Press, 1993).

———, *Road to Divorce: England 1530–1987* (Oxford: Oxford University Press, 1993).

———, *Uncertain Unions: Marriage in England 1660–1753* (Oxford: Oxford University Press, 1992).

Straub, Kristina, *Sexual Suspects: Eighteenth-Century Players and Sexual Ideology* (Princeton, NJ: Princeton University Press, 1992).

Stuart, Dorothy Margaret, *Dearest Bess: The Life and Times of Lady Elizabeth Foster* (London: Methuen, 1955).

———, *Molly Lepell, Lady Hervey* (London: George G. Harrap & Co., 1936).

Survey of London, vol. 45, *Knightsbridge*, ed. John Greenacomb (London: Althone Press, 2000).

Tasch, Peter A., *The Dramatic Cobbler: The Life and Works of Isaac Bickerstaffe* (Lewisburg, PA: Bucknell University Press, 1971).

Taylor, John, *Records of My Life* (New York: J. & J. Harper, 1833).

Trefman, Simon, *Sam. Foote, Comedian* (New York: Columbia University Press, 1971).

Trowbridge, William R. H., *Seven Splendid Sinners* (New York: Brentano's, 1924).

Trumbach, Randolph, *Sex and the Gender Revolution*, vol. 1, *Heterosexuality and the Third Gender in Enlightenment London* (Chicago: University of Chicago Press, 1998).

Turner, David, *Fashioning Adultery: Gender, Sex and Civility in England 1660–1740* (Cambridge: Cambridge University Press, 2002).

Valentine, Alan, *The British Establishment, 1760–1784* (Norman: University of Oklahoma Press, 1970).

Vickery, Amanda, *The Gentleman's Daughter: Women's Lives in Georgian England* (New Haven and London: Yale University Press, 1998).

Vincent, Arthur, ed., *Lives of Twelve Bad Women* (Boston: L. C. Page and Co., 1897).

Walters, John, *The Royal Griffin: Frederick, Prince of Wales, 1707–1751* (London: Jarrolds Publishers, 1972).

Werkmeister, Lucyle, *The London Daily Press, 1772–1792* (Lincoln: University of Nebraska Press, 1963).

White, T. H., *The Age of Scandal: An Excursion through a Minor Period* (London: Jonathan Cape, 1950).

Woodhouse, Diana, *The Office of the Lord Chancellor* (Oxford and Portland: Hart Publishing, 2001).

Wroth, Warwick, *The London Pleasure Gardens of the Eighteenth Century* (New York: Macmillan, 1896).

Young, Sir George, *Poor Fred: The People's Prince* (Oxford: Oxford University Press, 1937).

IV. Secondary Sources (articles)

Andrew, Donna T., "'Adultery-à-la-Mode': Privilege, the Law and Attitudes to Adultery (1770–1809)," *History* 82 (1997): 5–23.

Bataille, Robert A., "Hugh Kelly, William Jackson, and the Editorship of the *Public Ledger*," *Publication of the Bibliographical Society of America* 79 (1985): 523–527.

Blake, James Kingsley, "The Lost Dukedom, or the Story of the Pierrepont Claim," *Papers of the New Haven Colony Historical Society* 7 (1908): 258–287.

Boulton, Jeremy, "Itching after Private Marryings? Marriage Customs in Seventeenth-Century London," *The London Journal* 16 (1991): 15–34.

Brabner, Joyce, "I, Libertine: Making the List," WBUR Online Arts (1 June, 2002) http://publicbroadcasting,net/wbur/arts.

Clavin, Jim, "A Salute to Jean Shepherd," http://www.flicklives.com.

Dean, Frank, "He Talks by Night," *Scene* (1962).

Henderson, Carter, "Night People's Hoax on Day People Makes Hit with Book Folks," *Wall Street Journal*, 1 August 1956.

Kinservik, Matthew J., "Satire, Censorship, and Sodomy in Samuel Foote's *The Capuchin* (1776)," *Review of English Studies* 54 (2003): 639–660.

Morris, Marilyn, "The Royal Family and Family Values in Late Eighteenth-Century England," *Journal of Family History* 21 (1996): 519–532.

Rogers, Nicholas, "Pigott's Private Eye: Radicalism and Sexual Scandal in Eighteenth-Century England," *Journal of the Canadian Historical Association* 4 (1993): 247–263.

Senelick, Laurence, "Mollies or Men of Mode? Sodomy and the Eighteenth-Century London Stage," *Journal of the History of Sexuality* 1 (1990): 33–67.

Shearer, Harry, ed., "I, Libertine: *Satyr* meets Jean Shepherd," *Satyr* (1963).

Tillyard, Stella, "Celebrity in Eighteenth-Century London," *History Today* 55 (2005): 20–27.

Trumbach, Randolph, "London's Sodomites: Homosexual Behavior and Western Culture in the Eighteenth Century," *Journal of Social History* 11 (1977).

———, "Sodomitical Subcultures: Sodomitical Roles, and the Gender Revolution of the Eighteenth Century: The Recent Historiography," in R. P. MacCubbin, ed., *'Tis Nature's Fault: Unauthorized Sexuality during the Enlightenment* (Cambridge: Cambridge University Press, 1985).

Turner, David M., "Popular Marriage and the Law: Tales of Bigamy at the Eighteenth-Century Old Bailey," *London Journal* 30 (2005), 6–21.

Wagner, Peter, "The Pornographer in the Courtroom: Trial Reports about Cases of Sexual Crimes and Delinquencies as a Genre of Eighteenth-Century Erotica," in *Sexuality in Eighteenth-Century Britain*, ed. Paul-Gabriel Boucé (Manchester: Manchester University Press, 1982), 120–140.

Werkmeister, Lucyle, "Notes for a Revised Life of William Jackson," *Notes and Queries* n.s. 8 (1961): 43–47.

Wilcock, John, "The Village Square," in *The Village Voice Reader* (New York: Doubleday, 1962), 77–80.

NOTES

INTRODUCTION

1. *Westminster Magazine,* January 1776, 53–54.
2. Claire Gervat, *Elizabeth: The Scandalous Life of the Duchess of Kingston* (London: Century, 2003), 145.
3. *"The Production of a Female Pen": Anna Larpent's Account of the Duchess of Kingston's Bigamy Trial of 1776,* ed. Matthew J. Kinservik, Miscellaneous Antiquities, no. 17 (New Haven, CT: The Lewis Walpole Library, Yale University 2004), 83. Subsequent citations will be given in the text.
4. Reproduced in Anne Blandford's commonplace book, Osborn Collection, c341, Beinecke Library, Yale University, 1791, 151ff.
5. Edward Pigott, Diary, Osborn Collection fc80, 1770–1783, Beinecke Library, Yale University.
6. For a richly illustrated history of Westminster Hall, showing both its everyday appearance in the eighteenth century and its ornamentation for state trials, see Dorian Gerhold, *Westminster Hall: Nine Hundred Years of History* (London: James & James Ltd., 1999), esp. 45–60.
7. *Morning Chronicle,* 19 April 1776.
8. *St. James's Chronicle,* 16–18 April 1776.
9. Pigott, Diary, no. 349.
10. *St. James's Chronicle,* 16–18 April 1776.
11. James Boswell, *Private Papers of James Boswell,* ed. Geoffrey Scott and Frederick A. Pottle, 18 vols. (New York, 1928–1934), 11: 252–253.
12. *An Authentic Detail of Particulars Relative to the Late Duchess of Kingston. The Third Edition, With Considerable Additions* (London, 1790), 87.
13. Hannah More, *Letters of Hannah More,* ed. R. Brimley Johnson (London: John Lane and the Bodley Head Ltd., 1925), 43.
14. Quoted in *St. James's Chronicle,* April 16–18, 1776.
15. Alan Valentine, *The British Establishment, 1760–1784* (Norman: University of Oklahoma Press, 1970), 1: 177.
16. *The Court of Adultery. A New Edition, with Additions* (London: M. Smith, 1778), 8–9.
17. *Universal Magazine,* 1777, 124–126, quoted in Donna T. Andrew, "'Adultery à la Mode': Privilege, the Law and Attitudes to Adultery 1770–1809," *History* 82 (1997): 5.

18. Nicholas Rogers, "Pigott's Private Eye: Radicalism and Sexual Scandal in Eighteenth-Century England," *Journal of the Canadian Historical Association* 4 (1993): 252.

19. Anna Clark, *The Sexual Politics of the British Constitution* (Princeton, NJ: Princeton University Press, 2004), 15–16.

20. *Covent Garden Magazine; or, Amorous Repository: Calculated Solely for the Entertainment of the Polite World,* March 1774, 90.

CHAPTER 1

1. Philip Dormer Stanhope, Earl of Chesterfield, *Letters Written by the Late Right Honourable Philip Dormer Stanhope, Earl of Chesterfield, to his Son,* 7th ed. (London, 1776), 1: 164.

2. Mary Delany, *Autobiography and Correspondence of Mrs. Delany,* ed. Chauncey Woolsey, 2 vols. (Boston: Roberts Bros., 1880), 1: 554.

3. Quoted in Claire Gervat, *Elizabeth: The Scandalous Life of the Duchess of Kingston* (London: Century, 2003), 44.

4. Ibid., 132.

5. Ibid., 126.

6. In a letter to the Duke of Portland, she writes, "Monday the Lords are Suummond on the Dutchess's business. Tryall or not Tryall." Nottingham, PwF 2809, 18 November 1775.

7. Nottingham, PwF 2810, 14 December 1775.

8. For this anecdote and for an overview of Mansfield's character and professional reputation, see James Oldham, *English Common Law in the Age of Mansfield* (Chapel Hill and London: University of North Carolina Press, 1992), chap. 1.

9. *Characters, Containing an Impartial Review of the Public Conduct and Abilities of the Most Eminent Personages in the Parliament of Great Britain* (London, 1777), 4.

10. *St. James's Chronicle,* 18–21 November 1775.

11. *An Authentic Detail of Particulars Relative to the Late Duchess of Kingston. The Third Edition, With Considerable Additions* (London, 1790), 77.

12. *St. James's Chronicle,* 18–21 November 1775.

13. Ibid., 7–9 December 1775.

14. Lord Hailsham, *A Sparrow's Flight* (London: Collins, 1990), 397; quoted in Diana Woodhouse, *The Office of the Lord Chancellor* (Oxford and Portland: Hart Publishing, 2001), 5.

15. Nottingham, PwF 2813, 26 March 1776.

16. *St. James's Chronicle,* 12–14 December 1775.

17. Ibid., 12–14 December 1775.

18. Ibid., 14–16 December 1775.

19. Horace Walpole, *The Correspondence of Horace Walpole,* ed. W. S. Lewis, 47 vols., (New Haven: Yale University Press, 1937–1983), 17 December 1775, 24: 151.

20. *St. James's Chronicle*, 2–4 April 1776.

21. *Authentic Detail of Particulars*, 250–251.

22. *The Trial of His R. H. the D. of C. July 5th, 1770, for Criminal Conversation with Lady Harriet G—r.* (London, 1770), 58.

23. *An Epistle from Mrs. B—y to his R—l H—ss the D— of C—d, or, Beauty Scourging Rank* (London: W. Batteson, 1772), 18.

24. Lawrence Stone calls divorce proceedings the "soft-core pornography of the late eighteenth century" in *Road to* Divorce: *England 1530–1987* (Oxford: Oxford University Press, 1993), 44. See also David M. Turner, *Fashioning Adultery: Gender, Sex, and Civility in England, 1660–1740* (Cambridge: Cambridge University Press, 2002), chap. 6; and Peter Wagner, "The Pornographer in the Courtroom: Trial Reports about Cases of Sexual Crimes and Delinquencies as a Genre of Eighteenth-Century Erotica" in *Sexuality in Eighteenth-Century Britain*, ed. Paul Gabriel Bouce (Manchester: Manchester University Press, 1982), 120–140.

25. Quoted in Christopher Hibbert, *George III, A Personal History* (London: Viking, 1998), 171.

26. *Characters*, 15.

27. *Town and Country Magazine*, 4 (November 1772): 568–571.

28. *The Ciceroniad* (London, 1777), 25–26.

29. Richard Arthur Roberts, ed., *Calendar of Home Office Papers of the Reign of George III, 1773–1775* (London: 1881), 498.

30. Pierre Grosley, *A Tour to London; or, New Observations on England and its Inhabitants*, trans. Thomas Nugent, 2 vols. (London, 1772), 2: 223–224.

CHAPTER 2

1. Quoted in Lewis Melville [pseud.], *Trial of the Duchess of Kingston* (Edinburgh and London: William Hodge & Company, Ltd., 1927), 251.

2. Claire Gervat, *Elizabeth: The Scandalous Life of the Duchess of Kingston* (London: Century, 2003), 24.

3. *The Plays of Sir George Etherege*, ed. Michael Cordner (Cambridge: Cambridge University Press, 1982), 331.

4. Quoted in Gervat, *Elizabeth*, 21.

5. *Epistle to Dr. Arbuthnot*, ll. 309–310; quoted in *The Poems of Alexander Pope*, ed. John Butt (New Haven, CT: Yale University Press, 1963).

6. Quoted in Amanda Vickery's *The Gentleman's Daughter: Women's Lives in Georgian England* (New Haven and London: Yale University Press, 1998), 55.

7. Details of Collier's and Moseley's courtship are recounted in Lawrence Stone, *Uncertain Unions: Marriage in England 1660–1753* (Oxford: Oxford University Press, 1992), 68–77.

8. E. Cother, *A Serious Proposal for Promoting Lawful and Honourable Marriage*, 2nd ed. (London: 1751).

9. Bernard Mandeville, *Pretty Doings in a Protestant Nation* (London, 1734), 7.

10. Pierre Grosley, *A Tour to London; or, New Observations on England and its Inhabitants*, trans. Thomas Nugent, 2 vols. (London, 1772), 1: 158.

11. *Book of Common Prayer* (Oxford, 1743).

12. Gervat, *Elizabeth*, 29.

13. Stone, *Uncertain Unions*, 3.

14. For a fuller explanation of spousal law and other forms of marriage, see Martin Ingram, *Church Courts, Sex and Marriage in England, 1570–1640* (Cambridge: Cambridge University Press, 1987), 189–218.

15. All quotations are from Thomas Onslow, *The L—d's Protest against the Marriage Contract* (London, 1733), 5.

16. *The Mock-Marriage: or, A Lady and no Lady* (London, 1733), 7.

17. Frances Burney, *The Early Journals and Letters of Fanny Burney*, vol. 1, *1768–1773*, ed. Lars E. Troide (Oxford, Clarendon Press, 1988), 18.

18. Details of Rudd's case are recounted in Stone, *Uncertain Unions*, 158–160.

19. For fuller discussions of marriage law in eighteenth-century England, see Lawrence Stone, *Road to Divorce: England 1530–1987* (Oxford: Oxford University Press, 1993); Ingram, *Church Courts;* and R. B. Outhwaite, *Clandestine Marriage in England, 1500–1850* (London: The Hambledon Press, 1995).

20. Sir Tanfield Leman, Baronet, *Matrimony Analysed* (London: 1755), 9.

21. Jean-Bernard Le Blanc, *Letters on the English and French Nations* (London, 1747), 60–61.

22. Henry Gally, *Some Considerations upon Clandestine Marriages* (London, 1750), 2.

Chapter 3

1. Lewis Melville [pseud.], *Trial of the Duchess of Kingston* (Edinburgh and London: William Hodge & Company, Ltd., 1927), 232.

2. Augustus Hervey, *Augustus Hervey's Journal*, ed. David Erskine (London: William Kimber, 1953), 37.

3. Ibid., 40.

4. Ibid., 41. Because Hervey wrote his journal between 1767 and 1770, a time when his marriage to Elizabeth was still ostensibly secret, he took care to refer to her as "Miss Chudleigh," not "my wife."

5. John Walters, *The Royal Griffin: Frederick, Prince of Wales, 1707–1751* (London: Jarrolds Publishers, 1972), 149.

6. Elizabeth Chudleigh's Letters, Beinecke, Osborn MSS 17935 (6 February 1779).

7. Charles E. Pearce, *The Amazing Duchess*, 2 vols., 2nd ed. (London: Stanley Paul & Co., 1911), 1: 117.

8. Judity Schneid Lewis, *In the Family Way: Childbearing in the British Aristocracy, 1760–1860* (New Brunswick, NJ: Rutgers University Press, 1986), 157.

9. Dorothy Margaret Stuart, *Dearest Bess: The Life and Times of Lady Elizabeth Foster* (London: Methuen, 1955), 32.

10. Melville, *Trial*, 253.

11. Margaret Barton, *Tunbridge Wells* (London: Faber and Faber, 1937), 252.

12. Claire Gervat, *Elizabeth: The Scandalous Life of the Duchess of Kingston* (London: Century, 2003), 36.

13. This anecdote is more famous than reliable. Pearce points out that it was first printed in a 1773 pamphlet of Chesterfield's witticisms and ascribed it to the story of "Miss A—h," not Elizabeth Chudleigh (1: 126).

14. Elizabeth Montagu, *The Letters of Mrs. Elizabeth Montagu*, 4 vols. (London, T. Caldwell and W. Davies, 1813), 3: 72.

15. Amanda Vickery, *The Gentleman's Daughter: Women's Lives in Georgian England* (New Haven and London: Yale University Press, 1998), 124.

16. Christopher Hibbert, *George III, A Personal History* (London: Viking, 1998), 99.

17. Melville, *Trial*, 233.

CHAPTER 4

1. Thomas Benge Burr, *The History of Tunbridge-Wells* (London, 1766), 116.

2. Samuel Richardson, *The Correspondence of Samuel Richardson*, ed. Anna Laetitia Barbauld, 6 vols. (London: Richard Phillips, 1804), 3: 314.

3. Ibid., 3: 317.

4. For a full discussion of the many ways in which couples tried to resolve marital difficulties, including informal separations of this sort, see Joanne Bailey, *Unquiet Lives: Marriage and Marriage Breakdown in England, 1660–1800* (Cambridge: Cambridge University Press, 2003), chap. 3.

5. Horace Walpole, *The Correspondence of Horace Walpole*, ed. W. S. Lewis, 47 vols. (New Haven, CT: Yale University Press, 1937–1983), 3 May 1749, 20: 46.

6. Ibid.

7. Elizabeth Montagu, *The Letters of Mrs. Elizabeth Montagu, part the second*, 4 vols. (London, 1813), 3: 158.

8. For a full discussion of masquerade costumes, see Aileen Ribeiro, *The Dress Worn at Masquerades in England, 1730–1790, and its Relation to Fancy Dress Portraiture* (New York: Garland, 1994).

9. John Brown, *An Estimate of the Manners and Principles of the Times*, 2 vols. (London: 1757), 1: 45.

10. Walpole, *Correspondence*, 17 May 1747, 20: 57.

11. Walpole, *Correspondence,* 23 June 1750, 9: 107.

12. *Lord Hervey and His Friends, 1726–38* (London: John Murray, 1950), 256.

13. Quoted in Claire Gervat, *Elizabeth: The Scandalous Life of the Duchess of Kingston* (London: Century, 2003), 55.

14. Lady Jane Coke, *Letters from Lady Jane Coke to Her Friend Mrs. Eyre at Derby 1747–1758,* ed. Mrs. Ambrose Rathbone (London, 1899).

15. Quoted in Gervat, 55.

16. Thomas Whitehead, *Original Anecdotes of the Late Duke of Kingston* (Bath, 1792).

17. M. R. J. Holmes, *Augustus Hervey: A Naval Casanova* (Edinburgh: Pentland Press, 1996), 91.

18. The details of this trip are recorded in the testimony of Judith Philips (formerly Mrs. Amis) at the bigamy trial in 1776. See Lewis Melville [pseud.], *Trial of the Duchess of Kingston* (Edinburgh and London: William Hodge, 1927), 260–266.

CHAPTER 5

1. *The Complete Works of Shakespeare,* ed. David Bevington, 5th ed. (New York: Pearson Longman, 2004), 346.

2. Claire Gervat, *Elizabeth: The Scandalous Life of the Duchess of Kingston* (London: Century, 2003), 63.

3. John Brown, *An Estimate of the Manners and Principles of the Times,* 2 vols. (London: 1757), 158.

4. Count Frederick Kielmansegge, *Diary of a Journey to England in the Years 1761–1762* (London: Longmans, Green, and Co., 1902), 280.

5. Horace Walpole, *The Correspondence of Horace Walpole,* ed. W. S. Lewis, 47 vols. (New Haven, CT: Yale University Press, 1937–1983), 27 March 1760, 9: 277.

6. Ibid., 24 April 1776, 24: 198.

7. Philip Dormer Stanhope, Earl of Chesterfield, *Letters Written by the Late Right Honourable Philip Dormer Stanhope, Earl of Chesterfield, to his Son,* 7th ed. (London, 1776), no. cdxciii (August or September 1765), 3: 1326.

8. Quoted in Carola Hicks, *Improper Pursuits: The Scandalous Life of Lady Di Beauclerk* (London: Macmillan, 2001), 63.

9. Elizabeth Carter, *A Series of Letters between Mrs. Elizabeth Carter and Miss Catherine Talbot,* 4 vols. (London, 1809), 2: 352.

10. Ibid., 2: 365.

11. Quoted in Christopher Hibbert, *George III, A Personal History* (London: Viking, 1998), 50.

12. Quoted in Hibbert, *George III,* 77.

13. Marilyn Morris, "The Royal Family and Family Values in Late Eighteenth-Century England," *Journal of Family History* 21 (1996): 522.

14. Kielmansegge, *Diary of a Journey*, 281–282.
15. Details of Grafton's divorce are found in Lawrence Stone, *Broken Lives: Separation and Divorce in England, 1660–1857* (Oxford: Oxford University Press, 1993), 139–161.
16. Quoted in Stone, *Road to Divorce: England 1530–1987* (Oxford: Oxford University Press, 1993), 337.

Chapter 6

1. M. R. J. Holmes, *Augustus Hervey: A Naval Casanova* (Edinburgh: Pentland Press, 1996), 237.
2. Lewis Melville [pseud.], *Trial of the Duchess of Kingston* (Edinburgh and London: William Hodge & Company, Ltd., 1927), 246.
3. Ibid., 246.
4. Ibid., 247.
5. Ibid., 234.
6. Horace Walpole, *The Correspondence of Horace Walpole*, ed. W. S. Lewis, 47 vols. (New Haven, CT: Yale University Press, 1937–1983), 9 August 1768, 39: 105.
7. Melville, *Trial*, 247.
8. Ibid., 248.
9. Ibid., 247.
10. Ibid., 247.
11. Lady Mary Coke, *The Letters and Journals of Lady Mary Coke*, ed. James Archibald Home, 4 vols. (Edinburgh, 1889–1896; rpt. Bath: Kingsmead Bookshops, 1970), 2: 330–331.
12. Quoted in Claire Gervat, *Elizabeth: The Scandalous Life of the Duchess of Kingston* (London: Century, 2003), 85.
13. LMA/DL/C/176, ff. 83–85.
14. Ibid., ff. 86–88.
15. Ibid., f. 86.
16. Ibid., f. 88.
17. NA/C/12/1051/2, f. 2.
18. Melville, *Trial*, 250.
19. Ibid., 250.
20. LMA/DL/C/203, ff. 79–81.
21. Ibid., f. 80.
22. Ibid., f. 80.
23. Quoted in Gervat, *Elizabeth*, 87.
24. LMA/DL/C/555/50 (1–14).
25. LMA/DL/C/277, no. 16.
26. LMA/DL/C/277, no. 19.
27. LMA/DL/C/277, no. 15.
28. Holmes, *Augustus Hervey*, 237–238.
29. Melville, *Trial*, 227.

30. Quoted in Gervat, *Elizabeth*, 88–89.
31. Lady Mary Coke, *Letters and Journals*, 3: 124–125.
32. Walpole, *Correspondence*, 20 February 1768, 23: 93.
33. Melville, *Trial*, 289.
34. Thomas Whitehead, *Original Anecdotes of the Late Duke of Kingston* (Bath, 1792), 12–14.
35. Ibid., 13.
36. Ibid., 13.
37. Frontispiece to the Henry E. Huntington Library's copy of *The True, and Genuine Account of the Proceedings and Trial of the Duchess of Kingston* (London: 1776).
38. *The Case of the Duchess of Kingston* (London, 1775), 10.
39. BL Add 35509 (Hardwicke Papers, vol. CLXI), ff. 305–306. Letter from Elizabeth Chudleigh to Sir Robert Murray Keith (December? 1775).
40. Melville, *Trial*, 77.
41. *Lloyd's Evening Post*, 13–15 March 1769.
42. Ibid., 17–20 March 1769.
43. Lady Mary Coke, *Letters and Journals*, 3: 145.
44. Whitehead, *Original Anecdotes*, 60.
45. Quoted in Gervat, *Elizabeth*, 91.

CHAPTER 7

1. Thomas Whitehead, *Original Anecdotes of the Late Duke of Kingston* (Bath, 1792), 119.
2. Ibid., 179.
3. Nottingham, NeC3273 (3 August 1773).
4. Nottingham, NeC3246 (18 September 1773).
5. Nottingham, NeC3268 (19 September 1773).
6. Horace Walpole, *The Correspondence of Horace Walpole*, ed. W. S. Lewis, 47 vols. (New Haven, CT: Yale University Press, 1937–1983), 1 October 1773, 32: 146.
7. Walpole, *Correspondence*, 22 October 1775, 28: 225.
8. Nottingham, NeC3274 (undated; late September 1773).
9. Claire Gervat, *Elizabeth: The Scandalous Life of the Duchess of Kingston* (London: Century, 2003), 109.
10. BL Add 35509 (Hardwicke Papers, vol. CLXI), ff. 305–306. The recipient is probably Sir Robert Keith, and the letter seems to have been written in December 1775.
11. *"The Production of a Female Pen": Anna Larpent's Account of the Duchess of Kingston's Bigamy Trial of 1776*, ed. Matthew J. Kinservik, Miscellaneous Antiquities, no. 17 (New Haven, CT: The Lewis Walpole Library, Yale University, 2004), 95.
12. Charles E. Pearce, *The Amazing Duchess*, 2 vols., 2nd ed. (London: Stanley Paul & Co., 1911), 2: 125.

13. Roy Porter, *English Society in the Eighteenth Century* (London: Allen Lane, 1982), 57.

14. *Connecticut Gazette*, 17 May 1755; quoted in James Kingsley Blake, "The Lost Dukedom, or the Story of the Pierrepont Claim," *Papers of the New Haven Colony Historical Society* 7 (1908): 258–287; see 281–282n.

15. Blake, "Lost Dukedom," 264.

16. Ibid., 272.

17. Ibid., 275–276.

18. Ibid., 281.

19. Whitehead, *Original Anecdotes*, 40–42.

20. NA/C/12/1051/2.

21. Nottingham, PwF 2,802 (11 July 1774).

22. BL Add 35509 (Hardwicke Papers, vol. CLXI), ff. 305–306.

23. George E. Cockayne, *The Complete Peerage*, 13 vols. (London: St. Catherine Press, 1929), 7: 309n.

24. Whitehead, *Original Anecdotes*, 187–188.

25. NA/C/24/2450.

26. NA/C/12/1051/2, f. 5.

27. Ibid., ff. 2–3.

28. Ibid., f. 6.

29. Nottingham, PwF 2,802 (11 July 1774).

30. See Lawrence Stone, *Road to Divorce: England 1530–1987* (Oxford: Oxford University Press, 1993), 143–148.

31. Stone, *Road to Divorce*, 40; John R. Gillis, *For Better, For Worse: British Marriages 1600 to the Present* (New York and Oxford: Oxford University Press, 1985), 99.

32. David M. Turner, "Popular Marriage and the Law: Tales of Bigamy at the Eighteenth-Century Old Bailey," *London Journal* 30 (2005): 6–21.

33. *Lloyd's Evening Post*, 4–6 June 1775.

34. John Taylor, *Records of My Life* (New York: J. & J. Harper, 1833), 413.

35. Ibid., 414.

36. Quoted in Gervat, *Elizabeth*, 132. The Lord Chancellor's ruling is preserved in NA/C/33/444, ff. 606–607.

CHAPTER 8

1. The most recent biographical treatments of Foote are Simon Trefman, *Sam. Foote, Comedian* (New York: Columbia University Press, 1971) and Philip Highfill, Kalman Burnim, and Edward Langhans, *Biographical Dictionary of Actors, Actresses, Musicians, Dancers, Managers, and Other Stage Personnel in London, 1660–1800*, 17 vols. (Carbondale and Edwardsville: Southern Illinois University Press, 1973–1993), 5: 5.

2. William Cooke, *Memoirs of Samuel Foote, Esq.*, 3 vols. (London: R. Phillips, 1805), 1: 61n.

3. Ibid., 2: 4.

4. John Wells Wilkinson, *The Life and Works of Samuel Foote. Part One. The Dineley—Goodere—Foote Family* (preserved in an MS in the Henry E. Huntington Library; shelf mark HM 19996), 2: 969–980.

5. Wilkinson claims that Foote and the Duke of Kingston had a common ancestor, Sir Henry, the father of Grace Pierrepont, who married into the Manners family. See Wilkinson, *Life and Works*, 1: 13.

6. For details of Foote's involvement with Smart, see Christopher Mounsey, *Christopher Smart, Clown of God* (Lewisburg, PA: Bucknell University Press, 2001), 125–126.

7. Quoted from Cooke, *Memoirs*, 3: 159.

8. James Boswell, *Life of Johnson*, ed. George Birkbeck Hill and L. F. Powell, 6 vols. (Oxford: Oxford University Press, 1934), 3: 69–70.

9. L. W. Conolly, *The Censorship of English Drama 1737–1824* (San Marino: Huntington Library Press, 1976), 26.

10. Unless otherwise indicated, the details of the suppression of *A Trip to Calais* are derived from the accounts in Trefman, Conolly, and Cooke.

11. Quoted from Foote's open letter to the Lord Chamberlain, *St. James's Chronicle*, 1–3 August 1775.

12. Samuel Foote, *A Trip to Calais* and *The Capuchin*, ed. George Colman (London, 1778), 69–70.

13. Quoted from Foote's open letter to the Lord Chamberlain, *St. James's Chronicle*, 1–3 August 1775.

14. Horace Walpole, *The Correspondence of Horace Walpole*, ed. W. S. Lewis, 47 vols. (New Haven, CT: Yale University Press, 1937–1983), 7 August 1775, 28: 218.

15. The estimate comes from William J. Burling, *Summer Theatre in London, 1661–1820, and the Rise of the Haymarket Theatre* (Madison and Teaneck: Fairleigh Dickinson University Press, 2000), 122 and 135.

16. *St. James's Chronicle*, 1–3 August 1775.

17. Walpole, *Correspondence*, 7 August 1775, 28: 218–219.

18. Cooke, *Memoirs*, 1: 210–211.

19. Quoted from *The Case of the Duchess of Kingston* (London, 1775), 18–19.

20. BL Add 35 612 (Hardwicke Papers v. CCLXIV), ff. 293–294 (15 August 1775). The writer is M. Jeffreys, the recipient is unknown.

21. David Garrick, *The Letters of David Garrick*, ed. George M. Kahrl and David M. Little, 3 vols. (Cambridge, MA: Belknap Press, 1961), 3: 1020–1021.

22. Quoted from *St. James's Chronicle*, 12–15 August 1775.

23. Ibid.

24. Quoted from *St. James's Chronicle*, 15–17 August 1775.

25. Mason refers to Pope's "Letter to a Noble Lord" (1735), a satire written to his nemesis, Augustus's father. Walpole, *Correspondence*, 22 October 1775, 28: 224–225.

26. Ibid.
27. *The Devil: A Poetical Essay* (London: J. Dodsley, 1776), 22–23.
28. Garrick, *Letters*, 3: 1031.

CHAPTER 9

1. This print is preserved in the Harvard Theatre. Collection extra-illustrated edition of Dr. Doran, *Their Majesties Servants* (London: J. C. Nimmo, 1888), 3: 134.
2. *St. James's Chronicle*, 14–15 September 1775.
3. *The Case of the Duchess of Kingston* (London, 1775), 12–13.
4. *St. James's Chronicle*, 15–17 August 1775.
5. Donna T. Andrew and Randall McGowen, *The Perreaus and Mrs. Rudd: Forgery and Betrayal in Eighteenth-Century* London (Berkeley: University of California Press, 2001), 55–56.
6. *St. James's Chronicle*, 19–22 August 1775.
7. *St. James's Chronicle*, 15–19 September 1775.
8. Nottingham, PwF 2810, 14 December 1775.
9. Nottingham, PwF 2809, 18 November 1775.
10. HLRO, Main Papers, ff. 3868–3869, 11 December 1775.
11. Nottingham, PwF 2813 (26 March 1776).
12. HLRO, LGC/5/2 (Papers of the Lord Great Chamberlain), f. 364.
13. Ibid., ff. 365–367.
14. Ibid., f. 389.
15. Ibid., f. 394.
16. Ibid., ff. 386–388.
17. Ancaster had anticipated that the trial would last for four days and he had the tickets printed on differently colored paper for each day. When it became clear that the trial would go beyond four days, he had tickets for a fifth and sixth day printed. In the event, the trial lasted only five days. The House of Lords Record Office contains a rare sixth-day ticket (HLRO Main Papers, HL/PO/RO/1/28).
18. Nottingham, NeC2798, 8 April 1776.
19. Nottingham, NeC2688, 25 March 1776.
20. BL, Add MSS 47791 (Northcote's Life, vol. 2, 1777–1780), ff. 19–20.
21. BL, Egerton MSS 3524 (Thoresby Park Papers, vol. IX), f. 5 (Richard Heron to Elizabeth, 17 January 1775).
22. BL, Egerton MSS 3524 (Thoresby Park Papers, vol. IX), ff. 6–7 (Elizabeth to Richard Heron, 15 February 1775).
23. Dorian Gerhold, *Westminster Hall: Nine Hundred Years of History* (London: James & James, 1999), 56.
24. M. D'Archenholz, *A Picture of England*, 2 vols. (London, 1789), 2: 6.
25. Lewis Melville [pseud.] *Trial of the Duchess of Kingston* (Edinburgh and London: William Hodge & Company, Ltd., 1927), 58. Unless otherwise indicated, all quotations from the trial come from Melville and will be given in the text.

26. *A Brief for Her Grace the Duchess of Kingston; Containing the Points of Law, and Cases Adjudged, On which her Grace's Defence will Rest* (London, 1776), 7.

27. Technically, Elizabeth's case presented a matter of "collateral estoppel" as the ruling in the jactitation suit was closely related, but not identical, to the issue of bigamy.

28. Matthew J. Kinservik, ed., *"The Production of a Female Pen": Anna Larpent's Account of the Duchess of Kingston's Bigamy Trial of 1776,* Miscellaneous Antiquities, no. 17 (New Haven, CT: The Lewis Walpole Library, Yale University 2004), 87.

29. Edward Pigott, Diary, Osborn Collection, fc80, Beinecke Library, entry no. 349.

30. Quoted in Charles E. Pearce, *The Amazing Duchess*, 2 vols., 2nd ed. (London: Stanley Paul & Co., 1911), 2: 226–227.

31. Walpole, (17 April 1776) 24: 192–193.

32. Pigott, Diary, f. 349.

33. Kinservik, "*Production of a Female Pen*," 88.

34. Ibid., 89.

35. *St. James's Chronicle*, 16–18 April 1776.

36. Pigott, Diary, Osborn Collection, fc80, Beinecke Library, entry no. 349.

37. *Public Ledger*, 18 April 1776.

38. Kinservik, "*Production of a Female Pen*," 90–91.

39. De Grey's opinion is preserved in HLRO, Shelf Mark: 4/0/13.

40. *St. James's Chronicle*, 18–21 April 1776.

41. *Public Ledger*, 20 April 1776.

42. *An Authentic Detail of Particulars Relative to the Late Duchess of Kingston. The Third Edition, With Considerable Additions* (London, 1790), 87.

43. Melville, *Trial*, 271.

44. Kinservik, "*Production of a Female Pen*," 95.

45. Hannah More quoted in Pearce, *Amazing Duchess*, 2: 281.

46. D'Archenholz, *Picture of England*, 1: 15–16.

47. Kinservik, "*Production of a Female Pen*," 96.

48. Ibid., 97.

49. Pigott, Diary, entry no. 349.

50. D'Archenholz, *Picture of England*, 2: 8.

51. *St. James's Chronicle*, 25–27 April 1776.

52. Alan Valentine, *The British Establishment, 1760–1784* (Norman: University of Oklahoma Press, 1970), 1: 177.

53. *The Laws Respecting Women, as they Regard their Natural Rights, or their Connections and Conduct* (London, 1777), 321. This author also notes that Elizabeth's case is an important precedent, establishing a peeress's right to claim benefit of clergy.

54. Robert Sandeman, *The Honour of Marriage Opposed to all Impurities: An Essay* (London: 1777), 39.

CHAPTER 10

1. The details of Sangster's and Foote's appearances on 6 May are derived from Foote's deposition in his libel suit against the *Public Ledger* (NA/KB1/20/Part 4) and from Lord Mansfield's manuscript notes on Foote's attempted sodomy trial, reprinted in James Oldham, *The Mansfield Manuscripts and the Growth of English Law in the Eighteenth Century*, 2 vols. (Chapel Hill: University of North Carolina Press, 1992), 2: 1004–1009.

2. Martin Battestin, *Henry Fielding, A Life* (London and New York: Routledge, 1989), 459.

3. Unless otherwise noted, information on the criminal trial process comes from J. M. Beattie, *Crime and the Courts in England, 1660–1800* (Princeton, NJ: Princeton University Press, 1986).

4. Netta Murray Goldsmith, *The Worst of Crimes: Homosexuality and the Law in Eighteenth-Century London* (Aldershot: Ashgate Publishing Ltd., 1998), 44.

5. Ibid., 99.

6. Randolph Trumbach, "Sodomitical Subcultures: Sodomitical Roles, and the Gender Revolution of the Eighteenth Century; The Recent Historiography," in R. P. MacCubbin, ed., *'Tis Nature's Fault: Unauthorized Sexuality during the Enlightenment* (Cambridge: Cambridge University Press, 1985), 113.

7. David Garrick, *The Private Correspondence of David Garrick*, 2 vols., ed. James Boaden (London: H. Colburn and R. Bentley, 1831–1832), 1: 472f., quoted in David Garrick, *Letters of David Garrick*, ed. George M. Kahrl and David M. Little, 3 vols. (Cambridge, MA: Belknap Press of Harvard University Press, 1961), 2: 801n.

8. Simon Trefman, *Sam. Foote, Comedian* (New York: Columbia University Press, 1971), 176–177.

9. This letter was written by Elizabeth on 26 April 1776 to Maria Vittoria Colonna, the Marquise de los Balbasos. A copy of it is preserved in Horace Walpole, *The Correspondence of Horace Walpole*, ed. W. S. Lewis, 47 vols. (New Haven, CT: Yale University Press, 1937–1983), 32: 299–300. The original is in French; the translation is mine.

10. *Public Advertiser*, 27 April 1776, quoted in Claire Gervat, *Elizabeth: The Scandalous Life of the Duchess of Kingston* (London: Century, 2003), 155.

11. Walpole, *Correspondence*, 24 April 1776, 24: 196.

12. Anonymous [William Jackson], *Asmodeus* (London, 1776), 4.

13. Hannah More, *Letters of Hannah More*, ed. R. Brimley Johnson (London: John Lane and the Bodley Head Ltd., 1925), 43.

14. *Private Papers of James Boswell*, ed. Geoffrey Scott and Frederick A. Pottle, 18 vols. (New York, 1928–1934), 11: 259.

15. Ibid., 11: 275.

16. For a discussion of popular representations of sodomy in the eighteenth century, see Cameron McFarlane, *The Sodomite in Fiction and Satire 1660–1750* (New York: Columbia University Press, 1997).
17. All the information regarding the initiation of the libel suit is from the deposition of Foote, Hamilton, and Hawkins, NA/KB1/20/Part 4.
18. *London Chronicle*, 16–18 May 1776.
19. NA/KB1/20/Part 4.
20. William Cooke, *Memoirs of Samuel Foote, Esq.*, 3 vols. (London: R. Phillips, 1805), 1: 224–226.
21. *London Chronicle*, 18–21 May 1776.
22. Ibid.
23. *St. James's Chronicle*, 18–21 May 1776.
24. Oldham, *Mansfield Manuscripts*, 1007.
25. *Public Ledger*, 29 May 1776.
26. *St. James's Chronicle*, 11–13 June 1776.
27. *Monthly Review* 54 (1776): 240.
28. *Public Ledger*, 17 May 1776.
29. William Jackson, *Sodom and Onan, A Satire* (London, 1776), 7.
30. Ibid., 26–27.
31. *Public Ledger*, 10 July 1776.
32. The grand jury indictments and the writ of certiorari are preserved in NA/KB/10/40, nos. 34 & 35.
33. *Public Ledger*, 10 July 1776.
34. Ibid.
35. *Gentleman's Magazine* 46 July 1776, 334.

CHAPTER 11

1. William Cooke, *Memoirs of Samuel Foote, Esq.*, 3 vols. (London: R. Phillips, 1805), 1: 224–226.
2. *Atys: Or, a Letter to Momus* (London: C. Moran and Richardson & Urquhart, 1767), 6.
3. *Public Ledger*, 12 July 1776.
4. Ibid.
5. Ibid., 13 July 1776.
6. *Town and Country Magazine*, July 1776, 376.
7. Horace Walpole, *Book of Materials*, Lewis Walpole Library, Yale University, 2: 55, preserved in the Lewis Walpole Library.
8. *Nocturnal Revels: Or, The History of King's-Place*, 2 vols. (London, 1779), esp. chaps. 12–13.
9. Samuel Foote, *The Capuchin*, ed. George Colman the Elder (London, 1778), 98.
10. *St. James's Chronicle*, 17–20 August 1776.
11. All quotations to this scene are from the censor's manuscript copy of *The Capuchin*, preserved in the Larpent Collection of plays in the

Henry E. Huntington Library, MS no. 413, ff. 51–52. For a complete transcription of the scene, see Matthew J. Kinservik, "Satire, Censorship, and Sodomy in Samuel Foote's *The Capuchin* (1776)" *Review of English Studies* 54 (2003): 639–660, esp. 651–652.

12. *St. James's Chronicle*, 17–20 July 1776.

13. *London Chronicle*, 29–31 October 1776; quoted in David Garrick, *Letters of David Garrick*, ed. George M. Kahrl and David M. Little, 3 vols. (Cambridge, MA: Belknap Press of Harvard University Press, 1961), 3: 1138n1.

14. Garrick, *Letters*, 3: 1137.

15. J. S. Cockburn and Thomas A. Green, *Twelve Good Men and True: The Criminal Trial Jury in England, 1200–1800* (Princeton, NJ: Princeton University Press, 1988), 322n15.

16. NA/KB28/299/No. 3.

17. William Hawkins, *Pleas of the Crown*, 2: 400; quoted in J. M. Beattie, *Crime and the Courts in England, 1660–1800* (Princeton, NJ: Princeton University Press, 1986), 356.

18. *London Chronicle*, 7–10 December 1776.

19. All trial testimony is derived from Mansfield's manuscript notes, found in James Oldham, *The Mansfield Manuscripts and the Growth of English Law in the Eighteenth Century*, 2 vols. (Chapel Hill: University of North Carolina Press, 1992), 2: 1004–1007. Because Mansfield's notes are sketchy, I have taken some liberties with punctuation and paragraphing in reproducing them here. However, I have neither added words nor altered the order of speeches.

20. For instance, see Randolph Trumbach, ed., *Sodomy Trials, Seven Documents* (New York and London: Garland Publishing, Inc., 1986).

21. Foote had ridiculed the financial downfall of Fordyce's brother, Alexander, in one of his most popular plays, *The Bankrupt* (1773).

22. *Town and Country Magazine*, 1776 Supplement, 694.

23. *Lloyd's Evening Post*, 9–11 December 1776; quoted in Oldham, *Mansfield Manuscripts*, 1009n5.

24. *St. James's Chronicle*, 7–10 December 1776.

25. Ibid., 19–21 December 1776.

CHAPTER 12

1. John Forster, *Biographical Essays*, 3rd ed. (London: J. Murray, 1860), 461.

2. Arthur Murphy, *Plays by Samuel Foote and Arthur Murphy*, ed. George Taylor (Cambridge: Cambridge University Press, 1984), 173, 227.

3. Hester Lynch Piozzi, *Autobiography, Letters, and Literary Remains of Mrs. Piozzi (Thrale)*, ed. A Hayward, 2 vols. (London: Longman, Green, Longman, and Roberts, 1861), 1: 310–311.

4. Charle Macklin, "Memoranda and Anecdotes," The Folger Shakespeare Library, Washington, D. C. Macklin's "Memoranda and Anecdotes" are preserved in the Folger Shakespeare Library, call no.: Y.d. 515 (1–11), 8–9.

5. *Aristophanes, Being a Classic Collection of True Attic Wit, Containing the Jests, Gibes, Bon-Mots, Witticisms, and Most Extraordinary Anecdotes of Samuel Foote, Esq.* (London, 1778), xxx.

6. The subpoena, along with the affidavits of Mary Tempelman and Thomas Hawkins the Younger, are preserved in NA/ KB1/21/part 3.

7. NA/KB21/41 (Rule book, fair copy).

8. NA/KB/1/20/part 4.

9. William Cooke, *Memoirs of Samuel Foote, Esq.*, 3 vols. (London: R. Phillips, 1805), 1: 234–235.

10. BL Add 36593, f. 135.

11. Cooke, *Memoirs*, 1: 237.

12. Details of Morlet's delivery of the letter come from an account included as exhibit A in Bristol's appeal to the jactitation suit; LMA/ DL/C/558/12.

13. Horace Walpole, *The Correspondence of Horace Walpole*, ed. W. S. Lewis, 47 vols. (New Haven, CT: Yale University Press, 1937–1983), 32: 299–300; translation by Claire Gervat, *Elizabeth: The Scandalous Life of the Duchess of Kingston* (London: Century, 2003), 156.

14. *Westminster Magazine, or The Pantheon of Public Taste* 4 (1776): 369.

15. *Public Ledger*, 5 July 1776.

16. LMA/DL/C/558/54.

17. The documents related to the appeal are preserved in LMA/DL/ C/178, ff. 124–135.

18. NA/C/33/448, f. 484 (7 May 1777).

19. When Elizabeth did respond to the Chancery suit on 23 June 1777, she pleaded the probate of the duke's will as a bar to prosecution, lied about the details of the original jactitation ruling, and refused to respond to accusations of collusion in obtaining that ruling (NA/ C/12/1051/2, ff. 8–9).

20. BL Add 73563, f. 3.

21. BL Add 73563, ff. 5–6.

22. BL Add 73563, ff. 75–77.

23. Bettesworth's ruling is preserved in LMA/DL/C/178, ff. 133–135.

24. BL Add 73563, ff. 21–22, 10 March 1778.

25. James Kingsley Blake, "The Lost Dukedom, or the Story of the Pierrepont Claim," *Papers of the New Haven Colony Historical Society* 7 (1908): 258–287.

26. BL Add 73563, ff. 25–26, 20 March 1778.

27. BL Add 73563, ff. 29–30, 15 April 1778.

28. LMA/DL/C/559/01.

29. BL Add 73563, ff. 17–18, December 1777.

30. Gervat, *Elizabeth*, 214–215, 235.

31. Walpole, *Correspondence*, 33: 572, 6 September 1787.

32. For the rumors, see Simon Trefman, *Sam. Foote, Comedian* (New York: Columbia University Press, 1971), 263 n85; the 1779 payment is mentioned in a letter to Bell Chudleigh of 19 October 1779 preserved in the Beinecke Library (Osborn Folder 3211); and the claim that he worked for her in the late 1780s is made in William Sampson, *The Trial of the Rev. William Jackson at the Bar of the King's Bench in Ireland for High Treason* (Dublin: P. Byrne and H. Fitzpatrick, 1795), 34.

33. For details on this episode in Jackson's career, see Lucyle Werkmeister, "Notes for a Revised Life of William Jackson," *Notes and Queries* n.s. 8 (1961): 43–47.

34. Details of the Royalty Theatre fiasco are recounted in the entry on John Palmer in Philip Highfill, Kalman Burnim, and Edward Langhans, *Biographical Dictionary of Actors, Actresses, Musicians, Dancers, Managers, and Other Stage Personnel in London, 1660–1800*, 17 vols. (Carbondale and Edwardsville: Southern Illinois University Press, 1973–1993), 5: 11 and in Watson Nicholson, *The Struggle for a Free Stage in London* (1906; New York: Benjamin Blom, 1966).

35. BL Egerton MSS 3524 (Thoresby Park Papers, Vol. IX, ff. 100–101), 10 October 1788.

36. The best account of Jackson's spy mission is found in Marianne Elliott, *Partners in Revolution: The United Irishmen and France* (New Haven, CT: Yale University Press, 1982), 62–74.

37. Details are derived from Sampson, *Trial*.

Epilogue

1. Many of the details about Shepherd's career, including full-text reproductions of the printed accounts of the *I, Libertine* hoax cited here can be found on Jim Clavin's website, "A Salute to Jean Shepherd" http://www.flicklives.com.

2. Shepherd is best known today for writing the screenplay of the classic holiday film, *A Christmas Story*. He is also the film's narrator.

3. Harry Shearer, ed., "I, Libertine: *Satyr* meets Jean Shepherd," *Satyr* (1963).

4. Frank Dean, "He Talks by Night," *Scene* (1962).

5. Quoted in Carter Henderson, "Night People's Hoax on Day People Makes Hit with Book Folks," *The Wall Street Journal*, 1 August 1956.

6. Frederick R. Ewing [pseud.], *I, Libertine* (New York: Ballantine Books, 1956). Quotation is from the book cover.

7. John Wilcock, "The Village Square" in *The Village Voice Reader* (New York: Doubleday, 1962), 79.

8. Joyce Brabner, "I, Libertine: Making the List," WBUR Online Arts (1 June 2002) http://publicbroadcasting,net/wbur/arts.

9. Ewing, *I, Libertine*, 137.

10. Ibid., 151.
11. Charles E. Pearce, *The Amazing Duchess*, 2 vols., 2nd ed. (London: Stanley Paul & Co., 1911), 14–15.
12. Claire Gervat, *Elizabeth: The Scandalous Life of the Duchess of Kingston* (London: Century, 2003), 246.
13. Stella Tillyard, "Celebrity in Eighteenth-Century London," *History Today* 55 (2005): 24.
14. See Laurence Senelick, "Mollies or Men of Mode? Sodomy and the Eighteenth-Century London Stage," *Journal of the History of Sexuality* 1 (1990): 66–67; Kristina Straub, *Sexual Suspects: Eighteenth-Century Players and Sexual Ideology* (Princeton, NJ: Princeton University Press, 1992), 64; Netta Murray Goldsmith, *The Worst of Crimes: Homosexuality and the Law in Eighteenth-Century London* (Aldershot: Ashgate Publishing, Ltd., 1998), 104; and Rictor Norton, *Mother Clap's Molly House: The Gay Subculture in England, 1700-1830* (London: Gay Men's Press, 1992), 180.
15. Dean, "He Talks by Night."

INDEX